Published With The New York Times and The Washing...

D0745161

MORNING EDITION

Mastering Reading and Language Skills with the Newspaper

Ethel Tiersky
Robert Hughes

National Textbook Company
NTC a division of *NTC Publishing Group* • Lincolnwood, Illinois USA

About the Authors

Ethel Tiersky is associate professor of English at Harry S. Truman College in Chicago. *Morning Edition* is the thirteenth textbook that she has coauthored. With National Textbook Company, she has previously published two texts: *In the News: Mastering Reading and Language Skills with the Newspaper* (using articles from the *International Herald Tribune*) and *Read All about It: Mastering Reading Comprehension and Critical Thinking Skills* (using articles from *USA Today*).

Professor Tiersky holds a B.S. in education from Northwestern University and an M.A. in English from the University of Chicago. Her teaching experience has included primary grades, eighth- and ninth-grade English, adult education, and college-level English and ESL.

Robert Hughes holds a Ph.D. in English from Northwestern University and is associate professor of English at Harry S. Truman College in Chicago, where he teaches composition, ESL, and reading. Professor Hughes has contributed articles to *Newsweek, Parents,* and the *Chicago Sun-Times,* as well as literary essays to *Nineteenth-Century Literature, The Southern Literary Journal*, and *Essays in Literature.*

Articles from the *International Herald Tribune* are republished by permission of the International Herald Tribune, 181 avenue Charles-de-Gaulle, 92200 Neuilly-sur-Seine, France; The New York Times; and The Washington Post, the copyright proprietors.

1997 Printing

Published by National Textbook Company, a division of NTC Publishing Group, 4255 West Touhy Avenue, Lincolnwood (Chicago), Illinois 60646-1975 U.S.A.

CONTENTS

Introduction   **v**

Focus on the Newspaper: How to Read the Newspaper for Information and Enjoyment   vii

Section One: News/Features   1

1. Families in Upheaval Worldwide   2
2. Kobe Quake: A Nightmare Come True   7
3. Scottish Village Sticks By Its Benefactor, Crooked He May Be   12
4a. For Dalai Lama at 60, Bittersweet Success   17
  b. Mother vs. Tibetan Monks   17

Focus on the Newspaper: News/Features   24

Section Two: Opinion   27

1. Trans-Pacific Pitching   28
2. Unfair Doubts about the Nanny   32
3. In Rush for Gold, a Rain Forest Dies   37
4. Six Enviro-Myths You Can Stop Believing   42

Focus on the Newspaper: Opinion   48

Section Three: Business   51

1. 'Green' Clothes Take Root   52
2. The American Fast-Food Dream   56
3. Prenuptial Accords: Walking down the Aisle and Reading Fine Print   62
4. Cigarette Makers See Future (It's in Asia)   68

Focus on the Newspaper: Business   73

Section Four: Profiles   75

1. If It's a Laughing Matter, Call In Julie Hette   76
2. Walden Revisited: The Perils of Country Houses   81
3. Art as Memory: Filmmaker's Vietnam   87
4. Kenya City Learns to Accept a New Kind of Mayor   92

Focus on the Newspaper: Profiles   98

Section Five: Arts/Entertainment   101

1. George Eliot, Voice of a Century: A Biography   102
2. Race to Save Prague's Face   107
3. Disney Assailed for Pocahontas Portrayal   112
4. After an Epoch of Nagging, Christo Wraps Reichstag   118
5a. In Stone Age Cavern, a Stunning Menagerie   123
 b. Stone Age Picassos: 30,000-Year-Old Trove   123
Focus on the Newspaper: Arts/Entertainment   129

Section Six: Science/Health   131

1. Why Rock Fans Faint: Science Finally Comes to Its Senses   132
2. In Iceman's Outfit, Cultural Clues   136
3. Chain Reaction in the Orbital Junkyard   142
4. In a Newfound Tomb in Egypt, a Fresh Look at Ramses II's Era   148
Focus on the Newspaper: Science/Health   154

Section Seven: Sports   157

1. A Novice Angler in Arctic Russia   158
2. Rodeos of the American West Spur Imitators Far, Far South   163
3. An Adventurer's Life: Always New Heights   168
4. Bannister and Peers: Heroes Made by Dreaming the Impossible Dream   174
Focus on the Newspaper: Sports   179

Comprehension Check   181

INTRODUCTION

Morning Edition is a reading skills text built around articles from the *International Herald Tribune.* Readers who are familiar with *In the News* will be pleased to see this all-new volume featuring 31 recently published articles.

The *International Herald Tribune,* edited in Paris, France, is read around the world. Many of its articles originally appeared in *The New York Times* or *The Washington Post.* They are examples of the finest in American journalism. Other articles were written by *International Herald Tribune* journalists, who provide insightful coverage of happenings around the globe.

The articles in *Morning Edition* have been carefully selected for high interest, international scope, and varied subject areas. In this text, you will read about a Spanish boy being raised as a reincarnated Tibetan monk, an American man who works as a nanny, a French woman who gets paid for laughing, an internationally famous artist who wraps buildings, and a Tyrolean "Iceman" who's in pretty good shape for someone five thousand years old! News, business, science, sports, entertainment—these subjects and more are covered in the text. The articles provide fascinating facts on a wide range of topics, information you will enjoy gathering and sharing.

As you explore the issues in *Morning Edition,* you will strengthen your reading skills. The exercises that accompany the articles are designed to help you better understand the articles' main points and their vocabulary and idioms. The reading strategies you learn can be applied to your independent reading of a wide range of texts, from magazines and popular fiction to textbooks and business reports.

Special attention is given to improving newspaper reading skills in the text's eight "Focus on the Newspaper" sections. The first Focus section provides an overview of the newspaper. The others, placed at the end of each section of the text, deal with specific parts of the newspaper or particular types of writing: "hard" news stories, features, opinion pieces, profiles, sports stories, reviews, business news, and so on. The Focus sections describe the kinds of information you can expect to find in the newspaper and provide hands-on practice in recognizing and analyzing various types of articles.

The material accompanying each article (or pair of articles) is organized as follows:

Previewing the Article

- Introduces the topic of the article and provides background information helpful in understanding the article

- Provides discussion questions to stimulate interest in the article and to activate prior knowledge about the topic

- Suggests specific information to look for as you read

Getting the Message

- Focuses on key points of the article, using a variety of exercise types including true/false, multiple choice, short-answer questions, and charts to complete

- Offers an opportunity to confirm your understanding of the article by comparing your answers with the Comprehension Check at the back of the book

Expanding Your Vocabulary

- Provides practice in determining the meanings of words and phrases through context
- Groups related words (about occupations, money, geographical features, etc.) to aid in comprehension and retention of vocabulary
- Encourages analysis of both denotations and connotations of words
- Helps to distinguish between homonyms and other easily confused words
- Provides practice in building vocabulary using word parts

Working with Idioms and Expressions

- Defines key idioms and expressions from the article
- Provides practice in using idioms and expressions in context

Analysis of Key Features

Each lesson includes a section titled "Making Sense of Sentences," "Analyzing Paragraphs," or "Focusing on Style and Tone." These sections examine more sophisticated elements of the article, such as

- sentences that include contrasting ideas, conditional clauses, participles used as adjectives, appositives, and other elements of complex and compound sentences
- inferences, figures of speech, and ironic and paradoxical statements
- paragraph development and the ways in which various paragraphs relate to each other and to the main point of the article
- elements of style, such as the nonfiction writer's use of storytelling techniques

Talking and Writing

- Suggests several topics relating to issues in the article for oral and/or written discussion
- Encourages thinking beyond the article to the implications and long-term significance of its message

We hope that you enjoy the articles in *Morning Edition* and the accompanying exercises and activities. We also hope that this text will inspire you to spend some time each day "seeing" the world through a newspaper.

How to Read the Newspaper for Information and Enjoyment

Daily newspapers offer you a whole world to explore. Within their pages, you will find articles that inform, educate, excite, anger, or concern you. By reading the newspaper, you can find out about what's happening throughout the world: locally, nationally, and internationally. In this Focus section, you will learn about some general features of newspapers to aid you in reading them on your own. You will also analyze your current newspaper reading habits.

Overview of the Newspaper

Newspapers use a number of devices to help their readers find information quickly. Here are some of them:

- boxes listing articles, found on the front page of the paper or the front page of a section
- an index (often on the front page or the second page)
- page headings
- headlines

Most newspapers are divided into sections, including news, business, and sports. The sections come in a regular order; for example, the sports section is often last. Sometimes newspapers have special sections, such as an entertainment or arts and leisure section on the weekend.

You will notice that articles often begin with a *dateline,* or name of the place where the article was written. You'll find datelines from all over the world.

Exercise 1: The Organization of the Newspaper

A. Look at a recent issue of a newspaper. Circle some examples of the devices that help you find information.

B. Look over the newspaper you usually read. List the order of the sections.

Exercise 2: Locating Things in the Newspaper

Look through a newspaper for the following information. Then tell the location (the section number and page) where you found each item.

1. the weather forecast
2. the score of a sports event
3. a story about business conditions

4. a dateline from a European country
5. a headline that includes the name of a country
6. information about a cultural event
7. a letter to the editor

Your Newspaper Reading Habits

You will find many different types of articles in a newspaper. News articles are typically at the front of the paper: these report current news and political events. Articles expressing opinions and taking positions on current issues are on the opinion pages. Feature articles give background information about the news and may express the viewpoint of the writer. They may be found throughout the paper.

When you read a newspaper, do you often read just particular kinds of articles, such as sports pieces? Or do you usually look through the entire newspaper to find what interests you? In this section, you will explore your reading habits so that you can make the best use of the newspaper.

Exercise 3: What Catches Your Interest?

Skim an entire newspaper, looking for articles that interest you. Read whatever catches your interest. On a separate sheet of paper, complete a chart like the following. Fill in the first two columns with information about each article you look at. Then check the appropriate column to show how much of the article you read.

Name of Article or Item	Type of Article or Item*	I Read the Headline Only	I Read the 1st Paragraph	I Quickly Skimmed It	I Read It Carefully

*Use these abbreviations: N = News story; F = Feature story; ED = Editorial/Opinion; C = Cartoon; P = Photo; A = Advertisement; O = other.

As you did the activity, did you read anything interesting that you might not have noticed if you followed your regular reading habits? Repeat exercise 3 several times as you work through this book. Do your reading habits change?

Exercise 4: Reviewing Your Newspaper Reading Habits

Think about the following questions. Write your thoughts in a notebook, or discuss them with a partner.

1. Do you follow the same pattern each time you read a newspaper? For example, do you always look at the back page first?

2. What kinds of articles do you usually read: "hard" news stories? sports stories? editorials? comics? Why?

3. How familiar are you with various sections of the newspaper? Can you find what you're looking for quickly?

4. What motivates you to read an article completely: your interest in the subject? a catchy headline? the length?

5. What is your main purpose in reading the newspaper? Does your purpose ever change?

6. Do you usually read the entire newspaper from front page to back page? If not, what are some reasons: lack of time? lack of interest? lack of familiarity with some topics? unfamiliar vocabulary?

7. Do you read more than one newspaper regularly? If so, what are the differences between the papers?

8. Do you think your newspaper reading habits will be the same in six months? in a year? Would you like to change your reading habits? Why or why not?

Analyzing Headlines

Headlines are designed to catch your eye and interest as you look through a newspaper. They typically summarize the focus of an article in a few words. Headlines help you predict the subject of an article and its main idea or viewpoint, so they are important in helping you use the newspaper for your own purposes.

Headlines pose special problems in reading. Often, short function words like *be* and *the* are left out. Also headlines often contain idioms, word play, or puns because headline writers are trying to be clever and attract reader interest. Note the following types of headlines.

- *Straightforward headlines.* Many headlines make a clear, direct statement about the subject of the article. For example, in the Opinion section of this text, "Six Enviro-Myths You Can Stop Believing" states the viewpoint presented and defended by the author of this ecology piece. In News/Features, "Families in Upheaval Worldwide" summarizes the main point supported by the evidence in the article.

- *Headlines using word play.* One of the headlines in the Science/Health section is "Why Rock Stars Faint: Science Finally Comes to Its Senses." This headline begins with a straightforward statement of its topic. But the clause after the colon uses word play. The expression *comes to its senses* is used both literally and figuratively. The literal meaning contrasts with the word *faint* in the first clause. The figurative meaning refers to the scientists' finally coming up with a logical, believable explanation for the fainting at rock concerts. Another example of word play is in the Sports section headline "Rodeos of the American West Spur Imitators." There is a pun on the verb *spur,* which means that the word is being used in two ways at once. *Spur* means to incite or urge on, to encourage or stimulate action. But it also has a more specific meaning related to cowboys. To *spur* a horse is to make the horse follow directions by pressing its side with spurs, spiked metal pieces worn on the rider's boots.

- *Headlines requiring background knowledge.* In the Sports section, one headline speaks of "dreaming the impossible dream." These words are from a song in the musical show *Man of La Mancha,* which is based on Cervantes' famous novel *Don Quixote de La Mancha.* But the reader who doesn't know the song misses the allusion. In Arts/Entertainment, one headline reads: "After an Epoch of Nagging, Christo Wraps Reichstag." This headline is meaningless to readers who have never heard of Christo or the Reichstag. Journalists often assume that readers have knowledge of well-known people, places, and events. But this assumed knowledge may not be there, especially when readers are dealing with a foreign language and culture. In this textbook, the "Previewing the Article" sections provide a bridge for readers who might otherwise miss some references. The exercises following the article also help readers to notice and understand cultural allusions and idiomatic expressions.

Exercise 5: Behind the Headlines

Look through a newspaper and select four headlines. Predict the subject of each article from the information in the headline. Then read the article to find its subject. How many of your predictions were accurate? Show the results of this experiment by completing a chart like this one.

Headline	Predicted Subject	Actual Subject

Exercise 6: Make the Headlines

Cut three articles from a newspaper. Cut off and save the headlines. Trade your "beheaded" articles with a classmate's. Read the articles you receive, and write your own headlines for them. Then compare the headlines you and your partner wrote with the original ones the newspaper printed. In each pair, which headline is better? Why?

INTERNATIONAL

Herald Tribune

Published With The New York Times and The Washington Post

SECTION 1

NEWS / FEATURES

1

Families in Upheaval Worldwide

2

Kobe Quake: A Nightmare Come True

3

Scottish Village Sticks By Its Benefactor,
Crooked He May Be

4A

For Dalai Lama at 60, Bittersweet Success

4B

Mother vs. Tibetan Monks

Focus on the Newspaper: News / Features

1. Families in Upheaval Worldwide

Previewing the Article

The great Russian novelist Leo Tolstoy once said, "Happy families are all alike; every unhappy family is unhappy in its own way." Perhaps that was true in the 19th century. However, according to the following article, it isn't true today.

To be happy, every family needs two key ingredients—love and money. Both seem to be in short supply all over the globe. When marriages break up, families must deal with both emotional and financial problems. The challenge is the same on every continent. And, in most households, it is the mother who must meet that challenge.

Before You Read

Discuss these questions and do the map search.

1. What does the headline mean? Define the word *upheaval.* Does it have positive or negative connotations? Does this word imply that recent changes in family life are good or bad?

2. The world's great land masses are divided into seven continents. Point these out on a map and give their English names.

3. Scan the article for names of countries, and then point them out on a map.

4. Discuss the role(s) of women in various countries you have lived in or visited. Do many women in these countries work outside the home to support their families? Is divorce common?

As You Read

Look for facts that suggest that many fathers are irresponsible.

Families in Upheaval Worldwide

Mothers Are Carrying Increasing Responsibility

By Tamar Lewin
New York Times Service

1 NEW YORK—Around the world, in rich and poor countries alike, the structure of family life is undergoing profound changes, a new analysis of research from numerous countries has concluded.

2 "The idea that the family is a stable and cohesive unit in which father serves as economic provider and mother serves as emotional care giver is a myth," said Judith Bruce, an author of the study. "The reality is that trends like unwed motherhood, rising divorce rates, smaller households and the feminization of poverty are not unique to America, but are occurring worldwide."

3 The report, "Families in Focus," was released Tuesday by the Population Council, an international nonprofit group based in New York that studies reproductive health. It analyzed a variety of demographic and household studies from dozens of countries around the world.

Among the major findings:

4 • Whether because of abandonment, separation, divorce or death of a spouse, marriages are dissolving with increasing frequency. In many developed countries, divorce rates doubled between 1970 and 1990, and in less-developed countries, about a quarter of first marriages end by the time women are in their 40s.

5 • Parents in their prime working years face growing burdens caring for children, who need to be supported through more years of education, and for their own parents, who are living longer.

6 • Unwed motherhood is increasingly common virtually everywhere, reaching as many as a third of all births in Northern Europe, for example.

7 • Children in single-parent households—usually families with only a mother present—are much more likely to be poor than those who live with two parents, largely because of the loss of support from the fathers.

8 • Even in households where fathers are present, mothers are carrying increasing economic responsibility for children.

9 The idea that families are changing in similar ways, even in very different cultures, should bring about new thinking on social policy, experts say, and in particular on the role government should play in supporting families.

10 The Population Council report says women around the world tend to work longer hours than men, at home and on the job.

11 In studies of 17 less-developed countries, women's work hours exceeded men's by 30 percent. Data from 12 industrialized countries found that formally employed women worked about 20 percent longer hours than employed men.

12 Women's economic contributions also are becoming increasingly important.

13 In Ghana, the report said, a third of households with children are maintained primarily by women.

14 In the Philippines, women were found to contribute about a third of households' cash income, but 55 percent of household support if the economic value of their activities at home, such as gathering wood or growing food, is included.

15 In the United States, a Louis Harris survey released earlier this month found that nearly half of employed married women contribute half or more of their family's income.

16 While the reason for entering the work force may vary from country to country, women everywhere are finding that to give their children an adequate life, they must earn more money, said Ms. Bruce, one of the report's authors.

17 "In traditional Bangladesh, it may be because the husband was much older, and died while the children were still young," she said. "In sub-Saharan Africa, a woman might have a baby premaritally and have no strong connection with the father, or she might have a husband who goes on to another polygamous marriage and supports the children of that union."

18 "In Asia," she added, "the husband may have migrated for better economic opportunities and stopped sending money after a year or two. And everywhere, parents are finding that there are fewer jobs that pay enough to support a family."

19 Even among rural people in less-developed countries, Ms. Bruce said, the need for a cash income is becoming more pressing.

20 "Parents all over the world have an increasing awareness that their children will need literacy and numeracy," Ms. Bruce said. "That means that instead of having their 6 year old working with them in the fields, they have to pay for school fees, uniforms, transportation and supplies."

21 The fact that many developing countries have cut their spending for public education as part of their debt-reduction plans creates further pressure on families, she said.

22 One apparent exception to the general trends is Japan, where single-parent households and unwed motherhood have remained relatively rare.

23 The Population Council report, written by Ms. Bruce, Cynthia B. Lloyd and Ann Leonard, found that while most countries have extensive data on women as mothers, there has been little research on men as fathers.

24 But studies have found that although fathers' income usually exceeds mothers' income, women usually contribute a larger proportion of their earnings to their household, while men keep more for their personal use.

25 Collecting child support is also difficult. Among divorced fathers, three-quarters in Japan, almost two-thirds in Argentina, half in Malaysia and two-fifths in the United States do not pay child support, the report said.

I. Getting the Message

After reading the article, choose the best answer for each item.

1. According to this article, one of the main causes of family poverty is _____.
   a. the rising birth rate
   b. families supported by only one parent
   c. women who contribute very little to family income

2. The changes in family life that this article describes _____:
   a. are occurring only in poor countries
   b. are related to the rising divorce rate
   c. are likely to improve family life

3. The Population Council studied families in many countries and concluded that _____.
   a. in rich countries, nearly all children live in two-parent families
   b. family structure is changing in the same ways throughout the world
   c. in poor countries, the average woman earns more than her husband

4. The author of this article _____.
   a. does not give any personal opinions about the changes described
   b. criticizes fathers for deserting their children
   c. praises women for working so hard at home and at outside jobs

5. One important benefit of studies about families is that they _____.
   a. prove that divorce is harmful to families
   b. prove that men are lazier than women
   c. point out family problems and suggest ways government can help

6. Sending children to school nowadays _____.
   a. improves the economic situation in most families
   b. increases the economic burden upon families of school-age children
   c. has no effect upon family finances

Check your answers with the key on page 181. If you have made mistakes, reread the article to gain a better understanding of it.

II. Expanding Your Vocabulary

A. Getting Meaning from Context

Find each word in the paragraph indicated in parentheses. Use context clues to determine the meaning of the word. Choose the best definition.

1. myth (2)	a. true story	b. story that isn't true
2. dissolving (4)	a. breaking apart	b. staying together
3. exceeded (11)	a. were less than	b. were more than
4. vary (16)	a. be different	b. be the same
5. migrated (18)	a. stayed at home	b. moved away

6. pressing (19)   a. pushing against   b. urgent
7. extensive (23)   a. a little   b. a lot of
8. proportion (24)   a. percentage   b. amount

B. Using Prefixes

Study the meanings of these prefixes. Then choose the correct prefixes to complete these words from the reading. The definition of each word is given in parentheses.

co-, con- with, together   **non-, un-** not   **pre-** before
demo- people   **poly-** many   **uni-** one
ex- out of, from, beyond

1. _____hesive   (united; won't come apart)
2. _____graphics   (statistics about population)
3. _____gamous   (having many marriages)
4. _____que   (only one of a kind)
5. _____ceed   (go beyond)
6. _____wed   (not married)
7. _____profit   (doesn't make a profit)
8. _____tribute   (give a part of a whole)
9. _____marital   (before being married)
10. _____nection   (attachment, bond)
11. _____forms   (clothing that's the same for everyone in a particular group)
12. _____tensive   (a lot)

III. Making Sense of Sentences

Find each phrase in the indicated paragraph of the article. Read the whole paragraph. Then choose the statement that best conveys the meaning of the phrase.

1. *a stable and cohesive unit (2)*
   a. The family members love each other.
   b. The family will not be separated by divorce.

2. *the feminization of poverty (2)*
   a. Poverty is becoming weaker and more timid.
   b. Many more women than men are poor.

3. *rising divorce rates (2)*
   a. The number of divorces is higher now than it was in the past.
   b. A bigger percentage of couples is getting divorced now than in the past.

4. *much more likely to be poor (7)*
   a. The children don't mind being poor.
   b. The children have a greater chance of being poor.

5. *loss of support (7)*
   a. The fathers aren't giving the family any money.
   b. The fathers are seldom at home to help with child care.

6. *increasing economic responsibility (8)*
   a. Mothers are expected to be very economical, to save a lot of money.
   b. Mothers are expected to contribute more money to the family income.

7. *social policy (9)*
   a. The study encourages thinking about ways to entertain families.
   b. The study encourages thinking about ways that government can help families deal with their problems.

8. *one apparent exception (22)*
   a. It seems that single-parent households are not very common in Japan.
   b. Japan definitely does not have a lot of single-parent families.

9. *relatively rare (22)*
   a. Single-parent households are very unusual in Japan.
   b. Compared to other countries, Japan has few single-parent households.

IV. Talking and Writing

Discuss the following topics. Then choose one of them to write about.

1. At one time, women were supposed to be taken care of all their lives, first by their fathers and then by their husbands. But that also meant that they were controlled by these men. Today, in many countries, women have financial and personal independence—and the responsibility of being self-reliant. In your opinion, which way of life is better for women?

2. Once, children were a financial asset to a family because they worked from a very young age. Today, many countries have child labor laws that strictly limit the amount and type of work children can do. Children are now expected to put most of their energy toward their education. Do you think it is better for children to be only students until they finish high school or college? Or do you think that teenagers who work gain valuable experience that helps them become successful adults?

3. Worldwide, a significant number of parents are unable to give their children good educational opportunities or a childhood without deprivation. What should governments do to help families meet the basic needs of all children?

2. Kobe Quake: A Nightmare Come True

Previewing the Article

"I thought it was the end of the world," said one survivor of the 1995 earthquake in Kobe, Japan. Shortly before dawn on January 17, 1995, a ferocious, 20-second tremor shook Japan's sixth largest city. More major tremors followed. Buildings collapsed. A highway turned on its side. Gas-line leaks led to huge fires. By week's end, about 5,000 people were dead, 300,000 people were homeless, and more than 70,000 buildings were destroyed. The cost of rebuilding? Some predicted as much as $400 billion!

An earthquake is a shaking or rolling of the earth's surface. Earthquakes are caused by sudden movements of huge blocks of rock along a crack called a *fault.* Earthquakes are actually quite common. Perhaps a million of them occur every year in various parts of the world. But most earthquakes take place beneath the surface of the ocean and cause no damage.

In heavily populated urban areas such as Kobe, earthquakes cause immense destruction, suffering, and inconvenience. In addition to their direct effects (such as causing buildings to collapse), earthquakes cause a lot of problems indirectly by disrupting transportation and communication systems and sources of water and energy.

Before You Read

Discuss these questions and do the map search.

1. Find Japan on a map of the world. Why is it called an *archipelago?* Look for Kobe on a map of Japan. It is on Honshu, the largest Japanese island.

2. Share experiences that you have had in an earthquake or in other extreme weather conditions such as a hurricane, tornado, or flood.

As You Read

Make lists of the following:

1. the indirect effects of the Kobe quake (What supplies and services did people lose?)

2. reasons why Kobe was an especially bad place for an earthquake to occur

Kobe Quake: A Nightmare Come True

By T. R. Reid
Washington Post Service

1 KOBE, JAPAN—Tall pillars of flame illuminated the night sky over this major port city early Wednesday, as emergency workers battled scores of fires in the aftermath of the ferocious earthquake that killed more than 1,700 people and destroyed thousands of buildings.

2 The death toll from the first tremor that struck before dawn Tuesday and a long series of aftershocks could go above 2,000, Kobe officials said, as rescue teams continued to find bodies under the rubble of the nearly 4,000 buildings that were demolished.

3 Nearly 100,000 people spent the night Tuesday in temporary housing in schools and public buildings.

4 The national police said that 1,712 people were known dead, 985 were missing and 6,334 were injured. The tolls were expected to rise as communications were restored.

5 The earthquake was the most lethal one in this land since 1948, when a quake of 7.1 magnitude on the open-ended Richter scale killed about 3,600 people in Fukui Prefecture, north of Osaka.

6 The earthquake Tuesday, with a magnitude of 7.2, struck at 5:46 A.M. The epicenter was on the island of Awajishima, just outside Kobe Harbor in the Inland Sea. But that open, rural island reported relatively minor damage.

7 Quakes of this magnitude often trigger tsunami, or tidal waves, which can be as destructive as the quakes themselves. There were no tsunami Wednesday, perhaps because the Inland Sea is almost surrounded by land.

8 The major destruction and loss of life occurred in the urban center of Kobe, a city of about 1.5 million and the chief port of Japan's industrial heartland that is roughly at the center of Honshu, the largest Japanese island. The first tremor, which lasted about 20 seconds, collapsed roads, knocked trains off their tracks, wrecked docks and severed communications.

9 The considerably larger city of Osaka, a major financial center that borders Kobe to the east, suffered less damage. Two ancient capitals of Japan, Kyoto and Nara, both nearby and both home to many antique structures and artistic treasures, were shaken as well, and some cultural monuments were damaged.

10 The quake was barely felt in Tokyo, 450 kilometers (280 miles) to the east.

11 In Kobe, fires evidently caused by broken gas lines continued to rage in the brisk night winds nearly 24 hours after the quake hit. With water lines broken in many areas of the city, fire fighters were handicapped in their efforts to douse the flames.

12 By the light of the wind-driven fires, rescue workers could be seen digging through rubble that had once been homes. At one home, a rescue team reported hearing a child's voice shouting, "Over here! Help!" But the voice gave out before workers could dig through the collapsed roof.

13 Like many Japanese cities, Kobe has large residential districts made up of relatively weak wooden homes with heavy tile roofs. This is exactly the wrong kind of structure to be inside when an earthquake hits. Government officials said the collapse of these homes and aged apartment buildings was the main reason for the large death toll.

14 As viewed from a street in Kobe, and from television network helicopters, the earthquake left a scattered pattern of damage rather than a broad swath of destruction.

15 On one busy central Kobe street, an entire building had collapsed onto the pavement. But considerably taller buildings on each side were left standing, their windows broken but their structures otherwise apparently sturdy.

16 Some train stations emerged whole from the tremor. At the Hankyu Railroad's Itami Station, however, the station building was flattened and a huge passenger car, tossed from the tracks, lay sidewise on the fallen roof.

17 Experts said this patchwork pattern of ruin reflected changing architectural standards over the previous few decades. As a major port, Kobe was virtually leveled by Allied bombing during World War II. Much of the city's current housing stock was built in a rush just after the war, when an impoverished Japan was more interested in getting its cities rebuilt quickly than in tremor-proof architecture.

18 Over the decades, however, the Japanese have worked at earthquake damage prevention. Many of the newer buildings in Kobe evidently withstood the quakes, while older structures and a 25-year-old section of the city's main expressway toppled crazily to the ground.

19 Japan, a relatively young and unstable archipelago in geological terms, has hundreds of earthquakes every year. In Tokyo, about three dozen are felt each year, and two or three annually are so severe as to be terrifying.

20 Every school and company has yearly earthquake drills. Most public buildings have hard hats hanging on the walls in case of an earthquake. People are taught to grab a helmet, if possible, and seek protection under a desk or a door frame from falling debris.

21 The Great Kanto Earthquake of 1923—Kanto meaning the eastern plain where Tokyo stands—is remembered as one of the great disasters of this ancient country. About 140,000 people died in Tokyo and Yokohama then, some from collapsing buildings and even more from the sea of fire that broke out afterwards.

22 In recent years, though, major Japanese earthquakes have all hit in relatively unpopulated rural areas.

23 The Kobe earthquake represents Japan's worst nightmare come true: a quake of major proportions in one of the nation's teeming, tightly packed major cities.

REUTERS/BETTMANN

The Hanshin Expressway in Kobe toppled on its side from the quake. The epicenter was just outside the city's harbor.

I. Getting the Message

After reading the article, choose the best answer for each item.

1. This article was probably written _____.
   a. immediately after the earthquake occurred
   b. about 24 hours after the earthquake occurred
   c. several days after the earthquake occurred

2. The greatest amount of damage occurred _____.
   a. at the epicenter of the quake
   b. in Osaka, a major financial center
   c. in the chief port city of Japan's largest island

3. Many of the buildings that collapsed were _____.
   a. built before World War II
   b. built soon after World War II
   c. built recently

4. To protect themselves during an earthquake, people are often told to _____.
   a. jump into a nearby body of water
   b. go inside a building with a heavy roof
   c. stand under a door frame

5. The deaths and destruction in Kobe were caused by _____.
   a. one powerful tremor followed by a huge tidal wave
   b. one powerful tremor, a long series of aftershocks, and huge wind-driven fires
   c. two powerful tremors, scattered small fires, and three huge tidal waves

Check your answers with the key on page 181. If you have made mistakes, reread the article to gain a better understanding of it.

II. Expanding Your Vocabulary

A. Getting Meaning from Context

Find each word in the paragraph indicated in parentheses. Use context clues to determine the meaning of the word. Match each word with its definition.

A	B
1. _____ tremor (2)	a. causing death; fatal
2. _____ aftershocks (2)	b. tidal wave
3. _____ demolished (2)	c. broken pieces of demolished buildings
4. _____ rubble (2, 12)	d. shaking; vibration
5. _____ lethal (5)	e. size; extent; amount
6. _____ magnitude (5, 6)	f. central point of an earthquake's shock waves
7. _____ epicenter (6)	g. fell down; caved in
8. _____ tsunami (7)	h. small tremors following a major earthquake
9. _____ collapsed (8, 15)	i. destroyed; ruined

B. Comparing Words about Measurements

Choose the answer that matches each measurement.

		a.	b.
1.	three dozen	a. 36	b. 30
2.	20 seconds	a. 1/3 of a minute	b. 1/2 of a minute
3.	10 kilometers	a. 6.2 miles	b. 62 miles
4.	1.5 million	a. 150,000,000	b. 1,500,000
5.	100,000	a. one million	b. one hundred thousand
6.	a decade	a. 10 years	b. 20 years
7.	two score	a. 60 years	b. 40 years
8.	magnitude of Kobe quake	a. 7.1	b. 7.2

III. Making Sense of Sentences

Sometimes writers use figurative (unreal) comparisons to give readers a mental picture of something. Find each figurative phrase in the indicated paragraph. Reread the paragraph. Then choose the statement that best conveys the meaning of the phrase.

1. pillars of flame (1)
   a. The flames were close to the ground.
   b. The flames reached high into the sky.

2. patchwork pattern (17)
   a. The areas destroyed by the earthquake were all in one section of the city.
   b. The Kobe quake left a scattered pattern of damage.

3. sea of fire (21)
   a. The fires were low and covered a large area.
   b. The fires reached high into the sky.

IV. Talking and Writing

Discuss the following topics. Then choose one of them to write about.

1. Have you ever visited or lived on an island? If so, describe it.

2. Have you ever been the victim of weather-related damage or injury? If so, tell what happened.

3. Imagine that a severe earthquake occurred in the city you are living in now. Would conditions be similar to those in Kobe? Describe the ways in which conditions might be better or worse.

3. Scottish Village Sticks By Its Benefactor, Crooked He May Be

Previewing the Article

A tiny Scottish village seems an unlikely setting for white-collar crime. But the following story of embezzlement took place in one of the most scenic, idyllic areas in all of Europe—the Scottish Highlands. The Highlands cover the northern two-thirds of Scotland with beautiful lakes, steep valleys, and lovely mountains such as the Cairngorms, mentioned in the article.

Stories about criminals are often sad. They describe the moral decline of the villain and the suffering of the victim(s). But most readers think this article is humorous. Why? For one thing, the villain actually helped many people. Also, the story is quite ironic. (*Irony* means that what happens is the opposite of what is usual and expected.)

The following definitions will help you read the article with greater understanding:

- A *kilt* is a short, pleated plaid skirt worn by highland Scotsmen.

- *Tweed* is a coarse wool fabric woven in Scotland (or copied elsewhere).

- *Walter Mitty* is the main character in a famous short story by the American author James Thurber. In real life, Mitty is ordinary, timid, and cowardly, but in his daydreams he is a glamorous hero.

- *Scotland Yard* is the name of the metropolitan police department of London.

- *Old Bailey* is London's main criminal court building.

Before You Read

Discuss these questions and do the map search.

1. What does the headline mean? What is a *benefactor?* How does this noun relate to the verb *benefit?* What does the phrasal verb *stick by* mean? What is the meaning of *crooked* in this headline? What is the literal meaning of the word? What does a criminal mean when he says he plans to "go straight"?

2. Find Scotland on a map of Europe. What island is it on?

3. Discuss the meaning of *irony* and give some examples.

As You Read

Look for the following in the story:

1. examples of irony

2. reasons why Mr. Williams became a criminal

Scottish Village Sticks By Its Benefactor, Crooked He May Be

By John Darnton
New York Times Service

1 TOMINTOUL, SCOTLAND—On a Saturday night at The Grouse's Nest, they're still willing to raise a glass or two to "Laird Williams," though now his title prompts laughter. And now they just call him "Tony."

2 There are those in this idyllic highland village in the Cairngorms (population, 320) who say they were never quite sure about Anthony Williams, the soft-spoken, monied aristocrat who arrived in 1986 with his impeccably dressed wife, Kay.

3 And there are others who say their suspicions were aroused over time, as the 55-year-old Mr. Williams, who appeared on weekends turned out in fine tweeds or sometimes in a kilt, bought up property after property, sinking so much money into Tomintoul that he single-handedly revived it.

4 But no one could have possibly guessed the truth—that the bespectacled man with bottomless pockets and an easygoing manner was not a laird at all but a bureaucrat living out a Walter Mitty fantasy that he was a highland nobleman and paying for it by embezzling funds from Scotland Yard.

5 About two weeks ago, a repentant-looking Mr. Williams, who had worked for the Metropolitan Police since 1959 and had risen to a $65,000 position as deputy director of finance, was brought into the Old Bailey and sentenced to seven and a half years in prison.

6 Estimates are that he poured nearly $5 million of stolen money into the village and gave jobs to 43 people. And now that he has fallen upon dark days at least some villagers are sticking by him.

7 "I found him a very charming man, very friendly—no put-on about him at all," said Georgie McAllister, 70, the custodian of the local museum whose family has been farming the surrounding hills for generations. "It's hard to understand why a clever person like him would do a thing like that. It's sad. Of course, it did benefit the village. A lot of the properties were beautifully restored."

8 A few doors down the square, Donald Corr sat inside his wood-carving shop and described how suspicions began to grow. "Everyone wondered where the money was coming from. Why was he spending it in a wee little place in the highlands? He wouldn't have gotten it back in 100 years."

9 According to the court, Mr. Williams stole more than $8 million over eight years. Most of it came from a secret fund that had been placed under his sole jurisdiction and that was supposed to be used to pay informers and conduct surveillance and other undercover activities against the Irish Republican Army.

10 Instead, it went to create one more British lord.

11 Mr. Williams bought a fine brick mansion at Haslemere in Surrey. He bought a whitewashed villa with a pool in the Costa del Sol, in Spain. He bought aristocratic titles at auctions, spending $95,000 to acquire the 15th-century Barony of Chirnside and then adding on 10 more Scottish titles.

12 But most of all, he sunk his ill-gotten gains into this village that captivated his heart with its fine stone cottages, its central green, and its breathtaking view of rolling emerald fields and pine forests disappearing into the distance like the spikes of an ancient army marching over the horizon.

13 He bought cottages and fixed them up. He purchased the pub and made it into a fine place to nurse a glass of Glenlivet, distilled only 10 miles (16 kilometers) to the north. And most of all, he bought the down-at-the-heels Gordon Arms and totally renovated it, transforming it from an eyesore into a first-class hotel with 30 handsomely furnished rooms, wood-paneled staircases, false bookshelves with spines of leather and an outstanding restaurant.

14 "I would offer him three choices for glasses—a middling one, a poor one, and fine crystal. Always, he chose the crystal. Nothing but the best," said David Abdy, who was chosen by Mr. Williams to oversee the renovations and run the businesses.

15 Mr. Williams told everyone, including Mr. Abdy and including even his own wife, that he inherited the money from a rich uncle in Norway. He was caught because his bank deposits were so large they ran afoul of new anti-laundering provisions. The bank notified the police, who discovered, to their unspeakable embarrassment, that the culprit was one of their own.

16 The Metropolitan Police commissioner, Paul Condon, publicly apologized for the lax supervision of his force. Under a hastily brokered arrangement, the police will take a financial bath. Mr. Abdy, a 27-year-old entrepreneur from Sheffield, acquired most of the properties for about half a million dollars, obtaining bank loans and striking deals with various creditors to pay only a part of what they are owed.

17 In the only interview he has given since his arrest a year ago, Mr. Williams told The Times of London: "I discovered this bloody great bucketful of money. I went from the need to pay off a few debts to what can only be described as greed. There are no excuses."

I. Getting the Message

Imagine that you are the one lucky London reporter who has been able to interview the prisoner, Anthony Williams. He makes the following statements to you. Decide if each one is true (T) or false (F).

1. _____ I worked for London's Metropolitan Police Department for many years.
2. _____ My wife encouraged me to take money from the special police fund.
3. _____ I acquired one of my titles from my British ancestors.
4. _____ At first I took money just to pay my debts, not to deceive people.
5. _____ The money I spent was supposed to be used to pay spies and informers.
6. _____ Everyone in Tomintoul believed that I was a rich aristocrat.
7. _____ I wanted to revive Tomintoul because my ancestors, members of the Scottish aristocracy, came from this area of the Highlands.
8. _____ All of the money I took from the fund was spent to help the village.

Check your answers with the key on page 181. If you have made mistakes, reread the article to gain a better understanding of it.

II. Expanding Your Vocabulary

A. Getting Meaning from Context

Find each italicized word or phrase in the paragraph indicated in parentheses. Use context clues to determine the meaning of the word or phrase. Choose the best answer to complete each sentence.

1. *The Grouse's Nest* (1) is a _____.
   a. bird sanctuary
   b. pub (tavern or bar)

2. *They were never quite sure about Anthony Williams* (2) means _____.
   a. some people in town didn't know who Williams was
   b. some people in town were suspicious; they thought Williams might be a liar

3. *Embezzling* (4) means _____.
   a. stealing
   b. depositing

4. *Dark days* (6) means _____.
   a. a lot of rainy weather
   b. hard times

5. Williams stole a lot of money before he was caught. This suggests that the words *sole jurisdiction* (9) probably mean _____.
   a. Williams served on a committee that handled the money
   b. Williams was the only person handling the money in the fund

6. *Glenlivet* (13) must be _____.
   a. a popular Scottish tea
   b. an alcoholic beverage

B. Studying Vocabulary about Occupations

Find each occupation from column A in the indicated paragraph of the article. Reread the paragraph. Then match each occupation with its definition.

	A		B
1. _____	bureaucrat (4)	a.	a person who reveals information for pay
2. _____	deputy director (5)	b.	someone who guards or maintains property
3. _____	custodian (7)	c.	someone who starts or manages a business
4. _____	informer (9)	d.	an assistant to or substitute for a public officer
5. _____	commissioner (16)	e.	a government official in charge of a department or district
6. _____	entrepreneur (16)	f.	an official who follows a fixed routine without regard for its appropriateness

III. Working with Idioms and Expressions

Find each italicized expression about money in the indicated paragraph of the article. Reread the paragraph. Then answer the questions.

1. How does a person with *bottomless pockets* (4) behave?
2. If you *pour money into* (6) a project, are you spending a little or a lot?
3. What are *ill-gotten gains* (12)?
4. Is a building that looks *down-at-the-heels* (13) in good or bad condition?
5. Do *anti-laundering provisions* (15) make it easier or more difficult for embezzlers to steal money without getting caught?
6. If someone has taken a *financial bath* (16), what has happened to the person?
7. What did Anthony Williams mean by a *bloody great bucketful of money* (17)?

IV. Making Sense of Sentences

Sometimes what happens in a news or feature story is exactly the opposite of what the reader would expect. This is called *irony*. In some cases, irony is what gives a story its value as news. In other cases, the irony makes the story more powerful. A sad example of irony occurred in 1995; the American actor Christopher Reeve, who once played the movie role of Superman, was paralyzed in a horseback-riding accident.

Which of the following statements involve irony?

1. An ordinary man named Tony Williams bought some titles at auctions and became the highly respected Lord Anthony Williams.

2. An employee of a police department, Williams stole money from a police department fund he was in charge of.
3. Williams embezzled funds for several years before he got caught.
4. Williams invested millions of dollars in a run-down hotel in a tiny Scottish village.
5. Williams lied to his wife, telling her that he had inherited the stolen money.

V. Talking and Writing

Discuss the following topics. Then choose one of them to write about.

1. Discuss your feelings about Anthony Williams. Can you understand why he embezzled so much money? Do you feel sympathetic toward him? Did his punishment fit the crime? After discussing these questions, write a letter to Scotland Yard. Tell whether you think Williams should serve his full seven-year sentence or not.

2. Although his story is funny, Williams is an example of a serious social problem—the betrayal of public trust. Discuss other examples you know about.

3. When Williams gets out of prison, what kind of work could he do to earn an honest living? What skills does he have that he could use to start a new career? If you were counseling him, what occupations would you recommend?

4A. For Dalai Lama at 60, Bittersweet Success
4B. Mother vs. Tibetan Monks

Previewing the Articles

The Buddhist religion originated in India around 500 B.C. with the teachings of the first *Buddha* (enlightened or awakened one). It is difficult to calculate the world's present Buddhist population. Many people who accept some Buddhist beliefs and practice some Buddhist rituals identify themselves as members of other religious groups. Still, some population experts say that there may be as many as 300 million Buddhists worldwide.

During the 20th century, the influence of Buddhism has declined in the East because of the spread of communism and secularism. However, in Europe and America, the Buddhist influence is expanding.

The two articles in this chapter focus on Tibetan Buddhism, also called Lamaism. This form of Buddhism started in Tibet in the seventh century and eventually spread throughout the Himalayan region. For centuries, the title and the power of Tibet's Dalai Lama (high monk) were handed down from one ruler to the next. Then, in 1950 the Chinese Communists took control of Tibet. For six years, Tibet was allowed to maintain its religious and political freedom. In 1956, China began to tighten its control. In 1959, the Dalai Lama, along with thousands of his followers, fled from Tibet and set up a government in exile. The Dalai Lama's government is not recognized by other nations, but the man and his teachings have won worldwide respect and love.

Article 4B deals with a concept that is important in Buddhism and several other Eastern religions. It is *reincarnation,* the belief that the soul of a person lives on after death and enters the body of another person or animal. (The word *reincarnation* means "return to the flesh or body.") Another name for this concept is *transmigration of the soul.*

Before You Read

Discuss the questions and do the map search.

1. What do the headlines on both articles mean? (Look also at the subhead on Article 4B.)

2. What do you know about Buddhist beliefs and ways of life? Do you know any Buddhists?

3. On a map of the world, point out the following cities, countries, and mountain ranges mentioned in the articles: Tibet, China, India, Nepal, Spain, England, Beijing, New Delhi, Tokyo, the Himalayas, and the Alpujarra Mountains.

As You Read

Look for examples of "bittersweet" situations faced by both the Dalai Lama and Maria Torres.

For Dalai Lama at 60, Bittersweet Success

Reuters

1   DHARAMSALA, India—When the Dalai Lama fled across the Himalayas into exile in the face of advancing Chinese troops in 1959, little did the youthful spiritual leader know he might never see his Tibetan homeland again.

2   Now turning 60 this week, Tibet's exiled high priest is torn between the satisfaction of having encouraged the spread of worldwide interest in Buddhism and the pain of realizing that he may be the last Dalai Lama to rule in the Tibetan capital's Potala Palace, where he was brought up.

3   "While I was leaving Lhasa to the border, then at that time many of us made a calculation that things would be solved within a short period," he said in an interview at his exile headquarters at Dharamsala in the foothills of the Himalayas.

4   "But after reaching India, then we began to realize that it may take a few decades," he added with a sad smile.

5   The 60th birthday of the 14th Dalai Lama will be marked by three days of celebrations in New Delhi this week, culminating in his birthday Thursday. The religious leader, who was enthroned at the age of 4, is believed by his followers to be the reincarnation of a long line of Tibetan high priests.

6   Scientists, philosophers and human rights activists will gather for a series of symposiums on world issues, underlining the fact that although the Nobel laureate has lost a kingdom, he now has the world as his stage.

7   The Dalai Lama, who won the Nobel Peace Prize in 1989, presides over Tibetan Buddhism at a time when the religion is attracting converts in the West, including the Hollywood actors Richard Gere and Harrison Ford, the Italian soccer star Roberto Baggio and the rock singer Tina Turner.

8   The Dalai Lama fled Tibet disguised as a soldier, but he is a fervent believer in nonviolence, which he says is the only way to recover Tibet in the face of the vastly stronger Chinese.

9   "When we talk of religion, it has no national boundary," said the Dalai Lama in the interview.

10   The Dalai Lama has traveled from Washington to Tokyo to garner international support for his cause, although his government in exile remains unrecognized by any other government and Beijing remains adamant that Tibet is an integral part of China.

11   He has spent his life in exile trying to keep the Tibetan culture and religion alive, particularly during the period of the Cultural Revolution in China when monasteries across Tibet were destroyed and thousands of monks were locked up or killed.

12   Now, although the Chinese have restored some of the monasteries, he says they are often more like museums for tourists than places of worship.

13   In addition, Tibet is still rocked by periodic anti-Chinese unrest.

14   While he admits that he has failed to reach any negotiated settlement with Beijing, the Dalai Lama still hopes to return to his home one day, possibly after political liberalization in China.

15   "I feel that in a few years' time I think the situation will change," he said. "So I am hopeful."

The Dalai Lama received the first Congressional Human Rights Award on July 21, 1989, in New York City.

Mother vs. Tibetan Monks

Having a Reincarnated Lama as Son Is Maternal Trial for Spanish Woman

New York Times Service

1 BUBION, Spain—In the brilliant sunshine and crisp air of the Alpujarra mountains in southern Spain, Maria Torres gazed over the terraced rooftops of stone houses stacked on the steep slope, the home of a small Buddhist community.

2 Miss Torres, 41, a travel agent who converted to Buddhism 20 years ago, said she was worrying about her son Osel, who is 10. She is struggling with Tibetan monks, who believe the boy is a reincarnated lama, to gain more control over his upbringing.

3 "I don't care how much of a lama he is, he still needs his mother," she said. "The monks are spoiling him rotten and he is turning into a little tyrant rather than a little Buddha."

4 Osel is the fifth of Miss Torres's eight children. When he was 14 months old, the Dalai Lama, the exiled leader of Tibet, proclaimed Osel the reincarnation of Thubten Yeshe, who died in California in 1984.

5 After Miss Torres and others saw what they thought were mystical signs, Osel was brought before a panel of masters for testing. He passed all the crucial tests, including identifying dozens of objects that had belonged to Lama Yeshe.

6 "I found myself swept up on the tail of a blazing comet who was my son and my master," Miss Torres said, explaining why she had agreed to allow Osel to be taken to Nepal and India to be reared as a lama. At first his family accompanied him, but she felt that her other children were suffering and returned with them to Spain.

7 She is now divorced from Osel's father, also a Spaniard. He wants Osel to continue his monastic education in southern India, but she wants him to spend part of the year with her. She thinks he needs her and his brothers and sisters. The monks say that she can visit Osel, but that he is not yet prepared to face the temptations of Western life.

8 In recent years, Buddhism has gained Western followers, but Osel is still one of only a few Western children who have been raised for the priesthood. "I was attracted to Buddhism because of its tolerance," Miss Torres said. "But I am now learning that these monks are not tolerant. He needs to know his own country and culture and can best teach the West about Buddhism as a Westerner, not as a European-appearing Tibetan."

9 "Being a lama is not a good situation for a child," she added. "He was surrounded by adults who prostrated themselves before him. He had everything he wanted—except his family."

10 The conflict began two years ago, when she became worried by reports from other Western Buddhists who had seen him that Osel cried at night out of loneliness. After the monks decided to shorten a home visit to Spain, Miss Torres flew to India and returned with her son.

11 Once back in Spain, he had problems playing with local children, who did not treat him like a king, she said. He did not know how to share with his brothers and sisters.

12 "When you're a tyrant, you don't make friends," she said, sighing, "although the monks claim the little lamas get over being brats."

13 But when she sent Osel to visit his father, who was living in a Buddhist community in England, he whisked the child to Nepal.

14 A temporary compromise was reached, with Osel's father agreeing to live with the boy in a Tibetan monastery in southern India. Miss Torres visits him for a month a year. The monks also agreed to let him have a teacher from Spain for language, history and culture.

I. Getting the Message

A. Finding Main Ideas

Answer the following questions about article 4A.

1. What does the Dalai Lama hope to achieve?

2. What prevents the Dalai Lama from returning to Tibet?

B. Supporting an Argument

After reading article 4B, consider the statements in this chart. Which support the argument that Osel should spend more time with his family in Spain? Which suggest that he should spend nearly all his time in the monastery? Put a check (√) in the appropriate column. If a statement is irrelevant, don't check either column.

Statements about Osel's Situation	Home in Spain	Monastery in India
1. While staying in the monastery, Osel has been crying at night.	_____	_____
2. If Osel becomes a lama, he will be one of only a few Western lamas.	_____	_____
3. If Osel is educated in the West, he will be better able to teach Buddhism to people in Europe.	_____	_____
4. In the monastery, the monks are spoiling Osel.	_____	_____
5. When he lives with his family, Osel encounters many temptations of secular life.	_____	_____
6. The lamas are willing to let one of Osel's parents live with him in the monastery.	_____	_____
7. There is strong evidence that Osel is, in fact, a reincarnated lama.	_____	_____

Check your answers with the key on page 181. If you have made mistakes, reread the article to gain a better understanding of it.

II. Expanding Your Vocabulary

A. Getting Meaning from Context

Find each italicized word in the indicated paragraph of article 4A. Use context clues to determine the meaning of the word. Then choose the best definition.

1. A person living in *exile* (1) _____.
   a. lives in his native country
   b. lives outside his native country
   c. is a tourist

2. A *calculation* (3) means _____.
   a. a mathematical estimate
   b. a wild guess
   c. a promise

3. *Activists* (6) are people who _____.
   a. are physically active and athletically talented
   b. promote the teachings of a particular religion
   c. work toward achieving certain political or social goals

4. *Converts* (7) are people who _____.
   a. are very religious
   b. adopt a new religion in place of their original one
   c. disguise themselves to escape persecution

5. *Restored* (12) means _____.
   a. converted a building into a store
   b. destroyed a structure
   c. returned something to its original condition.

B. Using Words about Religion

Use one of these words about religion to complete each sentence.

convert   monastery   monk   mystical   reincarnation   temptation

1. A _____, or lama, is a person who devotes his life to religion.

2. A community of Buddhist monks is called a _____.

3. An attraction that makes people want to do something they shouldn't do is called a _____.

4. Strange experiences of a religious nature are sometimes called _____.

5. Osel was not a _____ to Buddhism. He was a Buddhist from birth because his parents had accepted Buddhism.

6. Osel passed several tests that led the lamas to believe that he was the _____ of a dead lama.

III. Working with Idioms and Expressions _____

Find each italicized phrase in the indicated paragraph of article 4B. Choose the answer that best conveys the meaning of the phrase.

1. When Maria Torres says, *"I don't care how much of a lama he is"* (3), she means that _____.
   a. it doesn't matter to her
   b. she doesn't really believe her son is a reincarnated lama

2. "The monks are *spoiling him rotten"* (3) means that _____.
   a. they are abusing him
   b. they are giving him everything he wants and making him selfish and demanding

3. When Maria Torres says that she was *"swept up on the tail of a blazing comet"* (6), she probably means that _____.

    a. it was difficult not to go along with the monks' exciting plans for her son

    b. the monks forced her to give up the boy by setting fire to her house

4. "The monks claim the little lamas *get over* being brats" (12). In this quotation, *get over* means _____.

    a. recover from

    b. continue

5. In the preceding quotation, *brats* (12) means _____.

    a. agreeable, cooperative, disciplined children

    b. children who expect to get whatever they demand

6. A child who is *raised for the priesthood* (8) is _____.

    a. lifted to a position of wealth and power

    b. brought up (reared and trained) to become a religious teacher

IV. Making Sense of Sentences

The usual question pattern in English is *helping verb—subject—main verb.*

           helping sub- main
           verb   ject verb
Example: When did you visit your son?

But when the question word is the subject of the verb, statement word order is used.

           subject   verb
Examples: Who visited your son?

                 helping main
           subject verb   verb
What is making your son cry at night?

Imagine that you are the journalist interviewing Maria Torres in order to write article 4B. What questions would you ask to get the information in each paragraph listed below?

1. paragraph 3: _____ Why do you want your child to spend less time in the monastery? ____

2. paragraphs 5–6: _____

3. paragraph 8: _____

4. paragraph 9: _____

5. paragraph 10: _____

V. Talking and Writing

Discuss the following topics. Then choose one of them to write about.

1. Although there is great diversity of ideas among the various Buddhist traditions, core teachings shared by all Buddhists include transcending a fixation on the self and practicing nonaggression, compassion, and benevolence. Discuss the meanings and practice of these four ideas.

2. What are some of the temptations of contemporary secular life? How can a person who lives in the secular world manage to resist them?

3. If you were Osel's father or mother, would you want him to become a lama? How would you deal with the problem of raising a child who is your religious superior?

Focus on the Newspaper

Most people read a daily newspaper to find out what is happening in their community, their city, their country, and around the globe. Newspapers have daily headlines and accompanying articles about the most important events affecting readers' lives. Whether it's a development in international or national politics, the success of a space mission, or the result of an important election, the news pages present the important facts on the subject.

Hard News Articles

Typically the "hard" news stories are on the front pages of newspapers. Hard or pure news stories report basic facts about an event or situation. Here are some essential characteristics that distinguish pure news articles:

- They report the facts, usually without giving the writer's viewpoint.

- They are usually short and to the point.

- They are organized to give all the important information in the first few paragraphs.

Most hard news articles follow a standard format. The lead (opening) paragraphs provide the most important information. The reader can usually answer five key "W" questions—*who, what, where, when,* and sometimes *why* or *how*—very quickly by reading the first few paragraphs. Thus, by skimming the lead, the reader can quickly get the main idea of a story and decide whether or not to read on. Objective details about the story follow the lead, in descending order of importance. The article ends with the least important information. Often, this is historical background about the people, places, or events involved in the story. These concluding paragraphs can be cut if the newspaper needs the space for another article.

Exercise 1: The News in Depth

Choose a major news article from a daily newspaper. Read the article carefully. Then analyze it by answering these questions.

ANALYZING A NEWS ARTICLE

1. Who wrote the article? In what city, state, and country did the story originate?

2. Does the article answer the five "W" questions in the first few paragraphs? What are the answers?

3. Does the article include all the information you want to know about the topic? If not, what is missing?

4. Does a photo or illustration accompany the article? If so, what information does it provide? Is it clear? Is it interesting? Does it help the reader understand the main point of the article?

5. Can you detect any slant or bias in the article, for example, in word choice or selection of facts?

6. Does the information in this article differ in any way from what you heard on the radio, saw on television, or read in another newspaper about the same event? If so, what do you think is the reason for the difference?

7. Does the article deal with a controversial issue? If so, are the opposing points of view given equal space and objective presentation? Can you tell which side the journalist favors?

8. Do you consider this article a good example of clear, objective news reporting? If not, why not?

9. What are the strengths and weaknesses of the article?

10. If an editor had asked you to write this news story, what would you have done differently?

Feature Stories

Feature stories are quite different from hard news stories in both purpose and style. News stories present, as objectively as possible, the facts about the latest news events. Feature stories have a wide range of goals. Some feature stories explain, interpret, and/or provide background. Others (such as "Scottish Village Sticks by Its Benefactor . . ." and "Mother vs. Tibetan Monks" in this book) tell of interesting, unusual occurrences that may have no great significance to the reader. Feature stories sometimes have emotional, personal, and/or humorous slants. Some are written in a distinctive style.

While some feature stories are spin-offs of major news events of the day (for example, a story analyzing the unhappy childhood of a person accused of murder), other topics reappear predictably. On any holiday or historical anniversary, newspaper readers expect to find feature stories related to that subject. In the United States, Father's Day inspires articles about famous (or infamous) fathers. In newspapers around the world, the fiftieth anniversaries of important World War II battles and bombings led to features about people who suffered through these events.

Exercise 2: Categorizing Stories as "Hard" News or Features

With a classmate, look through the first six pages of a daily newspaper. Skim the first few paragraphs of each article and decide whether it is a hard news story or a feature. Discuss what elements of the article helped you to classify it.

Exercise 3: The Feature Story in Depth

Select a feature story from your local newspaper. After reading it carefully, answer these questions.

ANALYZING A FEATURE STORY

1. What does the first paragraph accomplish? Is its main purpose to answer the five "W" questions or to attract the reader's attention?

2. Does the article end with less important, background information, or does it end with a "punch"?

3. Does this feature story relate to a news event covered elsewhere in the paper? If so, what was that event? If not, why was the story printed?

4. Can you detect the author's attitude toward the story? If so, describe it.

5. Does the article explain something that you didn't understand before? If so, what does it explain?

6. Do you have an emotional reaction to the story? Do you find it funny or sad? Does it make you angry?

7. Does the article make you want to do something, such as change your behavior in some way or become involved in a cause?

INTERNATIONAL

Herald Tribune

Published With The New York Times and The Washington Post

SECTION 2

OPINION

1
Trans-Pacific Pitching

2
Unfair Doubts about the Nanny

3
In Rush for Gold, a Rain Forest Dies

4
Six Enviro-Myths You Can Stop Believing

Focus on the Newspaper: Opinion

1. Trans-Pacific Pitching

Previewing the Article

In 1995, professional baseball was in great need of a change. After a long strike by the players that wrecked the 1994 season, delayed the start of the 1995 season, and angered the fans, the game needed new life. It came in the form of Hideo Nono, the only Japanese player to pitch in the major leagues since 1965, when Masanori Murakami pitched for the Giants.

The following editorial about Hideo Nomo first appeared in the *New York Times.* Editorials represent the collective opinion of the newspaper staff rather than the viewpoint of an individual. Some people read one newspaper instead of another because they trust the judgment of that paper's editorial board, especially at election time when the newspaper editorials endorse certain political candidates.

Before You Read

Discuss these questions.

1. Do you play baseball? What do you think of the sport? What are its strengths and weaknesses from both a player's and a spectator's point of view?

2. What do you know about the history of baseball? It is traditionally called the "national pastime" of the United States. Do you agree with this description? Is baseball popular in countries other than the United States and Japan?

3. The headline mentions *pitching.* In baseball, the *pitcher* throws the ball to the *batter,* who attempts to hit it with a bat. The pitcher is usually considered the most important player in the game. The fact that Hideo Nomo is a pitcher makes his presence in the American game even more significant. Can you name any other famous pitchers?

As You Read

Most editorials are about international, national, and local politics. This one, however, is about a sport. As you read, ask yourself why the editors thought this subject was appropriate for an editorial.

Trans-Pacific Pitching

1 Two decades after Commodore Matthew Perry forced Japan out of isolation in 1854, the Japanese started playing baseball. This year Hideo Nomo, the 26-year-old imported pitching star of the Los Angeles Dodgers, has emerged to remind Americans that Japan's long-standing baseball pretensions must be taken seriously. By instantly becoming one of the best pitchers in the National League, Mr. Nomo has enlivened and internationalized the game in a sullen year. The secret of his success may be instructive.

2 When he was pitching for the Kintetsu Buffaloes, a team based in Osaka, he led his league in strikeouts and victories. His team was rarely on television and he played in relative obscurity. His only real fame stemmed from his decision to quit and join the Dodgers. Denounced then as an ingrate and a traitor, he is today a bigger hero in Japan than he would have been had he remained. Some are claiming that his performance shows the superiority of Japanese baseball techniques.

3 With his corkscrew windup and laconic style, he comes across as an exotic messenger from the Far East. But, at the risk of sounding chauvinistic, his achievement in the United States may be testimony to American ways no less than Japanese.

4 Mr. Nomo left the Kintetsu Buffaloes after fighting openly with the manager over demands that he pitch and practice more. He thus defied the tradition that players must serve as uncomplaining samurais. That assumption dates from the early days, when the training regimen of the country's best team was nicknamed "bloody urine," because the players practiced so hard that they urinated blood.

5 In Japan, Mr. Nomo came to believe instead in the weight-training methods of Nolan Ryan and the advice of other Americans who argued that Japanese players exhaust themselves into early retirement by constant practice, even on the day before pitching in a game. In the last year, Mr. Nomo began complaining of shoulder pain. But his request to ease up was rejected gruffly by his manager.

6 Analysts who have seen Mr. Nomo play in both the United States and Japan say that he is an even better player in America because he is finally pacing himself. The Dodgers have also apparently worked on his control and got him to stop unintentionally signaling that he is about to pitch one of his devastating forkballs. So his success may be testimony to the best of both worlds.

7 Bobby Valentine, the former Texas Ranger manager who now manages the Chiba Lotte Marines outside Tokyo, has said the top 20 pitchers in Japan are all major league quality "or above." There is talk in Japan of tightening up the rules to prevent more players from defecting overseas. It may be the only instance in modern history of Japan acting to crack down on exports to America. But opening up American baseball to more players from Japan, Cuba or elsewhere would be only proper for a game that claims to culminate each year in a World Series.

—*THE NEW YORK TIMES*

I. Getting the Message

After reading the article, choose the best answer for each item.

1. The editorial maintains that _____.
   a. Nomo has not been as successful as people said he would be
   b. Nomo has benefited from American training methods
   c. Nomo is the best pitcher ever to play in American baseball

2. According to the editorial, Americans _____.
   a. have always been eager to see Japanese baseball players
   b. have been slow to acknowledge Japan's seriousness about baseball
   c. have not accepted Nomo as a serious pitcher

3. The main idea of the editorial is that _____.
   a. major league baseball should be internationalized
   b. Americans are the best baseball players
   c. the number of Japanese playing on U.S. baseball teams should be limited

4. Japanese baseball fans _____.
   a. still consider Nomo a traitor
   b. always thought of Nomo as one of the best pitchers in Japan
   c. consider Nomo a hero

5. Nomo broke with Japanese baseball tradition by _____.
   a. pitching in a unique way
   b. practicing every day
   c. complaining to his Japanese manager

6. The article implies that American training methods _____.
   a. are lax and unproductive
   b. could be improved by changing to the Japanese way
   c. permit American players to have longer careers

Check your answers with the key on page 181. If you have made mistakes, reread the article to gain a better understanding of it.

II. Expanding Your Vocabulary

Find each word in the paragraph indicated in parentheses. Then choose the best definition.

1. pretensions (1)   a. rules   b. claims
2. obscurity (2)   a. state of being obvious   b. state of being little known
3. stemmed (2)   a. developed; came   b. prevented
4. ingrate (2)   a. an ungrateful person   b. a heroic person
5. exotic (3)   a. foreign; excitingly different b. familiar
6. defied (4)   a. challenged   b. obeyed
7. gruffly (5)   a. with a rough voice   b. in a gentle way
8. devastating (6)   a. ineffective and weak   b. destructive and effective
9. defecting (7)   a. deserting a country   b. deceiving

III. Working with Idioms and Expressions

Study the meanings of these phrasal verbs and other expressions. A form of each one appears in the indicated paragraph of the article.

take seriously (1)   consider seriously
come across (3)   appear
ease up (5)   lighten or reduce pressure on something
pace oneself (6)   go at a slow steady rate
tighten up (7)   make more strict or limiting
crack down on (7)   take action on; work hard to stop
open up (7)   make available or possible

Answer these questions.

1. How does Hideo Nomo *come across* to American spectators when he pitches?

2. How did Hideo Nomo's Japanese manager react when he asked if he could *ease up* on practicing?

3. Why do some Japanese want to *tighten up* rules about players leaving Japan to play on American baseball teams?

4. According to the editorial, why should Americans *open up* their sport to players from Japan and other countries?

IV. Analyzing Paragraphs

Answer these questions about the article.

1. Paragraph 1 begins with a detail about the history of Japanese baseball. Why does an article about a Japanese pitcher begin this way?

2. Why does paragraph 2 emphasize that Nomo was not a well-known pitcher when he played in Japan?

3. Paragraph 4 states that, in complaining to his manager about his training regimen, Nomo was not serving like an "uncomplaining samurai." A *samurai* was a member of Japan's ancient warrior class. What is implied here, but not stated explicitly, about the relationship that American athletes have with their managers?

4. According to paragraph 7, why is it ironic that some Japanese want to restrict the ability of players to get jobs playing baseball in the United States?

V. Talking and Writing

Discuss the following topics. Then choose one of them to write about.

1. As this article implies, American baseball players have more independence than Japanese baseball players. Can you think of any other areas of life (in the workplace, home, or school) where Americans have what people in other countries would consider a surprising degree of independence?

2. Hideo Nomo has helped to break many Americans' stereotypes about Japanese people and Japanese baseball. Can you think of any other ways that sports help to overcome prejudice? Are there any other athletes whose role has been similar to that of Hideo Nomo?

3. This editorial never mentions World War II; nevertheless, the war is in the background. How do you think Hideo Nomo's story reflects the changing attitudes of Americans and Japanese toward each other?

2. Unfair Doubts about the Nanny

Previewing the Article

In English the word is *nanny;* in Spanish it is *niñera:* in German, *Kindersmädchen;* in Polish, *niania.* But in any language, a person who is hired to take care of young children is generally a *woman.*

This column is a personal essay about what it is like to be a male nanny, or what the author jokingly calls a "manny." With wit and insight he describes several awkward moments in his professional life. Along the way, he explores some of the assumptions people make about the proper roles of men and women.

Note: *The Hand That Rocks the Cradle* was a 1992 suspense film starring Rebecca DeMornay as a violent, mentally disturbed nanny. The author refers to this film in paragraph 8.

Before You Read

Discuss these questions.

1. What do you know about nannies? Do you know a nanny? Have you ever had a nanny or been a nanny?

2. Child care is an increasingly important problem in many families. Hiring a nanny is one solution. What are some other solutions?

3. A nanny is widely considered to be a substitute mother, not a substitute father, because fathers usually do not spend as much time with their children as mothers do. Is this pattern changing? If so, why? Do you think fathers should be involved with their children?

As You Read

Ask yourself, "What would I think if I saw the author at work in a playground or other public place? Would I feel the way the people in the article do, or would I have a different attitude?"

Unfair Doubts about the Nanny

By John Searles

1 NEW YORK—The pinched-faced woman next to me in the bread café on 67th Street wants to know how much my baby weighs. I don't tell her that he's not my baby, because I'm tired of explaining.

2 Instead, I look at Sam's doughy year-old body. I have never been good at guessing weight, but I know Sam feels awfully heavy when I lug him around the city all day.

3 "Forty pounds," I tell her, none too confidently.

4 The woman's face pinches up still more. "Forty," she says. "I don't think so. Try somewhere around 20."

5 Sam squirms in my arms and I look at my watch. Ann, his mom, is due back from her hair appointment any minute. In the meantime, I bounce Sam, sip my coffee and wait.

6 "Honestly," the woman says to her friend. "What kind of parent doesn't know how much his child weighs?"

7 I want to tell her that I'm Sam's nanny, but I don't because I'm a guy—a "manny," you might say. Whenever someone learns that I'm taking care of Sam, they turn on me—telling me not to bounce him too much or he'll throw up, asking when I last changed his diaper, demanding that I give him another bottle.

8 You would think I was Rebecca DeMornay in "The Hand That Rocks the Cradle."

9 I have two younger sisters. I was a summer camp counselor for five years. I had a girlfriend with nephews. I read "What to Expect the First Year" and "What to Expect the Toddler Years." My experience with kids is probably just as good as, if not better than, any high school sitter or au pair. Still, I'm not the one thing most everyone thinks I should be for this job—a woman.

10 When I look up, Ann is walking through the door. She kisses Sam, then looks at me. "How was he?"

11 "Fine," I tell her. "How much does he weigh?"

12 "Twenty-three pounds. Why?"

13 I slide him into his pouch, feeling the weight. "No reason," I say.

14 I'm sitting on a bench in the Bleecker Street playground, eating a Moroccan chicken salad next to four Jamaican nannies, all twice my age. Sam is now a year and a half old, big enough to cross the playground's bouncy bridge himself. I watch him and the other children jump up and down.

15 "I didn't get paid until last Thursday," one woman says. She takes a bite of her tuna sandwich. "Oliver tried to stiff me on overtime."

16 Everyone nods, sympathetically.

17 "You guys get overtime?" I ask.

18 "After 40 hours," someone says. "Don't you pay your nanny that way?" one of them asks me.

19 "No," I tell them. "I AM the nanny."

20 They stare at me suspiciously.

21 Is it really that big of a deal? Women are mechanics, truck drivers, carpenters. Why can't a man be a nanny?

22 I began watching Sam as a favor to Ann when I was in graduate school. Before I knew it, though, I slipped into the nanny position almost full time. It's a job I like, and it helped pay for school. But why does everyone have a problem with it?

23 Insulted, I toss my lunch into the trash bin and let Sam lead me to the swings. I tell him to hold tight, and back and forth he goes.

24 "How old is he?" the woman at the next swing wants to know. She has a French accent and looks way too perky to be a new mother.

25 "About 17 months," I say. "And I'm 324 months."

26 She gives me a wary smile.

27 Her baby is in the bucket swing. Big brown eyes and wild curly hair.

28 "She looks like you," I tell her.

29 "Thanks," she says. "He has your blue eyes."

30 "Oh, no. He's not mine. I'm his nanny."

31 She keeps pushing her baby, unfazed. "A male nanny," she says. "How unique."

32 We look at the children, and I feel better. Across the playground, a girl in a denim jump suit falls off the bottom of the slide and bursts into tears. One of the nannies I lunched with rushes over and picks her up and brushes pebbles from her knees.

33 "Do you think she's all right?" I ask.

34 "She's fine," the French woman says. "Kids fall all the time."

35 But then Sam lets go of the swing. He does a somersault in the air and lands face down in the dirt.

36 "Sam!" I scream.

37 "My goodness," the woman says. I pick him up and wipe the dirt from his face. He looks like he is going to cry but laughs instead.

38 "You know," she says. "If you're going to take care of him, you really should be more careful."

39 Sam is almost 2 now. I've decided to go to his mother with my problem. We are riding the subway uptown. Ann is getting off at 42d Street. Sam and I are headed for the Central Park Zoo. Over the roar of the train, I ask, "What are the reasons you picked me to watch Sam?"

40 "What kind of question is that?" Ann says.

41 "I'm just wondering."

42 "Because he loves you," she says. "You make him laugh. You sing 'The Noble Duke of York' with him and 'I Know an Old Lady.' You read 'Where's Spot?' and 'Goodnight Moon' a thousand times."

43 "But I don't know how much he weighs. And I never can keep track of how many months old he is."

44 "So what?" she says. "I trust you. Besides, you guys are great friends."

45 At Times Square, the train comes to a stop. The doors open and Ann stands to get off. "Have fun, you guys," she calls back.

46 Sam and I wave out the window as she is swept into the crowd. The train picks up speed and Sam shouts, "All aboard!"

47 Next to us, an old woman is laughing. "What's his name?" she wants to know.

48 "Sam." I start to tell her that I'm his nanny, but then I remember what Ann just said.

49 "I'm his best friend," I say.

Mr. Searles is a New York writer and manny. He contributed this comment to The Washington Post.

I. Getting the Message

After reading the article, indicate if each statement is true (**T**) or false (**F**).

1. _____ The author believes that men should not work as nannies.

2. _____ The author believes he is a good nanny because he is a father himself.

3. _____ Most people the author meets seem to think that his occupation is very odd.

4. _____ Some people assume that he is Sam's father because he is a man.

5. _____ Ann thinks the author is a good companion for Sam because of his experience working with other children.

6. _____ One reason Sam likes the author is because the author has a good sense of humor.

7. _____ The author thinks he is good at what he does, but he feels irritated by the reactions of other people.

8. _____ The author is probably happy with Ann's answer to his questions about why she picked him to watch Sam.

Check your answers with the key on page 181. If you have made mistakes, reread the article to gain a better understanding of it.

II. Expanding Your Vocabulary

A. Getting Meaning from Context

Find each word or phrase in the paragraph indicated in parentheses. Use context clues to determine the meaning of the word or phrase. Then choose the best definition.

1. pinched (1)
   a. thin and tight
   b. attractive and pleasant

2. doughy (2)
   a. strong
   b. soft and heavy

3. lug (2)
   a. carry with difficulty
   b. carry a short distance

4. squirms (5)
   a. twists and turns
   b. falls asleep

5. au pair (9)
   a. experienced pre-school teacher
   b. live-in babysitter from a foreign country

6. pouch (13)
   a. a small stroller
   b. a kind of bag

7. overtime (15)
   a. pay for work past regular hours
   b. pay for vacation days

8. suspiciously (20)
   a. doubtfully
   b. excitedly

B. Defining Useful Vocabulary

Match each word with its definition.

	A		B
1. _____	toss	a.	watchful
2. _____	perky	b.	not disturbed
3. _____	wary	c.	throw lightly
4. _____	unfazed	d.	cheerful and confident
5. _____	somersault	e.	not like anything else
6. _____	unique	f.	a complete turn, end over end

C. Practicing Useful Vocabulary

Complete the sentences with words from column A of exercise B.

1. Letting go of the swing, Sam did a _____ in the air.

2. Few people are _____ when the author announces that he is a nanny.

3. The author is used to getting _____ looks from people who have never seen a male nanny.

4. The author is in the _____ situation of being a man in a female profession.

III. Working with Idioms and Expressions _____

Study the meanings of these idioms and expressions. A form of each one appears in the indicated paragraph of the article.

due back (5)   expected to return
get paid (15)   receive payment for work
that big of a deal (21)   such an important matter
have a problem with (22)   object to
back and forth (23)   in one direction and then the opposite direction
head for (39)   go toward
keep track of (43)   remember
get off (45)   leave (a train, airplane, elevator, etc.)
sweep into (46)   push into

Complete these sentences using the idioms and expressions.

1. As Sam swang _____, he unexpectedly fell to the ground.

2. The author found it difficult to _____ Sam's age and weight.

3. Ann was _____ from her hair appointment soon, so the author waited with Sam in the café.

4. Many people seem to _____ the author's job.

IV. Focusing on Style and Tone

This column is a nonfiction opinion essay that questions the assumptions people make about gender roles and the care of children. But, like many nonfiction writers, the author borrows some techniques from fiction to make his point more vivid and convincing. In this article, the author creates three dramatic scenes: in a café, at a playground, and on the subway. Each scene contains the important fiction elements of dialogue, character, and tension.

What is the author trying to show about the following characters and their attitudes?

1. the "pinched-faced" woman (in the café)
2. the French woman (at the playground)
3. Ann (on the subway)

V. Talking and Writing

Discuss the following topics. Then choose one of them to write about.

1. Do you think a man could be a good nanny? Why or why not? If you had to hire a nanny, would you consider a man for the job?

2. If you are a man, would you consider becoming a nanny? Why or why not?

3. Can you think of any professions other than child care that are dominated by women? Could men perform the work as well as women?

4. Near the end of the article, the author tries to get help from his employer to solve his "problem." What exactly is the problem? What is the solution? Do you think it is a good solution?

3. In Rush for Gold, a Rain Forest Dies

Previewing the Article

We usually think of the destruction of Native American tribal culture in South America as something that happened long ago, in the age of the 16th-century Spanish invaders. At that time, the armies of the gold-seeking *conquistadores* (conquerors) overpowered the Indians, sometimes enslaving or killing them, always pressuring them to accept European customs and beliefs.

But in this alarming article, the authors maintain that some of these same practices continue today. They argue that gold-mining companies are destroying tribal cultures in the Venezuelan and Brazilian rain forest. According to the authors, strip mining—a form of mining in which the surface of the land is torn away to obtain the gold underneath—threatens not only rare plant and animal species, but also precious and unique aspects of the human species.

The following historical information will help you read the article with greater understanding:

- *Sir Walter Raleigh* (1552–1618) was an English colonizer and writer.
- *El Dorado* was a mythical city of great wealth sought by 16th- and 17th-century explorers in the New World.
- *Hernán Cortés* (1485–1547) was the Spanish conqueror of the Aztecs in Mexico.
- *Francisco Pizarro* (1475–1541) was the Spanish conqueror of the Incas in Peru.

Before You Read

Discuss these questions.

1. What do you know about the first Europeans who came to the Americas after Columbus? What kind of relationship did they have with the Native American tribes?

2. Countless plants, animals, and humans lose their homes and their ability to survive when a rain forest is destroyed. In addition to these immediate effects, many scientists say that destruction of the rain forest can, over a period of many years, produce something called *global warming.* What is global warming? What causes it?

3. This article mentions the questionable relationship between some anthropologists and the tribes they are studying. Have you ever taken a class in anthropology? Can you name any famous anthropologists?

As You Read

This article appeared on the "Op-Ed" (opinion and editorial) page of the newspaper. The authors of the article are presenting a controversial opinion. As you read the article, ask yourself whether their arguments are convincing. Which parts of the article seem strong? Which parts seem weak? Why?

In Rush for Gold, a Rain Forest Dies

By Leda Martins and Patrick Tierney

1 PITTSBURGH—Four hundred years ago this month, Sir Walter Raleigh landed near the mouth of the Orinoco River, in what is now Venezuela, searching for the fabled city of El Dorado.

2 He predicted that the rugged lands he surveyed contained more "gold than either Cortés found in Mexico or Pizarro in Peru." He was right (or geology imitates art).

3 The Venezuelan government estimates that $90 billion in gold—perhaps 10 percent of the planet's reserves—lies in the Guiana Highlands of Brazil and Venezuela.

4 Although Raleigh never found El Dorado, more than 60 North American, European, Japanese and South African mining companies have picked up where he left off.

5 They have joined the Guiana Gold Rush, and are destroying the home of the last unassimilated Indian tribes in the New World and one of the planet's richest rain forests.

6 These companies are trampling the rights of Venezuela's Pemón Indians, like those from the village of Uaiparu, whose hunting and fishing lands were taken over by YellowJack Resources, a Canadian concern.

7 When Pemóns from another village, accompanied by three German reporters, went to investigate the site, a YellowJack employee offered to shove their car off a cliff with his tractor.

8 Since 1991, the Corporación Venezolana de Guayana, the agency of the Venezuelan state that oversees the forest, has handed out more than 3.5 million acres (1.4 million hectares) in mining concessions.

9 Lawyers in the country's attorney general's office call the corporation an illegal, carpetbagging entity that violates Venezuelan mining and environmental laws. The state's governor has also condemned the corporation, and it is under a congressional investigation.

10 Robert Friedland, the former principal owner of the Summitville gold mine in Colorado, has gone to Venezuela with $50 million he raised on the Vancouver stock market.

11 Summitville, which went bankrupt in 1992, is a toxic mess—a lake of cyanide, a ruined river and a polluted reservoir—that will cost more than $100 million to clean up.

12 Since 1993, Mr. Friedland has been vice president of Minas Guariche, a strip-mining operation that, ironically, is partly owned by the Venezuelan explorer and naturalist Charles Brewer-Carias, a highly respected research associate at the University of California and the New York Botanical Gardens.

13 Mr. Brewer has a reputation in North America as a savior of the Yanomami Indians, yet he has been running open-pit mines on more than 12,000 acres in the environmentally protected headwaters of the Cuyuni River. The Venezuelan police charged that in 1984 he was using unsalaried Miquiritares Indians in illegal mining operations in the Amazon forests.

14 "Brewer destroys not only nature but also the men who work for him," said Sergio Milano, an anthropologist and retired police official who carried out the investigation, referring to the loss of cultural identity among Indians who work the mines.

15 A Venezuelan congressional commission said that Mr. Brewer had used scientific expeditions as a cover for illegal mining. He has brought anthropologists from the University of California to the last uncontacted cluster of aboriginal villages in the Amazon without quarantine precautions or medical follow-up.

16 Three Venezuelan Air Force colonels asserted that these trips were "to extract gold."

17 Venezuela's assistant attorney general for indigenous affairs, Joséfa Camargo, said that the expeditions were conducted without the knowledge or permission of Venezuela's Indian affairs agency, as required.

18 A court is looking into the accusations, but no details of the inquiry have been released.

19 There is a reasonable way to tap the region's wealth. Strip mining the fragile soil clogs rivers with silt and creates pits of stagnant, malaria-producing water. But some gold deposits are in bedrock and can be removed with less damage if the work is done by companies that respect the forest and the indigenous people. Before more mining takes place, however, the Indians' rights to the land and minerals must be recognized.

20 This approach should also be tried in Brazil, particularly in the lands of the Macuxi Indians around Mount Roraima, the highest of the Guiana tabletops.

21 The ancestors of the Macuxi had the misfortune to welcome Sir Walter Raleigh. Since then they have paid a terrible price in invasions, epidemics and postponed promises. On the sad anniversary of the New World's oldest gold crusade, the Macuxi and the Pemón should be protected and given their lands.

Leda Martins, a Brazilian journalist, and Patrick Tierney, author of the forthcoming "Last Tribes of El Dorado: The Gold Wars in the Amazon Forest," contributed this comment to The New York Times.

I. Getting the Message

A. Finding Main Ideas

After reading the article, choose the best answer for each item.

1. This article is mainly about _____.
    a. gold-mining methods in the rain forest
    b. the fascinating culture of the Pemón Indians
    c. the destruction of something valuable because of greed

2. The Guiana Gold Rush is the creation of _____.
    a. one powerful U.S. company
    b. many companies from all over the world
    c. an illegal corporation in Brazil

3. The authors believe that the illegal mining in Venezuela _____.
    a. is both encouraged by a state agency in Venezuela and fought by the Venezuelan attorney general's office
    b. is not as extensive as the Venezuelan attorney general's office thinks
    c. would end if a massive education program were started for the Indian tribes

4. The authors think Charles Brewer-Carias _____.
    a. has a well-deserved reputation as a friend of Indian people
    b. uses his reputation to exploit Indian people
    c. is the only one currently using safe and sensible methods of gold mining

5. The authors believe that _____.
    a. no one should mine gold in the area
    b. gold should be mined in a different, safer way
    c. only Indian tribes have the right to strip-mine

6. The Native American tribes mentioned in the article are special because _____.
    a. they know how to get and maintain political power
    b. they have great economic power based on gold mines
    c. they are the last groups of native people who have had no significant contact with people from outside their land

B. Studying the Structure

Answer the following questions.

1. Reread the title. Does it seem appropriate for this article? Why or why not?
2. A *thesis statement* is a one-sentence statement of the main point of an article. Not all essays contain a thesis statement, but this one does. It is the last sentence of the article. Why did the authors put their thesis statement at the end of the article?
3. Reread the first few paragraphs of the article. Is this a strong beginning? Why or why not?

Check your answers with the key on page 181. If you have made mistakes, reread the article to gain a better understanding of it.

II. Expanding Your Vocabulary _____

Find each word in the paragraph indicated in parentheses. Use context clues to determine the meaning of the word. Choose the best definition.

1. rugged (2) a. strong; independent b. rough; harsh

2. unassimilated (5) a. not absorbed or taken in b. poor

3. trampling (6) a. helping; aiding b. crushing; destroying

4. carpetbagging (9) a. coming from the outside and cheating the local people b. investing in illegal stocks and bonds

5. cluster (15) a. group b. large city

6. quarantine (15) a. isolation to prevent spread of disease b. military defense

7. indigenous (17) a. native to a region b. criminal

8. fragile (19) a. fertile b. easily destroyed or broken

9. clogs (19) a. blocks up b. widens and deepens

III. Working with Idioms and Expressions _____

Study the meanings of these phrasal verbs. A form of each verb appears in the indicated paragraph of the article.

pick up (4)   continue
leave off (4)   stop
take over (6)   get control of; acquire
hand out (8)   give out; distribute

go bankrupt (11)   lose all one's money
carry out (14)   accomplish; complete
look into (18)   investigate
take place (19)   happen

Complete these sentences using the phrasal verbs. Be sure to use the correct form of each verb.

1. Some mining companies have _____ the land and rights of the Macuxi and Pemón Indians.

2. One owner of a mining company is accused of trying to establish a gold-mining operation in Venezuela because his U.S. company_____ .

3. The authors believe that one Venezuelan state agency has _____ too much land to the mining companies.

4. According to the authors, too much unrestricted gold mining has already been _____ by irresponsible foreign companies.

IV. Making Sense of Sentences ————————————————

In many sentences in this article, the word *that* introduces a noun clause or an adjective clause. A *noun clause* is the object of a verb. For example, in paragraph 16, the clause beginning with *that* is the object of the verb *asserted:*

> Three Venezuelan Air Force colonels asserted *that these trips were "to extract gold."*

An *adjective clause* acts like an adjective that directly follows the noun it describes. For example, in paragraph 19, the clause beginning with *that* describes the noun *companies:*

> But some gold deposits are in bedrock and can be removed with less danger if the work is done by companies *that respect the forest and the indigenous people.*

In each indicated paragraph, find a clause beginning with *that*. If it is a noun clause, write NC and the verb that it follows as the object. If it is an adjective clause, write AC and the noun it describes.

Paragraph	*That* clause	Type	Noun or Verb
2	that the rugged lands he surveyed contained more "gold than either Cortés found in Mexico or Pizarro in Peru"	NC	predicted
3			
8			
9			
11			
13			

V. Talking and Writing ————————————————

Discuss the following topics. Then choose one of them to write about.

1. Are there any other areas of the world where tribal cultures are endangered by Western technological culture? How can this kind of conflict be resolved?

2. This article is an example of the saying, "Money is the root of all evil." Can you think of any other examples of how greed affects humans and their environment?

4. Six Enviro-Myths You Can Stop Believing

Previewing the Article

How much do people really understand about the environmental crisis?

Not much, according to the writers of this column. People know that there is a crisis—that the environment is becoming endangered at an alarming rate. However, their understanding is confused by mistaken ideas. Many of these ideas come from television and radio, which often present information in extremely shortened form. Because the information is not presented in context, truth is often distorted. This article attempts to replace some common "enviro-myths," false ideas about the environment, with "enviro-facts."

The authors did their research well, so they understand their audience, the reader. The title of the column refers to six myths that "*you* can stop believing," because the authors have talked to many people about environmental issues. They know that most readers probably believe these myths. With good research and an understanding of what readers already know about a topic, an opinion article can be convincing.

Before You Read

Discuss these questions.

1. Quickly find and read the six short "enviro-myths" printed in italics. Do you think these statements are true? Why or why not?

2. What do you already know about the problem of pollution of the environment? Do you think government and industry are doing enough to fight the problem?

3. If you wanted to know more about the environmental crisis, how would you research the topic? Where can you find reliable news on a daily basis?

As You Read

This article deals mainly with widespread but *false* ideas about the environment. As you read, try to discover what the authors believe to be the *true* environmental problems of our earth.

Six Enviro-Myths You Can Stop Believing

By Robert M. Lilienfeld and
William L. Rathje

1 ANN ARBOR, Michigan—We recently participated in an environmental festival at the Mall of America in Bloomington, Minnesota, the largest indoor shopping center in America. After speaking with thousands of parents, children and teachers, we were appalled at the public's wealth of environmental misunderstanding.

2 We were equally chagrined by the superficiality of what we heard, and have coined a new term for this type of sound-bite-based, factoid-heavy understanding: eco-glibberish. Here are half a dozen examples.

3 *One: Recycling is the key.*

4 Actually, recycling is one of the least important things we can do, if our real objective is to conserve resources.

5 Remember the phrase "reduce, reuse and recycle"? Reduce comes first for a good reason: It's better not to create waste than to have to figure out what to do with it. And recycling, like

any other form of manufacturing, uses energy and other resources while creating pollution and greenhouse gases.

6 Rather, we need to make products more durable, lighter, more energy efficient and easier to repair rather than to replace. Finally, we need to reduce and reuse packaging.

7 *Two: Garbage will overwhelm us.*

8 The original garbage crisis occurred when people first settled down to farm and could no longer leave their campsites after their garbage grew too deep. Since then, every society has had to figure out what to do with discards. That something was usually unhealthy, odiferous and ugly—throwing garbage in the streets, piling it up just outside of town, incorporating it into structures or simply setting it on fire.

9 Today we can design history's and the world's safest recycling facilities, landfills and incinerators. America even has a glut of landfill capacity, thanks to the fact that we have been building large regional landfills to replace older, smaller local dumps.

10 The problem is political. No one

wants to spend money on just getting rid of garbage or to have a garbage site in the backyard. The obvious solution is to stop generating so much garbage in the first place. Doing so requires both the knowledge and the self-discipline to conserve energy and do more with less stuff.

11 *Three: Industry is to blame.*

12 No, it's all people's fault. Certainly industry has played a significant role in destroying habitats, generating pollution and depleting resources. But we are the ones who signal to businesses that what they are doing is acceptable—every time we open our wallets.

13 And don't just blame industrial societies. In his recent book "Earth Politics," Ernst Ulrich von Weizsäcker wrote that "perhaps 90 percent of the extinction of species, soil erosion, forest and wilderness destruction and also desertification are taking place in developing countries." Thus, even non-industrialized, subsistence economies are creating environmental havoc.

14 *Four: The earth is in peril.*

15 Frankly, the earth doesn't need to be saved. Nature doesn't give a hoot if

Recycling is a good habit, but it is not the key to solving our environmental problems.

human beings are here or not. The planet has survived cataclysmic changes for millions upon millions of years. Over that time, it is widely believed, 99 percent of all species have come and gone while the planet has remained.

16 Saving the environment is really about saving our environment—making it safe for ourselves, our children and the world as we know it. If more people saw the issue as one of saving themselves, we would probably see increased motivation and commitment to actually doing so.

17 *Five: Packaging is the problem.*

18 If you were to examine a dumpster of garbage from the 1950s and a dumpster of garbage from the 1980s, you would find more discarded packaging in the first one. Packaging has actually decreased as a proportion of all solid wastes—from more than half in the 1950s to just over one-third today.

19 One reason is that there was more of other kinds of wastes (old appliances, magazines, office paper) in the 1980s. But the main causes were two changes in the packaging industry.

20 First, the heavy metal cans and glass bottles of the 1950s gave way to far lighter and more crushable containers—about 22 percent lighter by the 1980s. At the same time, many metal and glass containers were replaced by paper boxes and plastic bottles and bins, which are even lighter and more crushable.

21 Second, the carrying capacity of packages—the quantity of product that can be delivered per ounce of packaging material—increased hugely. Glass, for example, has a carrying capacity of 1.2, meaning that 1.2 fluid ounces of milk or juice are delivered for every ounce of glass in which they are contained. Plastic containers have a carrying capacity of about 30.

22 *Six: Americans are wasting more.*

23 The myth has it that Americans are overconsumers, since the per capita creation of solid waste continues to climb. Each person generates about 4.4 pounds of garbage a day—a number that has been growing steadily. The implication is that we partake in an unstoppable orgy of consumption.

24 In reality, increases in solid waste are based largely on the mathematics of households, not individuals. That is because regardless of the size of a household, fixed activities and purchases generate trash.

25 As new households form, they create additional garbage. Think about a couple going through a divorce. Once there was one home. Now there are two. Building that second house or condo used lots of resources and created lots of construction debris.

26 Where once there was one set of furniture, one washing machine and one refrigerator, now there are two. Each refrigerator contains milk cartons, meat wrappers and packages of mixed vegetables. Each pantry contains cereal boxes and canned goods.

27 Census Bureau numbers tell this story: From 1972 to 1987, the U.S. population grew by 16 percent, while the number of households grew by 35 percent. Municipal solid waste increased by 35 percent, too.

28 If Americans were really creating more trash by overindulging, we would be spending more on trash-generating items: nondurable goods like food and cosmetics. These all generate lots of garbage, since they are used and discarded quickly, along with their packaging. But household expenditures for nondurable goods, as measured in constant dollars, declined slightly from 1972 to 1987.

29 Yes, the earth's resources are finite; habitats are being destroyed; bio-diversity is declining; consumption of resources is expanding. But we must be less willing to accept glib, ideological pronouncements of right and wrong, cause and effect. To truly change the world for the better, we need more facts, not simply more faith.

The writers publish "The ULS Report" (for Use Less Stuff), a newsletter about preventing waste. They contributed this comment to The New York Times.

I. Getting the Message

After reading the article, choose the best answer for each item.

1. At an "environmental festival," the authors discovered that _____.
   a. many people have a good understanding of environmental pollution
   b. many people are not interested in environmental problems
   c. many people misunderstand environmental issues

2. The authors say recycling isn't the key to saving our environment because _____.
   a. reducing garbage is more important
   b. recycling is of no importance
   c. it is more important to start new landfills

3. The problem of garbage disposal _____.
   a. is a new one caused by technology
   b. is as old as human settlements
   c. cannot be solved

4. The main cause of damage to the environment is _____.
   a. faulty packaging
   b. the automobile industry
   c. all people

5. The authors believe that the earth itself is not in danger because _____.
   a. worldwide pollution is decreasing
   b. recycling is working
   c. the earth survives changes that destroy individual species

6. According to the authors, underdeveloped countries _____.
   a. don't damage the environment
   b. damage the environment a great deal
   c. will damage the environment when they become industrialized

Check your answers with the key on page 181. If you have made mistakes, reread the article to gain a better understanding of it.

II. Expanding Your Vocabulary

A. Getting Meaning from Context

Find each word in the paragraph indicated in parentheses. Use context clues to determine the meaning of the word. Choose the best definition.

1. appalled (1)	a. shocked	b. encouraged	
2. chagrined (2)	a. disappointed	b. helped	
3. superficiality (2)	a. great intelligence	b. shallowness; lack of thoroughness	
4. overwhelm (7)	a. be valuable to	b. overpower	
5. discards (8)	a. things thrown away	b. important possessions	
6. odiferous (8)	a. looking attractive	b. smelling bad	
7. glut (9)	a. too much of something	b. too little of something	
8. generating (12)	a. creating	b. calculating	

B. Matching Opposites

Match each word with its opposite.

	A		B
1. _____	havoc	a.	manufacture
2. _____	depleting	b.	objective; factual
3. _____	cataclysmic	c.	carefully considered
4. _____	overindulging	d.	order
5. _____	ideological	e.	increasing
6. _____	glib	f.	controlling or limiting consumption
7. _____	nondurable	g.	very fortunate
8. _____	consumption	h.	lasting

C. Practicing Useful Vocabulary

Complete these sentences with words from column A of exercise B.

1. The environmental _____ created in economically poor countries includes destruction of forests and other habitats, erosion, and extinction of species.

2. Some manufacturers are _____ the earth's natural resources, but they are not the only ones to blame for the environmental crisis we all face.

3. Political, _____ thinking is not very helpful when trying to find clear, practical solutions to environmental problems.

4. _____ our appetite for consumer goods can only make the environmental problem worse.

III. Working with Idioms and Expressions _____

Study the meanings of these idioms, expressions, and terms related to the science of ecology. A form of each one appears in the indicated paragraph of the article.

Idioms

coin a term (2)   make up a new word
figure out (5 & 8)   conclude; decide
settle down (8)   live in one place
give a hoot (15)   care about
go through (25)   experience; live through

Expressions

factoid-heavy (2)   containing much false information that is presented as fact
eco-glibberish (2)   nonsensical but smooth-sounding talk about ecological problems
per capita (23)   by each individual person

Ecological Terms

greenhouse gases (5)   gases such as carbon dioxide that heat the earth's atmosphere in a potentially dangerous way
landfills (9)   areas of land covered with layers of garbage and soil
desertification (13)   creation of desert areas
subsistence economies (13)   economic systems in which people produce only enough for basic survival
biodiversity (29)   the existence of many species of plants and animals in an environment

Complete these sentences using the idioms, expressions, and ecological terms.

1. Because of _____, many areas of the world where plants once grew are now unusable by human beings.

2. As soon as human beings began to _____, they began to produce garbage.

3. People must learn to preserve the kind of environments that support human life, because nature itself doesn't _____ about whether the human race survives or not.

4. _____ are just as much to blame for the destruction of the environment as the economic systems of richer nations.

IV. Analyzing Paragraphs _____

Newspaper paragraphs are usually shorter than paragraphs in magazines, nonfiction books, and textbooks. A standard paragraph in an essay contains a stated or implied topic sentence and several sentences of development. But newspaper paragraphs often contain only two or three sentences.

The reason for this is that narrow newspaper columns make an essay-length paragraph look long and uninviting. Newspaper editors wish to highlight ideas so that articles can be read quickly. Paragraphs 3–6 of this article, which discuss enviro-myth one, might be combined into one paragraph in a book.

Consider the discussions of enviro-myths one, two, three, and four as single paragraphs. Write a summary of the main idea (a topic sentence) for each "paragraph" in your own words.

1. *Recycling is the key.* (paragraphs 3–6)

   Main idea: __Reducing garbage and reusing packaging are more important than recycling.__

2. *Garbage will overwhelm us.* (paragraphs 7–10)

   Main idea: _____

3. *Industry is to blame.* (paragraphs 11–13)

   Main idea: _____

4. *The earth is in peril.* (paragraphs 14–16)

   Main idea: _____

V. Talking and Writing _____

Discuss the following topics. Then choose one of them to write about.

1. Do you think the news media—television, newspapers, and radio—often present a false picture of important issues? Can you think of some examples?

2. In your opinion, what is the most important ecological issue in the area where you live? What can be done to improve the situation?

3. Sometimes it is hard to get reliable information on an issue because so many sources of information are *biased*—that is, they are not objective because they have interests to protect. What competing interests are involved in environmental issues?

Focus on the Newspaper

News stories are *objective* and do not overtly express a viewpoint. However, most newspapers have special pages reserved for presenting *subjective* material. These *opinion* pages contain several types of articles.

- **Editorials** express the opinions of the newspaper's editorial board and of other journalists who write for the paper. Often a newspaper is known for having a certain political slant. For example, it may tend to favor a particular political party, or it may generally agree with a conservative or liberal outlook. This slant, or viewpoint, is usually expressed in the newspaper's editorials.

  Where can you find editorials? They are printed on a page called the editorial page, which is usually located toward the back of the paper's first section. Editorials are printed below the newspaper's *masthead* (which includes the name of the paper, its publisher, and its editors). Most editorials are printed without bylines.

- **Letters to the Editor** also appear on the editorial page in most papers. They are submitted by readers who want to state their views on public affairs. These letters often respond to news and opinion pieces that have previously appeared in the paper. Sometimes they tell "the other side of the story" or correct the paper's errors.

- **Columns** are written under a byline and express a certain writer's point of view, not necessarily the opinion of the paper's editorial board. Big-city newspapers commonly carry the work of several columnists with somewhat different perspectives or areas of interest. *Syndicated* columnists have their columns published in many different papers at the same time. Guest columnists often include people who are not journalists but who have expertise in some field currently in the news. They present explanations and opinions about matters of current concern.

- **Political cartoons** use art to express a point of view on issues in the news.

The newspaper does not limit all expressions of opinion to the opinion pages. The editorial pages deal mainly with major news events and government actions. Opinions on other matters are scattered throughout the newspaper. **Reviews** provide evaluations of new books, plays, concerts, movies, and art exhibits. (Reviews will be discussed further in the Arts/Entertainment section.) Many people read newspaper reviews before deciding how to spend their leisure time. **Columns** in the business, sports, and other sections provide analyses, opinions, and predictions. Thus, newspapers provide opinions on many facets of life—including politics, finance, culture, entertainment, athletics, and more.

Editorials and Columns

While a headline in the news section might read "New Government Bill on Education," the opinion section would contain articles that evaluate the new education bill. A headline in the opinion section might read "Revisions Needed to Make Education Policy Effective." The headline and the accompanying article present a *judgment* on the event. They take a position on the issue in the news. Taking a clear position on an issue is what distinguishes opinion articles from other articles in a newspaper.

Sometimes opinion pages present opposing views on the same news event: "Bad Planning on Education Policy" one article may read, while another may say "New Education Bill a Good First Step." This helps readers see both sides of an issue and perhaps clarify their own ideas on the topic.

Exercise 1: What's the Opinion?

Analyze an editorial or column by answering these questions.

ANALYZING AN EDITORIAL OR COLUMN

1. Who wrote the article? Does it express the opinion of an individual or of the newspaper? How do you know?

2. What key words in the headline or first paragraph let you know the opinion expressed in the article?

3. What issue is discussed in the article?

4. Is the scope of the issue local, national, or international?

5. What is the opinion of the newspaper or the columnist about the issue?

6. What reasons does the newspaper or columnist give to support the position taken?

7. What is your opinion on the issue?

Letters to the Editor

The Letters to the Editor section provides readers with a place to express their ideas on issues in the news or on the opinions expressed in the newspaper.

Exercise 2: What Are People Talking About?

Look at current issues of a newspaper for letters to the editor. List three issues that currently interest people, judging from the letters to the editor.

Exercise 3: Get in the News

Write a short letter to the editor. Choose a subject in the news about which you have an opinion. Remember to express a clear main idea and provide reasons to support your opinion.

Political Cartoons

A political cartoon illustrates some aspect of a political issue, often in simplified terms. These cartoons can be very effective in dramatizing an issue. One device commonly used in political cartoons is *caricature,* in which the physical features of a person in the news are exaggerated.

Exercise 4: A Picture Is Worth a Thousand Words

Find a political cartoon in a recent newspaper. Answer these questions.

ANALYZING A POLITICAL CARTOON

1. Who drew the cartoon?

2. Who or what is pictured in the cartoon?

3. Is there a caption on the cartoon? Do the characters say anything? How do the words help you understand the cartoon?

4. What issue is presented in the cartoon?

5. What position does the cartoonist take on the issue?

6. Is the cartoon humorous or satirical? Explain your answer.

7. Did you find the cartoon hard to understand? If so, what information about current events do you need to understand the cartoon?

Exercise 5: Do You Get It?

Clip a different political cartoon from a recent newspaper. Discuss your cartoons in small groups. Use the questions in exercise 4 to help you analyze each cartoon's meaning.

INTERNATIONAL

Herald Tribune.

Published With The New York Times and The Washington Post

SECTION 3

BUSINESS

1
'Green' Clothes Take Root

2
The American Fast-Food Dream

3
Prenuptial Accords: Walking down the Aisle and Reading Fine Print

4
Cigarette Makers See Future (It's in Asia)

Focus on the Newspaper: Business

1. 'Green' Clothes Take Root

Previewing the Article

We recycle glass bottles and plastic bottles. We recycle newspapers and magazines. We recycle soft-drink cans and auto parts.

But underwear?

Some of us might not be prepared to go that far, but this article tells about a German fashion designer who has built an entire company based on recyclable clothing. Wearing recyclable clothing is a logical step for people who are anxious not to harm the environment. Discarded clothing is garbage, and clothing made of artificial fibers does not decay the way natural, living things do. So fashion designer Britta Steilmann has created clothes made entirely of natural materials.

The business question asked in the article is this: Can such a company succeed? Consumers usually think of price, durability, and style when they buy clothes. Will they also begin to think about how fast their clothes can decay in the pile of cut grass, weeds, and leaves ecologists call a "compost heap"?

The fact that such a company can exist at all shows that the passion for protecting the environment has reached into all corners of the business world.

Before You Read

Discuss these questions.

1. Do you sort glass, metal, plastic, and newspaper trash for recycling? How important do you think it is to do this?

2. What do you look for when you buy clothes? At the moment you buy a pair of socks, do you think about what you will do with them when you no longer wear them?

As You Read

Try to find two reasons why Britta Steilmann's company might become a big success and two reasons why it might not.

'Green' Clothes Take Root

Bloomberg Business News

1 BOCHUM, Germany—It takes exactly seven weeks for Britta Steilmann's underwear to decompose.

2 For this fashion designer, that's a sign of quality.

3 "It means they have no chemicals in them, nothing that provokes allergies, nothing that can damage your health," she said.

4 Ms. Steilmann, 29, the eldest daughter of Europe's largest apparel manufacturer, is determined to prove that it is possible—and profitable—to make clothes without polluting the environment.

5 To this end, she started her company, called It's One World, and added biodegradable clothes to Germany's long list of recyclable products.

6 Ms. Steilmann said she expected her line of plant-dyed knitwear, biodegradable underwear and organic-cotton jeans to show sales of 9 million Deutsche marks ($6.4 million) this year, up from 7 million DM last year.

7 Bernhardt Rupprecht, director of the ecology division at the management consulting firm HFU Unternehmensberatung, says eco-fashion can be a winner. "Ecology is very much a theme of the '90s," he said.

8 Others aren't so sure.

9 "The retail industry is far more interested in saving their margins than in saving the world," said a Frankfurt-based retail consultant, Anyolina Hobson.

10 A survey by the trade publication Textile Economy found that although 60 percent of German consumers said they would like to buy eco-lines, only 5 percent said they actually bought them, and only 38 percent said they would be willing to pay extra.

11 Nonetheless, sales of clothes classified by their makers as eco-friendly—a broad term encompassing natural-fiber fabrics free to one degree or another from damaging chemicals—exceeded 250 million DM last year.

12 The clothing companies Esprit and Marc O'Polo offer "green" fashion lines, as do such mail-order companies as Otto Versand GmbH and Klaus Steilmann GmbH, the parent company of Ms. Steilmann's It's One World.

13 In Germany, which has some of the world's most stringent environmental and recycling laws, most of the attention has been focused on Ms. Steilmann and her 3-year-old company in the heart of the once-vibrant textile region near Düsseldorf.

14 "She's made the issue popular because she has a name" that is well known, said Iris Staubesand, ecology director of Interessen Gemeinschaft für Damen Oberbekleidung, the organization that runs Germany's largest textile trade fair.

15 Ms. Steilmann, who introduced her fashion line in 1992, has some of the most stringent ecological standards in the business. Her cotton, for example, is only from plantations certified by the International Federation of Organic Agriculture Movement. It is not bleached or treated with synthetic, or glue-based, sizing agents. Shrinkage is controlled with a system that avoids the use of resins or ammonia.

16 "I follow a product from its planting to its recycling to make sure every aspect is developed properly," she said.

17 Ms. Steilmann's clothes are as free of synthetic material as she can make them.

18 Buttons are made of wood, horn, bone or mother of pearl; linings and thread of organic cotton; zippers of nickel-free copper and zinc; and elastic bands from natural rubber.

19 She says her underwear line will disintegrate if left outside on a compost heap for two months, though not if kept dry in a drawer.

20 "We've tried it," she said. "It's a form of quality control."

I. Getting the Message

After reading the article, choose the best answer for each item.

1. This article is mainly about _____.
   a. the importance of recycling
   b. an interesting new clothing company
   c. the European fashion market

2. Besides the benefit of not polluting the environment, another possible benefit of the new "eco-friendly" clothes is that _____.
   a. they are less expensive than regular clothes
   b. they are easy to make
   c. they won't damage a person's health

3. Part of Britta Steilmann's success may be due to the fact that _____.
   a. she is the daughter of Europe's largest apparel manufacturer
   b. she has studied ecology for many years
   c. her clothes are noted in Germany for their beauty

4. One sign that "eco-fashion" is becoming more popular is that _____.
   a. some other companies are also offering this type of clothing
   b. in a survey, many consumers said they had bought this type of clothing
   c. teenagers are starting to wear this type of clothing

5. The article mentions that some of the world's strictest laws protecting the environment are in _____.
   a. Russia   b. Poland   c. Germany

6. The clothes made by It's One World are manufactured according to very strict environmental standards because of _____.
   a. German laws
   b. Britta Steilmann's attention to details
   c. consumer pressure

Check your answers with the key on page 181. If you have made mistakes, reread the article to gain a better understanding of it.

II. Expanding Your Vocabulary

A. Getting Meaning from Context

Find each word in the paragraph indicated in parentheses. Use context clues to determine the meaning of the word. Choose the best definition.

1. decompose (1)   a. write   b. decay
2. biodegradable (5)   a. able to be biologically   b. able to decay naturally
                               understood
3. retail (9)   a. selling in stores   b. producing in factories
4. margins (9)   a. edges   b. profits
5. encompassing (11)   a. excluding   b. including
6. exceeded (11)   a. were less than   b. were greater than
7. stringent (13)   a. severe   b. unfair
8. vibrant (13)   a. loud   b. lively

B. Matching Opposites

Match each word with its opposite.

A	B
1. _____ certified	a. soothe; make content
2. _____ synthetic	b. labor
3. _____ disintegrate	c. condemned
4. _____ provoke	d. stretching
5. _____ management	e. natural
6. _____ eco-friendly	f. form; come together
7. _____ shrinkage	g. polluting

C. Practicing Useful Vocabulary

Complete these sentences with words from column A of exercise B.

1. It's One World only uses cotton from _____ organic farms.

2. The underwear produced by Britta Steilmann's company will not _____ if kept dry in a drawer, but it will if left on a compost heap for two months.

3. A _____ consulting firm said that ecology-conscious fashion will probably succeed.

III. Making Sense of Sentences

Writers often refer to things that other people have said. When they do, they can use either *direct speech* or *indirect speech.* In *direct speech,* the writer reports someone's original words, enclosing them in quotation marks. In *indirect speech,* the writer rephrases or summarizes someone's original words. No quotation marks are used.

Direct speech always uses the speaker's original words, including the verb tense. Indirect speech usually talks about the past, so the verb tense changes to the past. However, when indirect speech is used to report something that is still true, the verb may stay in the present tense.

Examples: "I like pizza," my friend said. *(direct speech)*

My friend said that she liked pizza. *(indirect speech; past tense)*

My friend said that she likes pizza. *(indirect speech; present tense)*

Rewrite these direct quotations from the article as indirect speech. Decide whether to use the present or past tense for each one.

1. "It means they have no chemicals in them, nothing that provokes allergies, nothing that can damage your health," she said. (3)
2. "Ecology is very much a theme of the '90s," he said. (7)
3. "The retail industry is far more interested in saving their margins than in saving the world," said a Frankfurt-based retail consultant, Anyolina Hobson. (9)
4. "I follow a product from its planning to its recycling to make sure every aspect is developed properly," she said. (16)

IV. Talking and Writing

Discuss the following topics. Then choose one of them to write about.

1. Do you think ecologically designed clothing will become popular? What facts can you think of to support your view?

2. Would you prefer to wear environmentally safe clothing? Would you pay a higher price for such clothes?

3. What are other examples of environmental awareness changing the business world?

2. The American Fast-Food Dream

Previewing the Article

The sign outside a typical McDonald's restaurant says "Billions and Billions Served." Next to it could be another sign: "Over Twenty Million Have Worked Here." In addition to Big Macs and Quarter Pounders, McDonald's has been serving up the American dream for immigrant workers in the United States. As this article shows, some of these workers have built solid careers from the modest beginning of near-minimum-wage, part-time jobs.

Many immigrants come to the United States with the dream of a better life through freedom and employment opportunities. By examining a Chicago McDonald's that hires many immigrants, the author of this article tells both a business story and a human-interest story: The first explains how McDonald's Corporation solved the problem of hiring and training workers who leave frequently. The second describes three ambitious, hard-working immigrants who overcame difficult backgrounds in their native lands and found economic success in the United States.

Before You Read

Discuss these questions.

1. Have you ever worked at a McDonald's or other fast-food restaurant? If so, describe your experiences to the class.

2. What is the "American dream"? Do you think it is the same for immigrants as it is for native-born U.S. citizens?

3. Do you like to eat at fast-food restaurants? From a customer's point of view, what are the benefits of fast food? What are the drawbacks?

As You Read

Ask yourself how the author gets your interest and holds your interest throughout the article. To do this, note the placement of information. What sorts of information come first, second, and so on?

The American Fast-Food Dream

Burger-Flipping Can Be Rewarding for Immigrants

By Barnaby J. Feder
New York Times Service

1 CHICAGO—Mark Ishaya was a toddler in Baghdad when his father died and his mother abandoned the family. He was a child laborer in a Lebanese oil filter factory when Palestine Liberation Organization guerrillas massacred co-workers as he hid in a cabinet.

2 Zdenka Bulic was 21 when she emigrated from Bosnia nine years ago, frustrated at the career roadblocks she faced as a Croat. David Núñez left his home in Mexico at the age of 16 in search of higher wages.

3 All three have ended up in management jobs at the McDonald's restaurant on Peterson Avenue on Chicago's north side, overseeing the 50 other immigrants on a staff of 55.

4 Their achievement testifies to the energy and talent of immigrants who use "burger flipping" jobs that most Americans deride as dead ends to lift themselves to modest prosperity.

5 Their success also reflects the effectiveness of systems that McDonald's Corp. and other fast-food chains have been forced to develop to integrate vast numbers of low-skilled workers into their work forces.

6 At least 20 million people have worked in a McDonald's since Ray Kroc opened his first McDonald's hamburger stand 40 years ago in the Chicago suburb of Des Plaines.

7 Behind that number is a corporate strategy of using armies of part-time workers. In addition, hourly pay for McDonald's crew members is typically only a bit higher than the $4.25 minimum wage, and fringe benefits are meager. Employees leave so frequently that this year McDonald's and its franchisees, which employ more than 500,000 workers in the United States and Canada, will have to hire well over that number of new employees to stay fully staffed.

8 But there is an upside to this upheaval. The leading fast-food chains have been forced to concentrate more than other businesses on designing their jobs and training programs with an eye toward quickly adapting large numbers of raw recruits.

9 Training programs at Peterson Avenue start with McDonald's-supplied videotapes, in either English or Spanish, ranging from general topics such as methods of dealing with customer complaints to the specifics of operating equipment. Written manuals repeat much information. In addition, experi-

David Núñez is first assistant manager at the Peterson Avenue McDonald's in Chicago.

Mark Ishaya became a store manager at the age of 18. He is now a supervisor for three Chicago McDonald's.

enced employees work shoulder-to-shoulder with new hires.

10 The management track starts with introductory week-long courses in operations and management for new assistant managers. Those promoted to second assistant become eligible for the Intermediate Operations Course, focusing on recruitment and retention of workers and advanced decision-making problems, and an equipment-maintenance and technology course.

11 First assistant managers, who have already received up to 2,000 hours of training, become eligible to attend the two-week Advanced Operations Course at Hamburger University, the company's national training center in Oak Brook, Illinois. Managers also take review courses and specialized offerings, such as courses on career development for women, blacks, and Hispanics.

12 Nowhere has the McDonald's system worked better for immigrants than at the Peterson Avenue restaurant, one of six franchises owned by a retired contractor, Ralph Wright, and his wife, Marilyn, an immigrant from Croatia. Native-born Americans rarely make up more than a handful of the employees there. These days Mr. Ishaya, Ms. Bulic, and Mr. Núñez are among the role models.

13 **Mark Ishaya.** His psychological ties to a perilous childhood remain strong. He dreams of returning to Baghdad some day to visit the grave of his father, who died when he was 2. The memories are vivid of the flight

with his grandparents and sister by car, camel and foot to Lebanon when he was 6 and from Lebanon to Greece nearly three years later when Palestinian and Syrian attacks engulfed their Christian community.

14 By the time Mr. Ishaya took the suggestion of some friends and applied to work with them at a McDonald's, the habit of hard work to help support one's family was already ingrained. Then 15, he lied about his age to obtain more hours.

15 "I was made manager of a McDonald's within months of graduating from high school," Mr. Ishaya said. "There I was, an 18-year-old, running a $1 million operation."

16 Mr. Ishaya, now 31, was transferred to the McDonald's on Peterson Avenue within two years. He soon fashioned the branch into a frequent winner of performance awards from the company and neighborhood trade groups. In 1993, he was promoted to a job supervising the restaurant on Peterson Avenue and two others, with a salary he describes as "about $45,000" annually. The fringe benefits include health care and a leased 1995 Ford Explorer.

17 One of the first lessons McDonald's taught Mr. Ishaya was that he was not as shy as he once thought. "After you deal with thousands of people of every race day-in, day-out, your personality changes," he said.

18 Mr. Ishaya said McDonald's had taught him the basics of American financial controls, inventory manage-

ment and marketing strategies. Above all, he learned a respect for employees and customers that he said was foreign to the Middle East.

19 **Zdenka Bulic.** Bosnia had not yet plunged into civil war when Ms. Bulic, now 30, came to Chicago to attend a relative's wedding, live with her cousin, Judy, for a year and perhaps go to school. Her parents both worked at an airplane factory and her family enjoyed a middle-class life. But it was already apparent that she would never be given a shot in Muslim-dominated Mostar at teaching math and science, her dream job.

20 In retrospect, it is no surprise that Judy promptly took her to work at McDonald's: Judy's sister is Marilyn Wright. Ms. Bulic was initially assigned to grillwork and began picking up Spanish from fellow crew members before she learned any English.

21 As Mr. Ishaya's successor as store manager at Peterson Avenue, Ms. Bulic arrives at 4:00 A.M. every fourth day to meet the McDonald's delivery truck and by 5:00 A.M. the rest of the time. She sometimes leaves as early as 3:00 P.M., but often gets caught up chatting with employees or customers.

22 "The concept of 100 percent customer satisfaction was new to me," said Ms. Bulic, who had worked briefly in a restaurant in Mostar before coming to the United States. "At home, we never even say 'please' or 'thank you' to customers."

23 The other eye-opener, she said, was the emphasis on teamwork. "The system is so organized and responsibilities are so broken out that it makes the role of teamwork clear," she said. "I had no clue about how much goes into it when I started."

24 Ms. Bulic, who now earns about $35,000 annually, has piled up such all-American assets as a Chevy Beretta automobile, and a small two-bedroom home in Elk Grove, Illinois.

25 **David Núñez.** Now 32, Mr. Núñez never had trouble finding work in his native Michoacán, a state just west of Mexico City. By the time he was 17, he had been laboring for more than a decade to help his family make ends meet.

26 On the recommendation of a friend, he left his first job here as a busboy at an upscale restaurant to clean tables and mop floors at McDonald's. It took two years before Mr. Núñez made the move from cleaning into the kitchen. Willingness to work rather than raw ambition has lifted him to his current job as first assistant manager at Peterson Avenue under Ms. Bulic.

STEVE KAGAN/NYT PICTURES

Store manager Zdenka Bulic enjoys serving customers at the Peterson Avenue McDonald's in Chicago.

I. Getting the Message

After reading the article, choose the best answer for each item.

1. This article is mainly about _____.
   a. the history of McDonald's Corporation
   b. the inspiring stories of three immigrants
   c. the need to raise the minimum wage

2. McDonald's has trouble keeping employees because _____.
   a. the work is too difficult
   b. many of them cannot speak English
   c. the hourly pay is low

3. The author thinks the success of Mark Ishaya, Zdenka Bulic, and David Núñez is due both to their abilities and to _____.
   a. well-developed systems of employee training
   b. good fringe benefits
   c. luck

4. The Peterson Avenue McDonald's won several performance awards because of _____.
   a. Mark Ishaya's management
   b. higher pay
   c. the number of workers employed

5. The most important thing that Mark Ishaya has learned while working for McDonald's is _____.
   a. respect for customers and employees
   b. the basics of American financial controls
   c. American marketing strategies

6. The main reason for David Núñez's success is _____.
   a. training in his native country
   b. hard work
   c. talent for management

7. The author notes that Zdenka Bulic "began picking up Spanish from fellow crew members before she learned any English." This detail illustrates _____.
   a. her poor English training in her native Bosnia
   b. how many immigrants work at the restaurant
   c. her need for English-language classes

Check your answers with the key on page 181. If you have made mistakes, reread the article to gain a better understanding of it.

II. Expanding Your Vocabulary

A. Getting Meaning from Context

Find each word in the paragraph indicated in parentheses. Use context clues to determine the meaning of the word. Choose the best definition.

1. toddler (1)	a. teenager	b. young child
2. deride (4)	a. laugh at	b. admire
3. meager (7)	a. attractive	b. scanty; not adequate
4. upheaval (8)	a. advantage	b. disruption; turmoil
5. track (10)	a. course; path	b. class
6. perilous (13)	a. full of memories	b. full of danger
7. fashioned (16)	a. wished	b. made
8. upscale (26)	a. elegant	b. large

B. Identifying Categories of Words

Find the word that doesn't belong in each category.

1. jobs in a restaurant

   busboy   maintenance   managing   counseling

2. tools used in worker training

   manuals   aerobics   videotapes   courses

3. rewards for work

   assets   salary   fringe benefits   wages

4. responsibilities of restaurant managers

   hamburger flipping   inventory management

   marketing strategies   worker retention

III. Working with Idioms and Expressions

Study the meanings of these phrasal verbs and other expressions. A form of each one appears in the indicated paragraph of the article.

Phrasal Verbs

end up (3)   reach a certain place or situation
testify to (4)   prove; show
plunge into (19)   begin with energy
pick up (20)   learn
pile up (24)   collect, buy

Other Expressions

dead end (4)   a position that has no hope of progress
shoulder-to-shoulder (9)   with united effort
give someone a shot (19)   let someone try
get caught up (21)   become involved
eye-opener (23)   surprise
have a clue (23)   understand
make ends meet (25)   live within one's income

Complete these sentences with phrasal verbs and expressions from the list.

1. Some hard-working immigrants do not look upon part-time "burger flipping" positions as _____ jobs, for they know they might _____ in well-paying managerial positions.

2. McDonald's training programs are designed so that new workers can _____ the basics of the job in a short time.

3. The emphasis on teamwork was an _____ to Zdenka Bulic. She didn't realize that workers in a fast-food restaurant have to work _____ in order to keep the operation running smoothly.

4. David Núñez had to work very hard to _____ in his native Mexico.

IV. Analyzing Paragraphs

Reread the indicated paragraphs. Then answer the questions.

1. Paragraphs 1 and 2 say nothing about McDonald's or about the problems of training a large workforce. Instead, they give brief backgrounds of three people. Is this a good way to begin the article? Explain your answer.

2. Paragraphs 5 through 11 discuss the overall strategy of McDonald's hiring and training program. What problem does McDonald's face? How has McDonald's solved it?

3. Paragraphs 18 and 22 contain similar comments made by Mark Ishaya and Zdenka Bulic about the American business attitude toward customers. What have they observed?

V. Talking and Writing

Discuss the following topics. Then choose one of them to write about.

1. Have you ever held a minimum-wage job? Do you think valuable lessons about working can be learned from such jobs? Explain your answer.

2. The author says that most Americans laugh at "burger flipping" jobs and call them "dead ends." If this is so, why do recent immigrants have a different attitude toward these jobs?

3. Prenuptial Accords: Walking down the Aisle and Reading Fine Print

Previewing the Article

Dikembe Mutombo, a professional basketball player with the Denver Nuggets, once asked his fiancée to sign a prenuptial (premarital) agreement promising to bear him a child within two years and then to return to work four months after childbirth. (She refused to sign the agreement.) Other engaged couples have hired lawyers to draw up contracts stipulating who will do the housework and how much time will be spent with in-laws.

These kinds of agreements may pave the way for a smoother marriage, but legally they are useless because there is no way for courts to force compliance. As the following article indicates, most prenuptial agreements are not about the marriage at all. They deal with division of money and property in case of death or divorce.

Who wants to think about divorce shortly before a wedding? Many people do, especially if they have valuable assets to protect or children from a previous marriage. Because of the high divorce rate in the United States, "prenups" are quite common among Americans. As the following article indicates, divorce laws differ from state to state. In community property states, divorcing spouses divide the assets of the marriage equally. But in states with equitable distribution laws, the division of assets is based upon each partner's contribution to the marriage. In this context, *contribution* refers not just to money but to time and effort spent, for example, on homemaking, child-rearing, and being a supportive spouse.

Before You Read

Discuss these questions.

1. Study the headline of this article. What do "walking down the aisle" and "reading fine print" mean? Discuss the literal and figurative meanings of these expressions.

2. Are prenuptial agreements common in any countries you have lived in?

3. What English expressions do you know that mean a married couple has separated or divorced?

As You Read

Make some notes on the following:

1. the kinds of people most likely to want a prenuptial agreement;

2. any expressions that you don't understand. (Then ask about their meaning in class, or look them up in a dictionary of idioms.)

Prenuptial Accords: Walking down the Aisle and Reading Fine Print

By Judith Rehak

1 A prospective husband wanted to be sure that if his marriage didn't work out, he could keep his treasured snowball collection, safely stored away in a freezer. A fiancée insisted on stipulating who would walk the dog. One man wanted the right to sue for divorce if his bride-to-be gained more than 15 pounds once she became his wife.

2 These are some of the wackier terms of prenuptial agreements. But make no mistake about it, what most of them are about is money—and how financial assets will be divided up if a couple divorces. And divorce with its attendant money problems is common in the United States and other economically developed countries, as the accompanying graphic illustrates.

3 Prenuptial agreements—or "pre-nups," as they are known in the American legal profession—are designed to address these problems as they arise. Prenups are negotiated by lawyers for the prospective spouses, and signed before they walk down the aisle. They have been gaining in popularity in the United States since the early 1980s, when more states began passing laws that affected who gets what financial assets in a divorce. The laws are based either on "community property" (split evenly) or on "equitable distribution" (in New York state, whatever a judge thinks is "fair").

4 The celebrity prenups make the headlines: When Ivana and Donald Trump, the real estate mogul, parted ways, there were postnups to the prenup, forbidding Mrs. Trump to speak publicly about the marriage; lawyers for Jacqueline Kennedy Onassis contested the prenuptial agreement between her and Aristotle Onassis af-ter his death, reportedly winning $26 million in an out-of-court settlement; the younger, and considerably less affluent husband of Joan Collins, the actress, tried unsuccessfully to invalidate their prenuptial agreement when they divorced.

5 But premarital agreements are also for lesser known, albeit wealthy folks. "It's because divorce has such great economic consequences, and serial marriage has become so prevalent," said William Zabel, a family law lawyer with Schulte Roth & Zabel, a New York law firm.

6 A typical candidate for a pre-matrimonial agreement is a man who has accumulated considerable wealth, and has already been burned once. "They want to make differing arrangements, rather than let a court decide," said Barbara Ellen Handschu, president of the New York chapter of the American Academy of Matrimonial Lawyers.

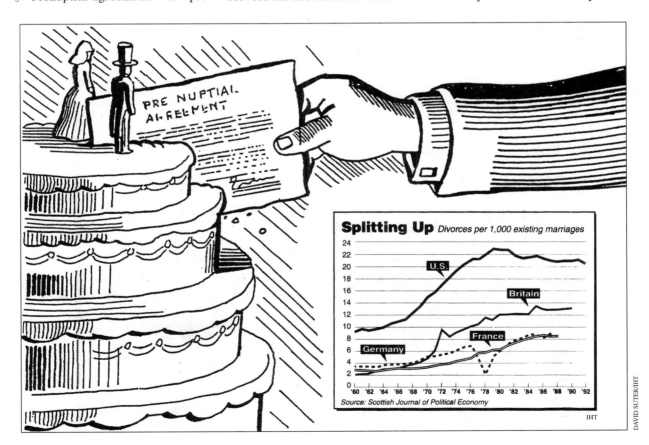

Splitting Up Divorces per 1,000 existing marriages

U.S.

Britain

France

Germany

Source: Scottish Journal of Political Economy

DAVID SUTER/IHT

IHT

7 Protecting children from a previous marriage is a strong motivation for prenuptial contracts. "Someone may have an estate of $1 billion and he may not want a second spouse to get a half a million. He may want more for his children," said Mr. Zabel. The effort to shield inheritances for children and grandchildren is making prenups more common among people in their 60s and 70s who are remarrying after a spouse has died.

8 Another situation that calls for premarital agreements occurs when a prospective spouse has, or is in line for, great inherited wealth, or a family business, especially if the prospective partner has little or nothing at all. (Lawyers say that the parents of the heir or heiress often press for a prenuptial agreement.)

9 But even when both parties have signed such an agreement, it can be upset in court if proper guidelines have not been followed. Never, ever, warn the specialists, should you use the same lawyer as your prospective spouse. Another red flag is a prenuptial agreement signed under "duress." The classic example is cited by Ms. Handschu: "An agreement stuck under somebody's nose on the day of the wedding—and it's usually a 'she'—and she signs, but doesn't even read it."

10 To avoid such problems, Ms. Handschu will not draw up an agreement once a wedding date has been set. "I figure there's a gun at their head, and that's duress," she said. Mr. Zabel counsels his clients never to send out wedding invitations until an agreement is signed.

11 But not everyone takes his advice. He recalled one episode where negotiations were still under way as 150 wedding guests were arriving at the mansion of a client. When an agreement could not be reached, the wedding was canceled.

12 A dispute can also break out over prenuptial agreements if a couple decides to divorce while living abroad, or when they hold different citizenships. Jeremy Levison, a partner with Collyer-Bristow, a London law firm that often handles divorces for British-American couples, noted that in Britain, prenuptial agreements were "just about ignored" by the courts because English law says that circumstances of a marriage change over time and therefore a judge should decide how financial assets will be divided.

13 That can lead to "forum-shopping," said Mr. Levison, since what matters is the law of the country where the couple is getting divorced. He gave the following example: "Mr. Ed Smith gets married to Mrs. Smith. He's worth $5 million and wants to protect that against eventual divorce, so he enters into a New York prenuptial contract. They live in England, have two children, and then decide to get divorced. English lawyers will say to Mrs. Smith, 'No, that contract is not valid, you should get a crack at it,' while Mr. Smith will want it to be an American case. The issue of where it will be held can be a lengthy battle."

14 As for the role of romance and everlasting love in this picture, there isn't any, say these lawyers, who consider prenups to be business agreements. Their justification: some 50 percent of all marriages in the United States end in divorce.

15 Moreover, they claim, the negotiations for a prenuptial agreement, which involve laying bare all one's finances, sometimes save a couple from a disastrous marriage. "It brings issues to a head which would have ended in divorce," said Mr. Zabel. "It turns out that the money means more than the marriage, and the person says, 'To hell with this, the money is more important than I am.'"

16 But there is still hope. "Many people sign an agreement, put it in a drawer and never look at it again," added Mr. Zabel. "They have a happy marriage, or contrary to what a spouse may be obligated to do, even if they're divorced, they may give more than they're required to."

I. Getting the Message

A. Reading for Details

After reading the article, indicate if each statement is true (T) or false (F). For help, check the paragraph number indicated in parentheses.

1. _____ Prenuptial agreements discuss financial matters only. (1)
2. _____ In the United States, divorce laws differ from state to state. (3)
3. _____ A spouse who signs a prenuptial agreement can still sue for more money if a divorce occurs. (4, 9, 12)
4. _____ Prenuptial contracts are equally popular among wealthy people and people with few financial assets. (5, 6, 8)
5. _____ Before signing a prenuptial agreement, a prospective spouse should hire his or her own lawyer to look it over. (9)

B. Using What You've Learned

Imagine that you are a lawyer and that these couples are your clients. Should you recommend a prenuptial agreement? Think about the information and opinions given by the lawyers in the article. Then write **yes** or **no** on the line before each sentence.

1. _____ A woman who expects to inherit a large business is marrying a doctor.
2. _____ The bride and groom are both successful businesspeople. They live in London and are British citizens.
3. _____ A millionaire widower with three grown children is marrying his 19-year-old secretary.
4. _____ Two American teachers in their late twenties are marrying for the first time. Their only assets are their engagement and wedding gifts.
5. _____ The bride and groom have invited 300 guests to their wedding, which is taking place this weekend.
6. _____ The bride-to-be owns a valuable collection of impressionist paintings.

Check your answers with the key on page 181. If you have made mistakes, reread the article to gain a better understanding of it.

II. Expanding Your Vocabulary

A. Studying Legal Vocabulary

Here are some legal terms from the article. If you are not familiar with their meanings, look them up in a dictionary. Then choose the best words to complete the sentences.

assets	contract	invalidate	settlement
case	estate	issues	stipulate
contested	inherit	negotiations	sue

1. An out-of-court _____ ends a lawsuit.
2. In a lawsuit, _____ matters are those the parties don't agree about.
3. A _____ is a legally binding agreement.
4. Lawyers help their clients during _____. They often encourage clients to compromise in order to reach an agreement.
5. A court _____ involves legal _____ or matters that are being disputed.
6. When a wealthy person dies, the _____ (money and property) usually become part of the dead person's _____.

B. Using Prefixes

The prefixes *pre-* and *pro-* sometimes mean "before in place or time." *Pro-* also conveys the idea of something ahead or projecting forward. The prefix *post-* means "after." Use *pre-*, *pro-*, and *post-* to complete these words. The definition of each word is given in parentheses.

1. _____ tect (to keep safe from harm)
2. _____ vent (to stop something from happening)

3. _____ marital (before marriage)
4. _____ nuptial (after the wedding)
5. _____ spective (likely to become)
6. _____ vious (something that happened earlier)

Discuss how the idea of *before* relates to words one, two, and five.

Note: The prefix *ante-* also means "before." *Prenuptial* agreements can be called *ante-nuptial* agreements.

C. Identifying Jobs, Roles, and Titles

Match each person with an appropriate definition. For context clues, refer to the paragraphs indicated in parentheses.

1. _____ celebrity (4)   a. a famous person
2. _____ client (10)   b. a leader in a particular industry
3. _____ fiancée (1)   c. the woman that a man is engaged to marry
4. _____ mogul (4)   d. someone who hires a lawyer
5. _____ partner (8)   e. a business associate who shares the company's risks and profits

III. Working with Idioms and Expressions

Find each expression in the paragraph indicated in parentheses. Choose the best definition.

1. parted ways (4)   a. divided assets   b. separated
2. been burned once (6)   a. been injured in a fire b. been hurt in some way
3. in line for (8)   a. standing in a line   b. likely to get something
4. red flag (9)   a. a warning of danger   b. a sign of celebration
5. get a crack at it (13) a. get to hit it   b. have a chance to try for it
6. to hell with this (15) a. I want this.   b. I don't want this.

IV. Analyzing Paragraphs

A. Finding the Paragraph's Purpose

Write the numbers of the paragraph(s) that give the following information.

1. a definition of a prenuptial agreement _____

2. information about who needs a prenuptial agreement _____

3. situations that can cause a "prenup" to be declared invalid in court _____

B. Using Transitional Words and Phrases

In the first sentence of a new paragraph, a writer often refers to information that was in the previous paragraph. For example, paragraph 2 of the article begins with the word "These," referring to the examples given in paragraph 1. The first sentence of each paragraph listed below contains a word or phrase that refers to an idea in the preceding paragraph. Write these linking words.

(5) _____   (10) _____

(8) _____   (12) _____

(9) _____   (13) _____

Discuss the purpose of using linking words.

V. Talking and Writing

Discuss the following topics. Then choose one of them to write about.

1. If you were asked to sign a "prenup," how would you feel about it? Under what circumstances would you agree or refuse to sign?

2. What tasks would you include in a prenuptial agreement dealing with the duties and responsibilities of each spouse? If you are contemplating marriage or are married, draw up a prenuptial or marital agreement that you and your partner could agree to and live happily with.

3. In your opinion, why is the divorce rate high in some countries and not in others? What factors affect the divorce rate?

4. Cigarette Makers See Future (It's in Asia)

Previewing the Article

"Thank You for Not Smoking."

A sign with this message often greets American smokers who want to light up a cigarette in a public place. But in other parts of the world, smokers live in a more smoking-friendly environment. In fact, according to this article, sales of cigarettes are rising in Asian countries and in much of the Third World—although they are declining in the United States, Western Europe, and other industrialized countries. The good news for the U.S. tobacco industry is that American-made cigarettes are especially in demand in Asia. The bad news for Asian countries is that smoking is very dangerous to people's health, so many Asian smokers will suffer greatly in the years to come.

American cigarettes, like American movies, music, and blue jeans, are an extremely successful export. But unlike popular art and fashion, they have deadly consequences for people.

Before You Read

Discuss these questions.

1. Do you smoke cigarettes? Why or why not?

2. Have you seen the Marlboro Man, a cigarette-smoking cowboy who appears on billboards and in other ads? Do you think this kind of advertising is effective?

3. What other popular habits can you think of that are both widespread and unhealthy?

As You Read

Look for reasons why American cigarettes are becoming more popular in some countries even though domestic brands are less expensive.

Cigarette Makers See Future (It's in Asia)

By Philip Shenon

New York Times Service

1 BANGKOK—The Marlboro Man has found greener pastures.

2 The cigarette-hawking cowboy may be under siege back home in the United States from lawmakers and health advocates determined to put him out of business, but half a world away, in Asia, he is prospering, his craggy all-American mug slapped up on billboards and flickering across television screens.

3 And Marlboro cigarettes have never been more popular on the continent that is home to 60 percent of the world's population.

4 For the world's cigarette-makers, Asia is the future. And it is probably their savior.

5 Industry critics who hope that the multinational tobacco companies are headed for extinction owe themselves a stroll down the tobacco-scented streets of almost any city in Asia.

6 Almost everywhere here the air is thick with the swirling gray haze of cigarette smoke, the evidence of a booming Asian growth market that promises vast profits for the tobacco industry and a death toll measured in the tens of millions.

7 At lunchtime in Seoul, throngs of fashionably dressed young Korean women gather in a fast-food restaurant to enjoy a last cigarette before returning to work, a scene that draws distressed stares from older Koreans who remember a time when it would have been scandalous for women from respectable homes to smoke.

8 In Hong Kong, shoppers flock into the Salem Attitudes boutique, picking from among the racks of trendy sports clothes stamped with the logo of Salem cigarettes.

9 In Phnom Penh, the war-shattered capital of Cambodia, visitors leaving an audience with King Sihanouk are greeted with a giant billboard planted right across the street from his ornate gold-roofed palace. It advertises Lucky Strikes.

10 According to tobacco industry projections cited by the World Health Organization, the Asian cigarette market should grow by more than a third during the 1990s, with much of the bounty going to multinational tobacco giants eager for an alternative to the shrinking market in the United States.

11 American cigarette sales are expected to decline by about 15 percent by the end of the decade, a reflection of the move to ban public smoking in most of the United States. Sales in Western Europe and other industrialized countries are also expected to drop.

12 But no matter how bad the news is in the West, the tobacco companies can find comfort in Asia and throughout the Third World, markets so huge and so promising that they make the once all-important American market seem insignificant. Beyond Asia, cigarette consumption is also expected to grow in Africa, Latin America, Eastern Europe and in the nations of the former Soviet Union.

13 Status appears to matter far more than taste. "There is not a great deal of evidence to suggest that smokers can taste any difference between the more expensive foreign brands and the indigenous cigarettes," said Simon Chapman, a specialist in community medicine at the University of Sydney. "The difference appears to be in the packaging, the advertising."

14 He said that researchers had been unable to determine whether the foreign tobacco companies had adjusted the levels of tar, nicotine and other chemicals for cigarettes sold in the Asian market. "The tobacco industry fights tooth and nail to keep consumers away from that kind of information," he said.

15 Most governments in Asia have launched anti-smoking campaigns, but their efforts tend to be overwhelmed by the Madison Avenue glitz unleashed by the cigarette giants.

16 With 1.2 billion people and the world's fastest-growing economy, China is the most coveted target of the multinational tobacco companies. Cigarette consumption, calculated as the number of cigarettes smoked per adult, has increased by 7 percent each year over the last decade in China. There are 300 million smokers in China, more people than the entire population of the United States, and they buy 1.6 trillion cigarettes a year.

17 Competing in many cases with domestically produced brands, the multinational tobacco companies are moving quickly to get their cigarettes into China and emerging markets in the rest of the developing world. Their campaign has been bolstered by the efforts of American government trade negotiators to force open tobacco markets overseas.

18 Since the mid-1980s, Japan, South Korea, Taiwan and Thailand have all succumbed to pressure from Washington and allowed the sale of foreign-brand cigarettes. Foreign cigarettes, shut out of Japan in 1980, now make up nearly 20 percent of the market.

19 "Worldwide, hundreds of millions of smokers prefer American-blend cigarettes," James W. Johnston, chairman of Reynolds Tobacco Worldwide, wrote in his company's 1993 annual report. "Today, Reynolds has access to 90 percent of the world's markets; a decade ago, only 40 percent. Opportunities have never been better."

20 Last year, Philip Morris, the company behind the Marlboro Man, signed an agreement with the government-controlled China National Tobacco Corp. to make Marlboros and other Philip Morris brands in China. The company's foreign markets grew last year by more than 16 percent, with foreign operating profits up nearly 17 percent. Operating profits in the domestic American market fell by nearly half.

21 Physicians say the health implications of the tobacco boom in Asia are nothing less than terrifying.

22 Richard Peto, an Oxford University epidemiologist, has estimated that because of increasing tobacco consumption in Asia, the annual worldwide death toll from tobacco-related illnesses will more than triple over the next two decades, from about 3 million a year to 10 million a year, a fifth of them in China. His calculations suggest that 50 million Chinese children alive today will eventually die from diseases linked to cigarette smoking.

23 "If you look at the number of deaths, the tobacco problem in Asia is going to dwarf tuberculosis, it's going to dwarf malaria and it's going to dwarf AIDS, yet it's being totally ignored," said Judith Mackay, a British physician who is a consultant to the Chinese government in developing an anti-smoking program.

24 The explosion of the Asian tobacco market is a result both of the increasing prosperity of large Asian nations—suddenly, tens of millions of Asians can afford cigarettes, once a luxury—and a shift in social customs. In many Asian countries, smoking was once taboo for women. Now, it is seen as a sign of their emancipation.

I. Getting the Message _____

After reading the article, indicate if each statement is true (**T**) or false (**F**).

1. _____ This article is mainly about the dangers of smoking.
2. _____ Cigarette advertising is very effective in Asian countries.
3. _____ Research shows that foreign cigarettes taste better to Asian smokers than native brands do.
4. _____ Asian governments, like many governments of Western countries, actively try to discourage smoking.
5. _____ The U.S. government has worked hard to open Asian markets to foreign cigarette companies.
6. _____ China is a bigger market for cigarettes than the United States is.
7. _____ Smoking is becoming more socially acceptable for women in Asia.
8. _____ Foreign cigarette makers have not yet discovered the big market for cigarettes in Asia.

Check your answers with the key on page 181. If you have made mistakes, reread the article to gain a better understanding of it.

II. Expanding Your Vocabulary _____

A. Getting Meaning from Context

Find each word in the paragraph indicated in parentheses. Use context clues to determine the meaning of the word. Choose the best definition.

1. craggy (2)   a. rough; rugged   b. ugly
2. mug (2)   a. cup   b. face
3. swirling (6)   a. moving; twisting and   b. imaginary; unreal
                       floating
4. throngs (7)   a. pairs   b. large crowds
5. logo (8)   a. price tag   b. brand name and/or
                                                 company symbol
6. bounty (10)   a. financial rewards   b. taxes
7. launched (15)   a. started   b. forbidden
8. coveted (16)   a. feared   b. wanted
9. succumbed (18)   a. yielded; given in   b. resisted

B. Defining Useful Vocabulary

Match each word with its definition.

	A		B
1. _____	distressed	a.	rapid increase
2. _____	trendy	b.	let loose
3. _____	emancipation	c.	forbidden
4. _____	shrinking	d.	freedom
5. _____	unleashed	e.	fashionable
6. _____	boom	f.	make something appear small
7. _____	dwarf	g.	getting smaller
8. _____	taboo	h.	unhappy; pained

C. Practicing Useful Vocabulary

Complete these sentences with words from column A of exercise B.

1. The death rate from cigarette smoking in Asia will someday _____ the death rate from better-known causes like tuberculosis and AIDS.
2. Older, more traditional Korean people feel _____ when they see young women smoking in public.
3. Because the population of China is so large and smoking is so popular there, China has become a _____ market for foreign cigarette manufacturers.
4. Smoking American brand-name cigarettes is a _____ habit in many parts of Asia.

III. Working with Idioms and Expressions _____

Study the meanings of these idioms and expressions. A form of each one appears in the indicated paragraph of the article.

greener pastures (1)   better places to live or do business
under siege (2)   in danger
put someone out of business (2)   stop someone from doing business
head for (5)   go toward
owe oneself (5)   should do for one's own benefit; should give oneself
find comfort in (12)   be satisfied or relieved about
fight tooth and nail (14)   fight very hard
shut out of (18)   excluded from; kept from entering
have access to (19)   be able to enter or use

Complete these sentences using the idioms and expressions.

1. Foreign cigarettes were once _____ Japan, but now they have a big percentage of the Japanese market.

2. Asian countries are _____ for American cigarette makers, whose sales are down in the United States.

3. There is some question whether cigarette manufacturers have changed the levels of tar and nicotine for cigarettes sold in the Asian market, but the cigarette companies _____ to keep such information a secret.

4. Cigarette companies may feel _____ by lawmakers and health advocates in the United States, but they are becoming more and more successful in Third World markets.

IV. Analyzing Paragraphs ——————————————————————

Statistics are necessary to every phase of business, so they are also vital to any business article. The writer of this article uses statistics to support many important points in the story. For example, the statistics in paragraphs 16, 19, and 22 show how profitable the Asian market will be for foreign cigarette companies and how disastrous cigarette smoking will be for the health of the Asian people.

Below are some statistics from these paragraphs. Each one illustrates a positive or negative consequence of cigarette sales. Write a phrase or two that explains the significance of each statistic. The first one has been done for you.

1. 1.2 billion people _____ the population of China, so a good market for cigarette sales ___

2. 7 percent a year over the last decade _____

3. 90 percent of the world's markets _____

4. 3 to 10 million a year _____

5. 50 million Chinese children _____

Find three other statistics in the article that illustrate facts about cigarette sales in Asia.

V. Talking and Writing ——————————————————————

Discuss the following topics. Then choose one of them to write about.

1. Smoking is more and more popular among American teenagers. In your opinion, why is this so?

2. Research has shown that smoking is addictive and causes a variety of serious illnesses that can lead to death. Do you think sales of cigarettes, like illegal drugs, should be banned completely? Why or why not?

Focus on the Newspaper

The business section of a newspaper contains information that affects people's economic lives. Individuals with money to invest can find information and advice that will help them earn money on investments in stocks, bonds, or real estate. Everyone can find information about employment trends and developing career areas. Since we live in a global economy, economic events in other countries that can affect business where you live are reported.

Topics of Business Articles

You will find a variety of articles in the business section, including:

- articles reporting the financial situation of companies, whether they are running at a profit or a loss
- articles reporting new products and technology developed or being developed by businesses and how these might affect the businesses
- information on whether currencies, such as the dollar, are going up or down in value
- articles on how political policies and elections are affecting business

All the articles help readers understand current business conditions.

Exercise 1: It's Your Business

Analyze a business article by answering these questions.

ANALYZING A BUSINESS ARTICLE

1. What is the headline? How does it help you predict the content and viewpoint of the article?

2. What is the purpose of the article? (to report conditions of a company, a new product, trends in the stock market, experts' opinions on economic conditions, and so on)

3. What is the main idea of the article?

4. Does the article make a prediction about the future? If so, what is the prediction?

5. Does the article give the reader any advice? If so, what is it?

Exercise 2: The Language of Business

Like all areas, business uses its own special vocabulary. To understand business articles, you need to know terms such as *recession, bonds, stocks, futures,* and *bull market.* Read two or three articles from the business section of a newspaper. Write down at least five sentences that include business terms you don't know, and underline the terms. Discuss the terms in class, and see if you can define them. Research the meanings of any terms you can't define.

Exercise 3: How's Business?

Scan the newspaper business section for a few weeks, looking for information about general business conditions in your area. As you read, look for answers to the following questions. Be prepared to discuss your conclusions with the class.

1. Is it difficult to find a job right now? Why or why not? In what fields are employment opportunities best?

2. What are some good investment opportunities now, according to the experts?

3. What economic problems does your area face at this time?

4. What is the overall economic outlook—optimistic or pessimistic?

Reading Stock Prices

Daily newspapers run long lists of the stock and bond prices of companies on the major exchanges. Investors who own any of these stocks or bonds can follow the fluctuating prices in the daily paper.

Exercise 4: The Ups and Downs

In class, practice reading the newspaper listing of stock prices. (Note that some newspapers provide a key to help you read the information.) Then choose the stock of a well-known company on one of the major exchanges. "Purchase" one hundred shares, and follow the closing price for any four days within a two-week period. At the end of the two weeks, "sell" the stock. During the period that you "own" the stock record the following information:

Name of stock purchased _____

Date of purchase _____   Price per share _____

Date _____ Closing price _____   Date _____ Closing price _____

Date _____ Closing price _____   Date _____ Closing price _____

Profit or loss (on 100 shares) _____

Do you know any reasons why the price went up or down?

INTERNATIONAL

Herald Tribune

Published With The New York Times and The Washington Post

SECTION 4

PROFILES

1

If It's a Laughing Matter, Call In Julie Hette

2

Walden Revisited: The Perils of Country Houses

3

Art as Memory: Filmmaker's Vietnam

4

Kenya City Learns to Accept a New Kind of Mayor

Focus on the Newspaper: Profiles

1. If It's a Laughing Matter, Call In Julie Hette

Previewing the Article

> The last time I saw Paris, her heart was warm and gay
> I heard the laughter of her heart, in every street café.

When songwriter Oscar Hammerstein II wrote the words above, he certainly didn't have Julie Hette in mind. Though this clever Frenchwoman has a personal goal of making "half of Paris laugh," her wish is more professional than romantic.

This article tells how Julie Hette has marketed a unique product: her laugh. There are probably as many ways of laughing as there are people, but Julie Hette actually gets paid for her style of laughter. Most of the profits to be made from humor are on the production side, but Julie Hette shows that money can be made on the consumption side as well.

Through this profile of the career of a self-styled "professional laugher," the author makes the reader reflect on the whole role of laughter in modern life.

Before You Read

Discuss these questions.

1. Look at the illustration accompanying the article. How are the onlookers reacting to the woman carrying the laughing mouth? What can you guess about the kind of laugh that Julie Hette has?

2. This article appeared in the newspaper on April 1. What minor holiday is celebrated on this date? Why is this an appropriate article for April 1?

3. Can you think of any situations in which a person might be hired to laugh?

As You Read

Pay close attention to the author's description of Julie Hette's laugh and others' reactions to it. Try to imagine what her laugh actually sounds like.

If It's a Laughing Matter, Call In Julie Hette

By Mary Blume
International Herald Tribune

1 PARIS—Julie Hette wears a serious suit and has a serious job as a receptionist at one of France's biggest corporations. She might even be called a serious young woman—she cries at movies and wants to devote her life to humanitarian causes—but, more than most people, she laughs.

2 She laughs at dinner parties and bar mitzvahs and film premieres. She recently pre-recorded April Fool's peals of laughter for a French radio station. She is a professional laugher, as far as she knows the only one in France, not the most giggly country in the world.

3 "The French are stiff and self-centered, they are open to nothing. Not to a smile, a laugh. Nothing." This makes work harder but success, more resonant. "I am very wholehearted," she says. "To bring laughter is fabulous."

4 She has been hired to laugh in Japan, so triumphantly that she now has a Japanese agent, and she has laughed on an American television program where she was introduced as the "French Toast." It all began in the east of France, where she grew up with a laugh so loud that schoolteachers sent her out of class and friends would say "shut up, you're bothering us." Even today, her mother, when they go to the movies together, sits a few rows away so as not to be ashamed.

5 Then one night she went to the circus and laughed at the clown, who responded by making her laugh again to the point where a whole number evolved and the circus director hired her to come back.

6 "I found it wonderful to be paid for what had always been forbidden." To train herself she went on the Métro to see if she could make straphangers laugh, which she did so successfully that she then had to train herself to stop. A voice teacher taught her how to control her breathing and she took an ad in a show biz magazine, L'Information du Spectacle, describing herself as a *"rieuse professionelle."*

7 She was 20 (she is now 33) and spent the next five years laughing full-time. "In the beginning I did it everywhere just to show I was a professional. I don't do that now, but if people suggest something interesting I say why not?"

8 She has of course read Bergson and also Heinrich Böll's short story about the professional laugher whose repertory is so vast that he has never heard his own laugh. Hette has no repertory but relies on variations of her own megadecibel hoot, which billows in a full-throated way and also grates like a dentist's drill. It has, she says, been compared to a jalopy that won't start.

9 Her first break came when a woman who had seen her ad hired her to laugh at her father's funny stories at a New Year's Eve party. The father was a high-up functionary with a penchant for terrible jokes. Hette took lessons in which fork to use and other branches of Neuilly etiquette, appeared at the grand and stuffy party and laughed herself silly to the host's great pleasure.

10 "It was a nice gift that girl made to her father, he was so happy that night," Hette said.

11 She has been hired to laugh at the graduation ceremony of France's grandest *grande école*, ENA, has done a lot of television and has become a fixture at openings of not-very-funny comic films. "This can be tricky because my laugh shouldn't drown out

the next gag. In French films this isn't much of a problem," she added.

12   One of her early successes came when Paco Rabanne hired her to laugh during his fashion show. "My laugh does have a metallic quality," she explained. In the current French presidential campaign she would never accept an offer from a candidate to laugh at his rival's electoral promises because she won't laugh to offend.

13   She has laughed at fancy dinners when the hosts are entertaining a dull provincial client and is proudest of a letter she got from a 75-year-old man who heard her on the radio and laughed for the first time in 20 years. For a while when she was new to the trade she went to the movies Sundays with an elderly man whose laugh was as wild as hers.

14   "His laugh was so irritating that he didn't dare go to the movies alone, so we went together and had tea afterwards. It didn't pay well but it was pleasant." These days her fees range from 1,500 to 2,500 francs ($300 to $500).

15   A speech expert told her that her laugh cannot leave people indifferent: it often irritates and people say "kindly shut up" or "do you want an aspirin?" Having been told she sounds like a chicken, she went to the Paris quai where animals are sold and laughed in front of a rooster. He crowed back. If she decides to practice when she is alone at a café, people tend to back away, thinking she is a street crazy, but, when she explains she is an *artiste* all is well.

16   Her dream is to be on a crane high over the Place de la Concorde, laughing as infectiously as she can to the crowd below. "To make half of Paris laugh, it would be fabulous."

17   But these are hard times. Recently, for training purposes she got on the Métro and laughed, which she hasn't done for eight years. "I realized how hard it is now. People are depressed and constantly harassed by panhandlers. They just aren't in the mood."

18   It's enough to make one cry.

I. Getting the Message

After reading the article, choose the best answer for each item.

1. Julie Hette thinks that French people _____.
   a. like to laugh
   b. have the best sense of humor among Europeans
   c. should laugh more

2. Julie Hette discovered that people noticed her laugh _____.
   a. when she was a child
   b. when she worked as a receptionist
   c. at a New Year's Eve party when she was an adult

3. The main point of this article is that _____.
   a. Julie Hette has made a great deal of money
   b. Julie Hette has an odd but interesting way to make money
   c. Julie Hette has a beautiful laugh

4. Julie Hette thinks her work is getting harder because _____.
   a. comedy is more popular than ever
   b. modern life makes people suspicious and depressed
   c. the competition in her artistic field is getting more and more intense

5. When Julie Hette practices her art in a public place, _____.
   a. people gather around and laugh along with her
   b. people compliment her on her lovely, melodious laugh
   c. people are irritated and think she is crazy

6. The author's attitude toward Julie Hette is best described as _____.
   a. interested and amused
   b. hostile and irritated
   c. ironic and critical

Check your answers with the key on page 181. If you have made mistakes, reread the article to gain a better understanding of it.

II. Expanding Your Vocabulary

A. Getting Meaning from Context

Find each word in the paragraph indicated in parentheses. Use context clues to determine the meaning of the word. Choose the best definition.

1.	wholehearted (3)	a. friendly and loyal	b. enthusiastic and sincere
2.	triumphantly (4)	a. with difficulty	b. successfully
3.	evolved (5)	a. developed	b. ended
4.	megadecibel (8)	a. very pleasing	b. very loud
5.	penchant (9)	a. liking; fondness	b. hatred
6.	stuffy (9)	a. rich	b. self-important
7.	provincial (13)	a. from the country	b. downtown
8.	indifferent (15)	a. having no opinion	b. no different

B. Reading for Suggested Meanings

Answer these questions.

1. In the first paragraph the adjective *serious* appears three times to describe Julie Hette. Why does the author use this word to introduce a woman known for her laughter?

2. In paragraph 8 the author notes that Julie Hette has read works by two authors: Henri Bergson (1859–1941), a French philosopher who wrote a famous essay on laughter, and Heinrich Böll, a contemporary Nobel Prize-winning German author of a short story about a professional laugher. What does this information tell us about Julie Hette?

3. In paragraph 8 the author says, "Hette has no *repertory* but relies on *variations* of her own megadecibel *hoot,* which *billows* in a *full-throated* way and also *grates* like a dentist's drill." Rewrite the sentence, using context clues to replace each italicized word with another word or phrase.

III. Analyzing Paragraphs

Reread the indicated paragraphs. Then choose the answer that best completes each sentence.

1. Paragraphs 1 through 3 do all but _____.
   a. introduce Julie Hette's profession
   b. mention some places Julie Hette is hired to laugh
   c. tell about Julie Hette's childhood

2. Paragraphs 4 through 7 do all but _____.

    a. show how Julie Hette became a professional laugher

    b. show why everyone encouraged Julie Hette to laugh

    c. show why people notice Julie Hette's laugh

3. Paragraphs 9 through 13 discuss how Julie Hette has been hired for all these reasons except _____.

    a. to laugh on dull, formal occasions

    b. to laugh at presidential candidates

    c. to laugh at unfunny jokes

4. Paragraph 15 shows that people react to Julie Hette's laugh in all these ways except _____.

    a. by backing away from her

    b. by telling her to be quiet

    c. by telling her to laugh some more

IV. Talking and Writing

Discuss the following topics. Then choose one of them to write about.

1. When and where is it appropriate to laugh? Have your ideas about this changed as you have gotten older?

2. Do people in some countries laugh more than people in other countries?

3. Julie Hette is critical of the French and thinks their sense of humor is lacking. What do you think about the sense of humor of most people from your country? Could it use improvement?

4. Julie Hette thinks that modern life is stressful and discourages laughter. Do you agree? Can a sense of humor thrive in hard times?

2. Walden Revisited: The Perils of Country Houses

Previewing the Article

Walden is the name of a wooded area and a pond near Concord, Massachusetts. But to students of American literature, the name means much more. In a one-room cabin beside Walden Pond, a brilliant naturalist and philosopher wrote one of the great American literary works. His name was Henry David Thoreau.

Thoreau's masterpiece, *Walden,* was an autobiographical book about nature and philosophy. In it, Thoreau urged his readers to simplify their needs. Then they wouldn't have to work at jobs they hated just to pay for unnecessary possessions. They'd have more time to do what was really important and interesting to them.

Thoreau wanted to try living simply, so he built himself a cabin near Walden Pond and lived there for more than two years. He paid no rent and spent very little money on food or other supplies. Besides fishing, cooking, gardening, and other activities to supply his basic needs, Thoreau spent his time studying nature and writing in his journal. From those journal notes came *Walden,* published in 1854.

As the following article indicates, Thoreau moved into his tiny cabin on July 4, 1845— Independence Day in the United States. He chose this date for a reason. At Walden, he was totally free to be himself and to pursue his own interests.

This article is not based upon an interview (although most profiles are). It is a profile in a more general meaning of the word. That is, it is a summary of a person's life and values.

Before You Read

Discuss these questions and do the map search.

1. Find Concord, Massachusetts, on a map of the United States.

2. Discuss the meanings of

   - the article's headline;

   - the word *unconventional.*

3. Thoreau was born in 1817 and died in 1862. Slavery was the major political and social issue in the United States during those years. What, do you think, was Thoreau's position on slavery?

As You Read

Look for answers to these questions.

1. Why was Thoreau called unconventional?

2. What made this article about Thoreau timely? What two events related to him were about to happen when this piece was published?

Walden Revisited: The Perils of Country Houses

By Suzanne Hamlin

New York Times Service

1 NEW YORK—On July 4, 1845, Henry David Thoreau celebrated quietly. On that day, the philosopher and naturalist moved into the cabin he had built on the side of Walden Pond in Concord, Massachusetts, and began to write the journal that would have a far greater impact on the world than the modest writer could have predicted.

2 Trying to live simply 150 years ago, the 28-year-old refugee from convention who was seeking solitude appears to have had the same problems as many country-house owners: a stream of guests, meal planning, curious neighbors, a garden needing constant tending and decorating decisions.

3 He thought he had dispensed the last consideration with dispatch: "It costs me nothing for curtains, for I have no gazers to shut out but the sun and moon and I am willing that they should look in."

4 But then it began. The entertaining! The visitors!

5 Unexpected guests started to come in droves, wrote Thoreau, the young schoolteacher and scholar (Harvard College, class of 1837) in "Walden," his journal of two years, two months and two days of roughing it in the woods. He had wanted quiet and time to think, away from the masses leading lives of quiet desperation. Instead, he became a captive host.

6 In "Walden: An Annotated Edition," to be published by Houghton Mifflin this month, a series of edifying notes has been added to the text by the editor, Walter Harding, a professor emeritus at the State University of New York who has studied Thoreau for 50 years. His notes make it clear that the eccentric young Thoreau and his homemade house became an attraction for the curious almost immediately.

7 Thoreau noted that "many a traveler came out of his way to see me and the inside of my house," including his family, friends, groups of schoolchildren, fellow philosophers, aimless tourists, trappers, hunters and the down and out from local almshouses who often, he found, were far more interesting than some of his more affluent drop-ins. "With respect to wit I discovered there was not much difference between the half and the whole."

8 Thoreau, shy and usually polite, had no tolerance for babble but was always responsive to thoughtful dialogue and particularly to children, who brought him flowers, weeds and dead animals they had found in the woods in an early version of show and tell. On the whole, they entertained themselves, unlike some of his adult "unreckoned guests," who expected to be directed on their day in the country. Some of the more shameless, Thoreau suspected, came when he was out walking in the woods and rooted through his drawers and cabinets.

9 Most of the drop-in guests came from nearby Concord and Lincoln, Massachusetts, or from Boston, about 12 miles (20 kilometers) away. "Girls and boys and young women generally seemed glad to be in the woods," Thoreau wrote. "They looked in the pond and at the flowers, and improved their time. Men of business, even farmers, thought only of solitude and employment, and of the great distance at which I dwelt from something or other; and though they said they loved a ramble in the woods occasionally, it was obvious that they did not."

10 Thoreau had excavated a cellar and built his 10-by-15-foot (3-by-4.5-meter) cabin on land lent to him by Ralph Waldo Emerson, a friend of his

NICULAE ASCIU/IHT

family, intellectuals of modest means who lived a mile away, in Concord.

11 He made some of the furniture and then filled in the gaps with castoffs, being careful to avoid an overdone look. ("Furniture! Thank God, I can sit and I can stand without the aid of a furniture warehouse.")

12 Completing the rustic ambiance, he added "a pair of tongs and andirons, a kettle, a skillet, and a frying pan, a dipper, a wash bowl, two knives and forks, three plates, one cup, one spoon, a jug for oil and a jug for molasses." Even the most obtuse visitor observed quickly that it would be difficult to stay for dinner.

13 Thoreau, a first-time householder, was determined to live on a strict budget and was not prepared to sacrifice writing time earning money "for fine cookery." He was convinced that "a man may use as simple a diet as the animals, and yet retain health and strength."

14 In the first eight months at Walden, Thoreau spent $8.74 for staples like rice, molasses, rye meal, corn meal, flour, sugar, lard, apples, salt, sweet potatoes, a pumpkin and a watermelon. The expense, which he thought was embarrassingly large, was reduced when he harvested his plot of beans and started to fish and to forage for wild greens and field corn. By conviction a vegetarian, he once splurged on a woodchuck but only because the little beast had ravaged his cornfield.

15 An impatient cook, he quickly discovered fast food: bread made from a Latin recipe, "which Marcus Porcius Cato gave about two centuries before Christ." The Walden flatbread was made with flour or meal and water, kneaded, molded and baked on a shingle over an outdoor fire. Although baking bread could be unpleasant in winter, at least, Thoreau noted, he had dispensed with the rising step. Yeast, he thought, was totally unnecessary and not, as local housewives had it, a health food: "after going without it for a year am still in the land of the living."

16 Thoreau's mother and sisters, worried that he wasn't eating properly, weekly brought him pies and cakes. But his diet was not nutritionally deficient, according to a detailed article in a 1977 edition of the Thoreau Society Bulletin called "T's Nutrition" by Daniel Wesolowski. Based on today's mantra of beans, greens and grains, the Walden diet appears almost prophetic.

17 For more than two years. Thoreau tilled the land, wrote, thought and walked. He took a getaway excursion to Maine and was jailed overnight for not paying poll taxes (the experience led to a series of lectures that became "Civil Disobedience"). Occasionally, he visited the always interesting Bronson Alcott family, fellow transcendentalists in search of a spiritual philosophy. Alcott's daughter, Louisa May, had been his pupil in the private school he had started in his early 20s with his brother, John.

18 When Thoreau went to Walden, his brother had recently died and his one and only proposal of marriage, to Ellen Sewell, had been rejected. Her father, a Unitarian minister, found the antislavery, freethinking Thoreaus to be troublesome rabble-rousers.

19 When Thoreau left the pond, it was not by desire but by request. Emerson, who was going abroad for a year, asked him to return to Concord to look after Mrs. Emerson and his two children. Later, Thoreau joined his father in the family's pencil manufacturing business while rewriting "Walden" for two years. (Thoreau lived with his parents and three unmarried sisters until he died of tuberculosis at 45.)

20 "The growing interest in Thoreau now is much like the 1960s," said Ellen Spear, the director of the 1,200-member Thoreau Society in Lincoln. Thursday, the group begins its annual four-day meeting, which is always held near Thoreau's birthday, July 12. The agenda includes lectures and a chance to wander through Walden Woods, a 2,680-acre area that encompasses the pond (overseen by the state of Massachusetts) and parts of both Lincoln and Concord. The site of Thoreau's cabin is now marked by stone posts. In a series of moves, it became a pig house and a shed before being dismantled for barn lumber.

I. Getting the Message

Many people have misconceptions about Thoreau and his life at Walden Pond. The information in this article disproves some of these misconceptions. Read each pair of sentences. Indicate which sentence states the truth (**T**) and which states a misconception (**M**).

1. a. _____ Thoreau was alone all of the time in Walden Woods.
   b. _____ Many people visited Thoreau at his cabin in the woods.

2. a. _____ Thoreau preferred the company of animals to that of human beings.
   b. _____ Thoreau enjoyed the company of children and his freethinking friends.

3. a. _____ Thoreau's family brought him pies and cakes every week.
   b. _____ Thoreau ate only what he could catch or grow.

4. a. _____ Thoreau made some of his furniture and brought some of it from town.
   b. _____ Thoreau built all the furniture in his cabin.

5. a. _____ Thoreau never left Walden Woods during the two years he lived there.

   b. _____ Thoreau visited friends and even took a trip to Maine during the years he lived in his cabin.

6. a. _____ Thoreau moved out of his cabin at the request of his friend Ralph Waldo Emerson.

   b. _____ Thoreau moved out of his cabin because he was tired of living in the woods.

Check your answers with the key on page 181. If you have made mistakes, reread the article to gain a better understanding of it.

II. Expanding Your Vocabulary

A. Recalling Words from the Reading

Choose the best word or phrase to complete each sentence. Do the exercise without looking at the article. Then check your answers by rereading the indicated paragraphs.

1. A lot of people came to Walden Pond to visit Thoreau. In fact, people came _____. (2, 5)
   a. in droves
   b. in solitude

2. People wanted to see Thoreau's cabin. They were very interested in it. In other words, they were _____ about it. (6, 9)
   a. curious
   b. obvious

3. A person who is not very smart is _____. (12)
   a. obese
   b. obtuse

4. Thoreau's handmade furniture fit in well in his simple country house. The cabin had a rustic feeling or _____. (7, 12)
   a. ambiance
   b. affluent

5. Because of the way he lived, many people considered Thoreau _____. (6, 15)
   a. eccentric
   b. impatient

6. Thoreau didn't use yeast when he made bread, so his bread didn't rise. He _____ that step in bread making. (15)
   a. disposed of
   b. dispensed with

B. Using Adjectives to Describe a Person

The adjectives listed below appear in the article. Which ones are used to describe Thoreau?

affluent	interesting	shameless
curious	modest	shy
eccentric	obtuse	spiritual
freethinking	polite	troublesome
impatient	prophetic	unexpected

III. Working with Idioms and Expressions ─────────────────

Study the meanings of these idioms and expressions. A form of each one appears in the indicated paragraph of the article.

with dispatch (3)   quickly
half-wit (7)   a foolish person
down and out (7)   destitute; people without money, friends, or prospects
drop-ins (7)   uninvited, unexpected guests
show and tell (8)   a school activity for children; bringing something from home to show in class and tell about
castoffs (11)   things that people throw away or give away

Answer these questions.

1. What decorating problem did Thoreau solve *with dispatch?*

2. What did children bring to Thoreau for *show and tell?*

3. Who were the *drop-ins* that came to Thoreau's cabin by Walden Pond?

4. Which did Thoreau find more interesting—the visitors who were *down and out* or his more affluent friends?

5. Is a *half-wit* a witty person?

IV. Making Sense of Sentences ─────────────────

Find each phrase in the paragraph indicated in parentheses. Use context clues to determine the meaning of the phrase. Then choose the statement that best expresses the meaning.

1. refugee from convention (2)   a. He rejected the conventions of society.
                                    b. Conventional society had rejected him.

2. quiet desperation (5)   a. Silence bothered them. They liked noise.
                                    b. They were silent about their unhappiness.

3. captive host (5)   a. He forced his guests to stay.
                                    b. He was forced to entertain unwanted guests.

4. edifying notes (6)   a. The notes are edible.
                        b. The notes explain and clarify.

5. no tolerance for babble (8)   a. He hated meaningless conversation.
                                 b. He hated the sound of water running.

6. of modest means (10)   a. He was modest about his wealth.
                          b. He wasn't wealthy.

V. Talking and Writing

Discuss the following topics. Then choose one of them to write about.

1. Compare these two quotations:

   • "Sell your clothes and keep your thoughts."

   • "Clothes make the man."

   Which one do you think was said by Thoreau? Do you agree with either one? Why or why not?

2. Do you have time to do the things that are meaningful to you, or are you living a life of "quiet desperation"? If so, what can you do to make more time for activities that are important to you?

3. The author makes two humorous comparisons:

   • the comparison between Thoreau's cabin and a country house

   • the comparison between Thoreau's bread and today's fast food

   Why are they funny?

3. Art as Memory: Filmmaker's Vietnam

Previewing the Article

Are you haunted by a memory? Sometimes the best way to get a memory out of your head is to share it with others. Many Americans have turned painful memories of their wartime experience in Vietnam into powerful antiwar books and films. So when the words *filmmaker* and *Vietnam* appear together, the horrors of quiet villages turned into fiery battle zones come quickly to mind.

But the movies of the young Vietnamese director Tran Anh Hung are not about the war. Hung has filmed his memories of Vietnamese family life and his observations of contemporary Vietnamese culture. His first film, *The Scent of Green Papaya,* won honors in France and the United States, but it was harshly criticized in Vietnam. This profile explains why.

Though the Vietnam War is not the subject of Hung's movies, it had a major impact upon his life and work. The war between North and South Vietnam began in 1957. By the time it ended in 1975, nearly two million Vietnamese (and about 58,000 Americans) had died. Because of the war, Hung lived most of his childhood as an exile. This fact has affected both his work and audience reaction to it.

This profile gives readers a clear picture of Tran Anh Hung, including his appearance and personality. The article also reveals Hung's goals and inner strength. The reader, of course, views Hung through the eyes of the interviewer. The interviewer's high expectations for Hung are obvious.

Before You Read

Discuss these questions and do the map search.

1. On a map of the world, find the three countries Tran Anh Hung has lived in: Vietnam, Laos, and France.

2. Discuss the meanings of these words: *criticism, ambiguity, dilemma.*

3. What is a *paradox?* Can you give an example of a paradox?

As You Read

Look for the following:

1. two reasons why many Vietnamese didn't like Hung's first movie

2. words that relate to movies (Later, check your list with the one in Exercise II C.)

3. clues that will help you decide if this interview was conducted in English, French, or Vietnamese

Art as Memory: Filmmaker's Vietnam

By Carey Zesiger

1 HO CHI MINH CITY—Tran Anh Hung settles himself in a chair at the coffee shop of the Kim Do hotel. Gaunt but energetic, he speaks softly and struggles at times to make himself heard over the din of voices and squeal of fax machines from the hotel lobby.

2 The setting is a far cry from the meditative calm of his childhood Saigon, so tenderly portrayed in his impressionist first film, "The Scent of Green Papaya." But the young director seems unfazed. After receiving an Academy Award nomination for best foreign film and France's César for his first effort, his cinematic future appears secure. Memories of his days of working part-time at the Musée d'Orsay bookstore in Paris to make ends meet are beginning to fade.

3 Hung has just finished filming "Cyclo," shot entirely on location in Ho Chi Minh City. He explains that he had originally intended to shoot "Papaya" there as well, but upon returning to Vietnam in 1991, he soon revised his plans. Confronted by the fact that the Saigon of his childhood no longer existed, Hung opted to try to re-create it in a studio in France.

4 "I realized that the city here did not offer the setting I wanted," he said. "What I wanted was not a documentary on the country, but more of a mental vision I had."

5 In his films and in life, Hung shows an exile's preoccupation with memory, engaged in a constant quest to recapture the past and come to terms with the present. He cites Akira Kurosawa's dictum, "To create is to remember," and explains, "You have experienced a certain number of things in your childhood and these remain the strongest. Afterward everything flows from this. It could be a feeling, a smell, anything. And when one goes after the deepening of this vague feeling, which is memory, you can build a screenplay or make a film."

6 The process of reconstructing an image of Vietnam in a distant land was not an entirely new experience for Hung, whose parents saw to it that neither he nor his younger brother ever forgot where they were from. Transplanted to Laos at the age of 4, Hung was uprooted and brought to France at age 12. Preserving Vietnamese family traditions became almost an obsession with his parents.

7 "In Laos we lived in a small Vietnamese community, a miniature, transposed Vietnam." He pauses a moment. "When you live in Vietnam you are not so much preoccupied with what you have, with the traditions, but when you are in Laos, so as not to lose [the past] your parents are obliged to repeat things over and over. The result is that I know more about certain things than some of the Vietnamese living in Vietnam."

8 His apparent confidence on this point may reveal a slight defensiveness. Despite his critical successes, he has not always found full acceptance among his countrymen. Some Vietnamese both here and abroad have taken issue with his ability to represent them on the big screen, criticizing the narrow, slice-of-life focus of his first film, which virtually ignored his country's war-torn history and presented what some considered a romanticized portrait of Vietnamese family life.

9 Hung chafes at such critiques. He argues that too much celluloid had already been devoted to the war, that he wanted to break away from the Hollywood mold by offering a more intimate view of the country and its people.

10 "It was a way for me to give an image of Vietnam that was totally different from anything one would have imagined, especially for Americans," he says. "Americans have an image of Vietnam that is totally warped by all of the war movies and I want to remind them that there is also a mother and a little girl who can have very simple everyday exchanges. . . . And it is in these moments that one finds humanity."

11 Some of the criticism has clearly struck home. "My position is difficult," he explains, "because I feel like people demand too much of me, that they ask for me to give the totality of Vietnam in one film."

12 In the West, for better or worse, he is viewed as a Vietnamese filmmaker, but in Vietnam he is still regarded as an outsider. In the end, he occupies an uneasy position between these two worlds that is difficult to resolve. It is an ambiguity that may be summed up for him in two words: *viet kieu* (overseas Vietnamese).

13 "For me, the difficulty is purely psychological. . . . I am seen as viet kieu, in other words a Vietnamese who is somehow impure, who is not entirely of Vietnam, who is in some ways a monster, a foreigner. I don't let myself get too depressed about this. I just ask that people understand that this is my life, that's all, and it's not my fault."

14 In "Cyclo," he has sought to deflect some of his critics by taking on a contemporary theme. Filming on location with a Vietnamese cast, the "realism" of his work should be less of an issue this time. When people see the film, he says, "If they say they don't recognize today's Vietnam, then I will have to say, I failed."

15 Hung attempts to capture the tumult of images and emotions he experienced upon his return to Vietnam in 1991. "This sensation provides the rhythm of the entire film," he says, creating a very different pace and style from that of his previous film. He plunged his cameras into the chaotic and notoriously unpredictable streets of Ho Chi Minh City.

16 Named for the bicycle rickshaw that plies the streets of both the old and the new city, "Cyclo" traces the story of a young cyclo driver whose vehicle is stolen. In order to climb out of debt and repay the owner of his vehicle, the character begins to explore the city's seamy underworld. One aspect of the story that particularly attracted Hung was the mobility of the cycle, its ability to cut across the geographical and social divides, "from the shantytowns beside the blackened rivers to the New World Hotel."

17 As in his first film, he intends to present a vivid slice of Vietnamese life, but this time he has angled his knife quite differently. In the first film he took a close-up look at the dynamics of family life; in the second the camera pulls back to reveal a wider social tableau. Trying to bring the same intimate feel and sensitivity to bear on a very different subject matter posed a serious challenge: "I hope the sensibility is the same, in that, if you have the sensibility to create something very gentle, then that same sensibility can make something violent, extremely brutal . . . . I hope to make a film that has a gentle manner, but depicts violence, which is paradoxical."

18 Paradox is an apt word for Hung and his oeuvre. Ambitious and bold, it is the work of a man who, though shy by nature, feels compelled to explain himself. He lives with the chronic fear of being misunderstood, a dilemma he shares with Vietnam and its people. In the end, this is perhaps the one thing that indisputably unites them. The strange yin and yang of gentleness and violence that he is at such pains to explain is Vietnam's paradox as well.

Carey Zesiger is a free-lance writer living in Vietnam.

I. Getting the Message

After reading the article, indicate if each item is true (**T**) or false (**F**).

1. _____ The subject of this profile is a Vietnamese movie actor.
2. _____ According to the article, Tran Anh Hung is still living in exile.
3. _____ Some Vietnamese criticize Hung because of what his films are *not* about.
4. _____ Hung's goal is to create the best movie ever made about the Vietnam War.
5. _____ Hung was once a rickshaw driver.
6. _____ Hung's second film is about life in Vietnam today.
7. _____ Hung often uses his own memories and feelings in his films.
8. _____ Hung doesn't care whether the Vietnamese like his movies or not.
9. _____ The author of this article thinks that Hung has a good future as a film director.
10. _____ The interview for this article took place in Hung's apartment.

Check your answers with the key on page 181. If you have made mistakes, reread the article to gain a better understanding of it.

II. Expanding Your Vocabulary

A. Getting Meaning from Context

Find each word or phrase in the paragraph indicated in parentheses. Use context clues to determine the meaning of the word. Choose the best definition.

1. din (1)
   a. loud noise
   b. soft music
2. preoccupation (5)
   a. past job
   b. complete attention given to one idea, thing, or person
3. critical (8)
   a. based on the judgment of critics
   b. disapproving of
4. criticizing (8)
   a. expressing approval of
   b. expressing dislike of
5. romanticized (8)
   a. made into a love story
   b. unrealistic; presented as better than it really was
6. chafes at (9)
   a. becomes irritated with
   b. agrees with
7. oeuvre (18)
   a. attitude
   b. work

B. Understanding the Exact Meaning

To understand an author's exact meaning, readers must notice *qualifying words:* adjectives or adverbs that limit or change the meaning of the words they describe.

Choose the correct meaning for each italicized phrase. For context clues, reread the indicated paragraphs.

1. The expression *critical success* (8) means that _____.
   a. the general public liked the movie very much
   b. reviewers and other film experts liked the movie

2. The author mentions Hung's *apparent confidence* (8). This phrase suggests that
_____.

   a. Hung looks confident, but he may not feel as confident as he looks
   b. Hung's confidence is easy to see

3. Hung's first film *virtually ignored* (8) his country's war-torn history. This means that
_____.

   a. the film completely ignored it
   b. the film ignored it most of the time

4. Many Vietnamese distrust Hung because they consider him an outsider, but Hung says, *"I don't let myself get too depressed about this"* (13). He means that
_____.

   a. it doesn't bother him at all; he never thinks about it
   b. he doesn't allow himself to become very unhappy about it

C. Studying Words about Moviemaking

How many words about moviemaking did you find in the article? Discuss the meanings of these terms:

big screen (8)	cinematic (2)	documentary (4)	on location (3)
camera (17)	close-up (17)	film (2)	shoot (3)
celluloid (9)	director (2)	Hollywood (9)	shot (3)

III. Working with Idioms and Expressions

Study the meanings of these idioms and expressions. A form of each one appears in the indicated paragraph of the article.

a far cry from (2)   very different from
make ends meet (2)   manage to live on one's income
come to terms with (5)   learn to accept
slice-of-life (8)   an intimate look at one aspect of people's lives
strike home (11)   be felt by the intended person
for better or worse (12)   under any conditions; no matter what happens
yin and yang (18)   two principles of Chinese philosophy. *Yin* is passive, dark, and feminine. *Yang* is active, bright, and masculine. Their interaction is believed to influence destiny.

Answer these questions.

1. Why is the hotel lobby *a far cry from* the Saigon of Hung's childhood?
2. What kind of work did Hung once do to *make ends meet?*
3. What does Hung have to *come to terms with?*
4. *For better or worse,* Hung is considered a Vietnamese filmmaker. What might be the advantages and disadvantages of that?

5. In the last paragraph of the article, why are gentleness and violence related to *yin and yang?* Which one is yin and which is yang?

IV. Making Sense of Sentences

One way to describe an idea is by contrasting it with another idea; that is, by showing how it is different from the other idea.

Answer the following questions about the use of contrast in this article.

1. In paragraph 1, what two examples of contrast can you find?

2. What is being contrasted in the second sentence of paragraph 9?

3. At the end of paragraph 16, a contrast is made in the direct quotation, using the words *from* and *to.* What is the meaning of the contrast?

4. What is the paradoxical contradiction Hung describes in paragraph 17?

V. Talking and Writing

Discuss the following topics. Then choose one of them to write about.

1. What, if anything, is missing from this profile? What would you like to know about Hung that the author didn't tell you?

2. Some Vietnamese criticize Hung for not dealing with the war in his films. Do you think it is fair to criticize a creative artist because of the subject matter he chose *not* to deal with? Is it fair to consider the subject matter at all in evaluating a work of art?

3. In this article, you read about Hung's *preoccupation* and his parents' *obsession.* Compare and contrast the meanings of these two words. Is it better to be preoccupied or obsessed? Which word has stronger negative connotations? Which one would you use to describe your own great interest in something or someone? Tell about a preoccupation or obsession that you once had or still have.

4. Kenya City Learns to Accept a New Kind of Mayor

Previewing the Article

She's 24 years old, female, and the mayor of a sizable city. This would be unusual almost anywhere, but it's especially so in Africa, where women have only recently begun to push their way into the world of politics.

Agatha Mbogo is mayor of the city of Embu in Kenya. The following profile tells readers how she managed to reach this high position and what she has accomplished since taking office. The author is quite politically correct in not giving personal information about the mayor's looks or love life. The information presented in this article is no different than what would be said about a male mayor. This, in itself, says much about women's progress in achieving equal treatment.

The election of Mbogo is encouraging to Kenyan women, but they have a long road to travel to reach political equality. The republic of Kenya is headed by a president, assisted by twenty cabinet ministers. No woman has ever held a cabinet position. The country's National Assembly (its legislative body) has two hundred members. Although 60 percent of Kenya's voters are female, women make up only three percent of the National Assembly.

Another barrier keeps some Kenyans from participating intelligently in the political process: a language barrier. Kenyans belong to about 40 different ethnic groups, most of which have their own language or dialect. Some Kenyans know only their local language. However, many also know Swahili, the national language, and most educated Kenyans speak English, the country's official language.

Before You Read

Discuss these questions and do the map search.

1. Find Kenya, Nairobi, and Embu on a map of Africa. Note that the equator runs through Kenya. What kind of climate would you expect to find there?

2. What do you know about the roles of women in Kenya and other African countries?

3. What does the word *revolutionary* mean? Give examples of different kinds of revolutions, both political and social.

As You Read

Look for answers to these questions.

1. Why is it important for Kenyan women to become politically active?

2. How did the author gather information for this profile? What types of people did he talk to?

Kenya City Learns to Accept a New Kind of Mayor

By Stephen Buckley
Washington Post Service

1 EMBU, Kenya—Unassuming and soft-spoken, Agatha Muthoni Mbogo, 24, defies the image of a revolutionary. Yet, six months ago, she did a most revolutionary thing: She ran for mayor of this city of 66,000 people and won.

2 Miss Mbogo's victory was even more startling because she was voted in by her colleagues on the District Council, all men. For the thousands of women in this farming area two hours northeast of Nairobi, Miss Mbogo suddenly became a symbol of the increasingly potent political force women have become in Kenya and across Africa.

3 The multiparty movement that gripped Africa during the late 1980s and early 1990s has galvanized women across the continent, leading to a bevy of political groups and spurring hundreds of women to run for office.

4 African women are still years from political equality with men, who continue to dominate local and national legislatures as well as most countries' major policy-making positions. But, for the first time, women like Miss Mbogo have gotten a foot in the door to political power.

5 Since 1992, when Kenya dropped its single-party system, women have won 50 local political posts, doubling the positions they held before. The League of Women Voters, founded in 1992, now has 7,882 members. Six women have been elected to the National Assembly, the most ever.

6 This political progress has been mirrored across the continent. Uganda has the first female vice president in its history. The foreign minister of Burundi is a woman. The prime minister of Rwanda, killed in last spring's massacres, was a woman. In Tanzania, at least 15 percent of the National Assembly seats must be held by women. South

Africa became one of the continent's first nations to explicitly protect women's rights in its constitution.

7 "Women across Africa have similar problems, and we realize that if we are going to solve those problems we must have representation in the making of our nations' laws and policies," said Lilian Mwaura, chairman of the National Council of Women of Kenya.

8 The increased activism has had a price, however, as governments frequently break up meetings of women's groups, and female politicians are often harangued about their personal lives.

9 None of that deterred Miss Mbogo, who said she has long dreamed of a career in politics. She launched that dream in 1992 by running for the Embu council, facing the daunting obstacles that often plague African women vying for political office.

10 She had little money. She had no political experience. She had no trans-

Mayor Agatha Muthoni Mbogo of Embu, Kenya, a city of 66,000 residents, greets a produce seller at the downtown market. While government circles remain dominated by men, women across Africa have succeeded at gaining greater access at all levels.

THE WASHINGTON POST

portation. She faced a torrent of questions about her personal life.

11 "My opponent kept insisting that I was going to get married to somebody in another town and move away," Miss Mbogo said. "I kept telling the people, 'Give me a try. Let us try a woman.'"

12 Miss Mbogo also faced ignorance among the town's women, many of whom initially balked at voting for her. She gave speeches before women's groups and trudged from door to door, spending hours at a time giving a combination speech and civics lesson.

13 "I was overjoyed when she won, because men elected her," said Lydiah Kimani, 47, an Embu farmer and political activist. "It was a step forward for us because it seemed to be a victory over this stereotype of 'women can't lead.'"

14 Civic education of African women has become a top priority for political activists. The League of Women Voters, for example, has held dozens of workshops in rural Kenya to help women understand the procedures and philosophical underpinnings of a multiparty system.

15 Jael Mbogo, 51, a veteran political activist, said that many women, especially in rural areas, had not been taught the basics of political participation.

16 They are taught to vote for the one who "gives you a half-kilo of sugar" during the campaign, said the activist, no relation to Agatha Mbogo. "We must teach them that it is better to learn how to catch a fish than for someone to put the fish in your hand."

17 Women politicians and activists say they are bucking deeply engrained cultural mores. Those mores teach that African women cook, clean, take care of children, plant and harvest crops and support their husbands. They typically do not inherit land, divorce their husbands, control their finances or hold political office.

18 Yet, political activism among Kenyan women is not a new phenom-enon. During the struggle for independence in the 1950s, Kenyan women often secretly outfitted fighters with weapons and spied on the positions of colonial forces.

19 But after independence, political leaders shut them out of power, a scenario repeated across the continent.

20 Today, women make up 60 percent of Kenya's electorate but only 3 percent of the National Assembly. They produce 60 percent of the nation's food, but earn one-third of the typical male worker's salary. No Kenyan woman has ever held a cabinet post.

21 Against that backdrop, Agatha Mbogo began her political career. After winning her council seat, she asserted herself by declining a spot on the education and social services committee after a colleague called it "a woman's committee." She instead joined the town planning committee, a much more visible assignment.

22 Then last year, she decided to challenge Embu's mayor, a veteran politician. Miss Mbogo said she had become frustrated because the donor groups that provide substantial aid to Kenya's rural areas "did not want to come here."

23 "We weren't seeing things done for the community," she said. "The donors' money seemed to be going to individuals."

24 After a fierce campaign, the council elected her, 7 to 6. She said women in Embu exulted. Men were puzzled; some were hostile. They asked, "How could all of those men vote for a woman?" she recalled.

25 Samuel Muraguri, 49, a council member, admitted that years ago, he would not have voted for a woman. "I grew up during a time when people did not accept that women could lead," he said. "That is what we learned in school. That is what we learned at home. Now, we have been educated."

26 Miss Mbogo has not met with the kinds of verbal and physical assaults that other female politicians have been subjected to. Some have said their supporters are sometimes attacked with machetes and clubs after rallies.

27 Last June, Kenyan police attempted to break up a women's political meeting near Nairobi, insisting it was illegal. When the 100 women, including a member of the National Assembly, refused to go, officers beat them with batons and fists, witnesses reported.

28 Agnes Ndetei, a National Assembly member who was not at that gathering, said she no longer held large political meetings. "I meet with two or three women at a time because that is the only way I can do it without the police bothering us," she said.

29 Miss Mbogo generally receives warm greetings from the men of Embu, and many say they are now glad the council chose her.

30 Donor groups are funding projects again in Embu. A new market is going up downtown. A 200-bed maternity ward is being added to the hospital. A dormitory-style home has been built for the dozens of street children who once terrorized the city.

31 Miss Mbogo is especially proud of the market and the maternity ward because "they touch areas that have an impact on women."

32 At the current market, hundreds of sellers, shaded by umbrellas, lay out fruits and vegetables on burlap sheets, Lucy Wanjiku, 35, who sells potatoes, said she liked the new mayor.

33 "I feel like if I have a problem, I can go to her office," she said. "The other mayor shouted. He did not want to hear my problems."

34 Nearby, Joseph Kariuku, 32, said he found Miss Mbogo a refreshing change. "I am tired of men," he said, watching over his pile of onions. "They give us so many promises, but they don't deliver the goods. As long as she keeps giving us what we want, she is all right."

I. Getting the Message ————————————————

A. Reading for Details

After reading the article, indicate if each statement is true (**T**) or false (**F**). For help, reread the paragraphs indicated in parentheses.

1. _____ Mbogo's behavior is like that of a typical revolutionary. (1)
2. _____ Before 1992, women held only 25 of Embu's political positions. (5)
3. _____ In Africa, women are making progress in obtaining political power. (6)
4. _____ In Tanzania, the law requires that women hold 15% or more of the seats in the National Assembly. (6)
5. _____ Mbogo became mayor because the citizens of Embu elected her to that position. (2, 13, 24)
6. _____ Mbogo didn't want to be on the education and social services committee because she is not really interested in the problems of women. (21, 31)

B. Finding Information

Does this profile give you the following information about Agatha Mbogo? Write **yes** or **no**. If you find the information, tell which paragraph you found it in. (**Note:** Some of the answers may be implied, not directly stated.)

1. Mbogo's age _____
2. Mbogo's educational background _____
3. the name of her political party _____
4. her marital status _____
5. the year that she became mayor _____
6. some reasons the citizens of the city like her _____

Check your answers with the key on page 181. If you have made mistakes, reread the article to gain a better understanding of it.

II. Expanding Your Vocabulary ————————————————

A. Getting Meaning from Context

Find each word in the paragraph indicated in parentheses. Use context clues to determine the meaning of the word. Choose the best definition.

1. startling (2)   a. surprising   b. expected
2. potent (2)   a. weak   b. strong
3. deterred (9)   a. discouraged   b. encouraged
4. vying (9)   a. competing   b. resigning from
5. opponent (11)   a. supporter   b. competitor; rival
6. civic (14)   a. basic; primary   b. pertaining to a city or citizenship

| 7. mores (17) | a. increased amounts | b. basic moral views of a group |
| 8. declining (21) | a. going down | b. refusing |

B. Using Vocabulary from the Article

Find each italicized word in the indicated paragraph. Reread the paragraph. Then answer the question.

1. In what sense is Agatha Mbogo a *revolutionary?* (1)

2. What is Mbogo a *symbol* of? (2)

3. What is political *activism?* (8)

4. What is one African *stereotype* about women that is mentioned in this article? (13)

5. What do African *mores* say about the proper roles for women? (17)

III. Working with Idioms and Expressions —————————————————

Study the meanings of these idioms and expressions. A form of each one appears in the indicated paragraph of the article.

get a foot in the door (4)   begin to make progress in something
have a price (8)   have a disadvantage; require a sacrifice
break up (8)   end by force
dream of (9)   hope to achieve in the future
a step forward (13)   slight movement toward a goal; a little progress
deeply engrained (17)   an integral part of something; not superficial
no longer (28)   not anymore
deliver the goods (34)   do what was promised

Answer these questions.

1. If you *get a foot in the door,* have you taken *a step forward?*

2. What did the Kenya police *break up?*

3. What do you think Kenyan women *dream of?*

4. Many citizens of Kenya feel that Mbogo *has delivered the goods.* Why do they feel that way?

5. Increased activism on the part of Kenyan women *has had a price.* What is it?

6. Are cultural mores *deeply engrained,* or are they easy to change?

7. Does Kenya still have a single-party political system, or does it *no longer* have that kind of system?

IV. Making Sense of Sentences _____

Reread the paragraphs indicated in parentheses, and find the noun or noun phrase that each italicized pronoun or adjective refers to. Write the noun or noun phrase.

1. *"this* farming area" (1–2) Embu, Kenya _____

2. *"who* continue to dominate" (4) _____

3. *"we* must have representation" (7) _____

4. "many of *whom"* (12) _____

5. *"they* are taught" (15–16) _____

6. *"who* was not at that gathering" (28) _____

7. *"she* said" (32–33) _____

8. *"I* am tired" (34) _____

V. Talking and Writing _____

Discuss the following topics. Then choose one of them to write about.

1. Do you know any stereotypes about college students? Discuss the characteristics often attributed to college students. Why do you think each stereotype developed? What is the difference between a *stereotype* and a *generalization?*

2. In your opinion, should women be involved in politics? Why or why not?

3. In your opinion, should there be any limits on the kinds of jobs women can hold? Is there any kind of work you believe women should *not* do? If so, why?

Focus on the Newspaper

The public is curious about people in the news. Whether these people are viewed as admirable or despicable, newspaper readers want to know all about them. A feature story that describes a person's lifestyle and attitudes is called a *profile*.

Some people are so prominent and important that they are always newsworthy. But most celebrity profiles are printed around the time of a news event involving that person. For example, a well-known entertainer is profiled when appearing in a new show; a famous athlete is profiled after winning a big game; political figures are profiled around election time; and accused criminals are profiled when their trial is in the news. A person who is not a celebrity may also be the subject of a profile if he or she has done something heroic or been involved in an interesting story.

The Subjects of Profiles

Profiles typically do the following:

- tell something about a person's personal life

- tell about the person's current work or production

- reveal the person's professional goals, style, sources of inspiration, and attitudes toward his or her career.

The information in a profile comes from a journalist's interview with the person. A profile usually contains many direct quotations, so that readers share the experience of hearing the subject of the profile talk.

A good profile makes readers feel that they know and understand the person being interviewed. Often, this leads to a better understanding and appreciation of the person's work.

Exercise 1: What's in a Profile?

Find a profile in a newspaper. Analyze the profile by answering these questions.

ANALYZING A PROFILE

---

1. Why did the newspaper run a profile on this person at this time?

2. Did you know anything about the person before you read the article? If so, did the article cause you to change your attitude toward this person? Did you find out anything new that surprised you about the person?

3. Did the article stimulate your interest in the person's work? Why or why not?

4. How does the author of the profile seem to feel toward the subject?

5. What influenced your impression of the subject the most: the quotations from the person being profiled or the comments of the writer of the profile?

6. What would you like to know about the subject that the article did not tell you?

Exercise 2: Comparing the Profiles in *Morning Edition*

After reading the profiles in this section, discuss these questions with a partner or write your answers to them.

1. Which of the profiles in this section did you find most interesting? Why?

2. Which profile do you think is the best? Why?

How Profiles Personalize the News

Like other feature stories, profiles make newspaper (and magazine) reading more interesting. They tie events to the people who are involved in them. By comparing a news story with a profile, you will discover elements of style and content that enable a profile to draw a clear picture of a person in the news.

Exercise 3: Comparing a News Story and a Profile

Find a news story and a profile of a related person in the same issue of a newspaper. Compare the two articles. Put a check (√) in the correct column to show which articles contained the following information.

Information	News story	Profile
1. the subject's age	_____	_____
2. the subject's marital status	_____	_____
3. a physical description of the subject	_____	_____
4. information about the subject's education or childhood	_____	_____
5. a direct quotation of the subject's words	_____	_____
6. information about the subject's future plans	_____	_____
7. information about a controversy involving the subject	_____	_____
8. the journalist's attitude toward the subject	_____	_____
9. the reason why the person is in the news now	_____	_____
10. clues or direct statements indicating that the journalist interviewed the subject face-to-face or over the phone	_____	_____
11. answers to the five "W" questions (*who, what, when, where, why*)	_____	_____

How to Write a Profile

Writing a good profile takes both skill and creativity. To find out how such a piece is put together, try writing one yourself. Follow these steps:

1. *Planning for the interview.* A good profile begins long before you sit down to write it. First, you must select an interesting subject—a person who is unusual in some way or who has had an unusual experience. Your subject must be accessible by phone or in person because it's difficult to write a good profile from secondary sources. You need an interview. Before the interview, write a list of questions. Good questions bring out not only the facts of the person's life but also values, opinions, and goals.

2. *Conduct the interview.* Go to the interview with a notepad, several pens or pencils, and (if possible) a tape recorder. Ask the subject's permission before taping. It's fine to adopt a conversational tone, but be sure that the subject, not you, does most of the talking. Include in your notes some of the subject's exact words so that you can quote the person directly. What does your subject look like? Take some notes on that. Also, if you are doing the interview in the subject's home or office, take notes on the surroundings, especially those that reveal something about the person's interests and habits.

3. *Write the profile.* Make the first paragraph an attention-getter. Start with an anecdote, a surprising fact, or a direct quotation. Use at least two direct quotes in the piece. Include a description of the subject's physical appearance. After you finish your story, give it a headline and dateline—and don't forget to give yourself a byline!

Published With The New York Times and The Washington Post

SECTION 5

ARTS / ENTERTAINMENT

1

George Eliot, Voice of a Century: A Biography

2

Race to Save Prague's Face

3

Disney Assailed for Pocahontas Portrayal

4

After an Epoch of Nagging, Christo Wraps Reichstag

5A

In Stone Age Cavern, a Stunning Menagerie

5B

Stone Age Picassos: 30,000-Year-Old-Trove

Focus on the Newspaper: Arts / Entertainment

1. George Eliot, Voice of a Century: A Biography

Previewing the Article

George Eliot stands alone as a towering figure of the 19th century in England. Although the 19th century produced many excellent female novelists, Eliot was the only woman writer who was also a revered intellectual.

This article is a review of a biography of Eliot. It communicates the enthusiasm felt by many readers of her work. George Eliot's struggle to establish herself as a writer in a male-dominated world is a fascinating story of great relevance to women's issues today.

This book review, like most film or theater reviews, does two things: First, it briefly summarizes the main idea of the work. Second, it tells the reviewer's opinion about the work. Book reviews are excellent sources of information as well as entertaining essays about topics of interest to the reader.

The following biographical information will help you read the article with greater understanding:

- *Queen Victoria* (1819–1901) was queen of England from 1837 to 1901.

- *Florence Nightingale* (1820–1910) was an English nurse and health-care reformer.

- *Henry James* (1843–1916) was a U.S. novelist who lived in England.

- *George Henry Lewes* (1817–1878) was an English writer and critic.

Before You Read

Discuss these questions.

1. What do you know about the role of women in the 19th century? How does this compare with the role of women today?

2. Have you ever read novels by George Eliot? What do you know about other 19th-century novelists such as Charles Dickens and Jane Austen?

3. Do you read book or film reviews regularly? Why or why not?

As You Read

Notice how much of the article summarizes the book and how much gives the reviewer's opinion about the book. What does this tell us about the reviewer's purpose?

George Eliot, Voice of a Century: A Biography

By Frederick R. Karl
Illustrated. 708 pages. $30
W.W. Norton

Reviewed by Christopher Lehmann-Haupt

1 At the peak of her achievement as a novelist, George Eliot "was one of the three most famous women in England, along with Queen Victoria and Florence Nightingale," Frederick R. Karl writes at the end of his monumental new biography, "George Eliot: Voice of a Century."

2 He continues, "Victoria gave her name to the century and Nightingale to the Crimean war, but Eliot gave the era its intellectual sweep, offered it moral stability and gave voice to the huge forces contesting one another."

3 Yet as Karl shows in abundant detail, Eliot's journey to renown was a long and difficult one. Not only did she start her life obscurely, as the youngest daughter of an estate manager near rural Coventry, she had to overcome every sort of obstacle to her development as a writer.

4 When she was 16, she took on the care of her beloved father's household after her mother died. Since she was "not physically prepossessing," as Karl puts it, she seemed destined for spinsterhood. ("She is magnificently ugly—deliciously hideous," a young Henry James would write to his father in 1869, when Eliot was 50. "Now in this vast ugliness resides a most powerful beauty which, in a very few minutes steals forth and charms the mind, so that you end as I ended, in falling in love with her.")

5 Moreover, her fiercely independent mind drove her against the currents of Victorian society. Early in 1842, when she was 22, she refused to accompany her father to church, an act that Karl interprets not only as a quest for religious independence but as a bid "for the freedom of a woman held in thrall to male domination."

6 Her rebellion set her on a course that culminated 12 years later when she eloped to the Continent with a married man, George Henry Lewes, an act that made her a social outcast in a society that cared profoundly about such conduct.

7 Fortunately, the intelligence that drove her to such conduct also worked on her behalf. Well read and adroit with languages, she won commissions to translate weighty philosophical works from German.

8 Contacts in London led to editorial work on the Westminster Review, a leading journal of the day. This put her in touch with people like Emerson, Herbert Spencer and eventually Lewes, who not only encouraged her to write fiction but also acted astutely as her literary agent.

9 In January 1858, she published her first book, a collection of three novellas under the title "Scenes of Clerical Life." In the next two decades she wrote "Adam Bede," "The Mill on the Floss," "Silas Marner," "Romola," "Felix Holt, the Radical," "Middlemarch" and "Daniel Deronda," among other works. The evolution from Mary Ann Evans to George Eliot was complete.

10 Her novels won her fame and wealth, but in Karl's version of her story she paid a considerable price in physical and psychological suffering. Frequently depressed and forever plagued with headaches and other physical ailments, she appears to have been someone who quite literally embodied her emotional conflicts.

11 Yet in Karl's view, the same conflicts account for her importance as a novelist and were the source of her ability to dramatize great moral dilemmas.

12 Karl, who has written biographies of Conrad, Kafka and Faulkner, undertook this life of Eliot in part because new material was available to him, and in part because he felt that Gordon Haight's "George Eliot" (1968), which he calls "the first authoritative biography," suffered from an "angle of vision" that is "narrow, squeezed, protective and carefully conventional." Karl opens up our perspective of Eliot by reading back from her fiction to her life, with many a warning of the dangers of such a maneuver.

13 The result is a dramatic psychological study that rarely drifts into the kind of trivial chronological detail that could easily have sunk a study of such great length.

Christopher Lehmann-Haupt is on the staff of The New York Times.

I. Getting the Message

After reading the article, choose the best answer for each item.

1. George Eliot is an important 19th-century figure because _____.
   a. she contributed greatly to the intellectual life of her time
   b. she was an important aide to the Queen
   c. she knew many famous people

2. The author of this book review thinks that _____.
   a. this book is a below-average biography
   b. this book is good, but others about Eliot are better
   c. this book is excellent

3. Before she started writing, George Eliot _____.
   a. had a life of wealth and ease
   b. encountered many difficulties
   c. lived in London and studied writing

4. George Eliot's refusal to attend church with her father was, according to the biographer, _____.
   a. an attempt to identify herself as a free woman
   b. a sign of her troubled family life
   c. the beginning of her difficulties with her father

5. According to the biographer, George Eliot's depression and headaches _____.
   a. kept her from being an even better novelist
   b. made her an interesting object for medical study
   c. helped her to portray moral and emotional conflict

Check your answers with the key on page 181. If you have made mistakes, reread the article to gain a better understanding of it.

II. Expanding Your Vocabulary

A. Getting Meaning from Context

Find each word in the paragraph indicated in parentheses. Use context clues to determine the meaning of the word. Choose the best definition.

1.	monumental (1)	a. architectural	b. important
2.	hideous (4)	a. ugly	b. hidden
3.	culminated (6)	a. ended	b. began
4.	adroit (7)	a. not straight	b. skillful
5.	astutely (8)	a. intelligently	b. greedily
6.	dramatize (11)	a. feel pain	b. show
7.	maneuver (12)	a. method	b. scholarship

B. Finding Opposites

Scan each paragraph indicated below for a word that means the opposite of the word listed. Use a dictionary if necessary.

1. stops (2)   _____

2. obscurity (3)   _____

3. easy (3) _____

4. hated (4) _____

5. agreed (5) _____

6. single (6) _____

7. figuratively (10) _____

8. insignificance (11) _____

9. odd (12) _____

III. Working with Idioms and Expressions

Study the meanings of these idioms and expressions. A form of each one appears in the indicated paragraph of the article.

at the peak of (1)   at the highest point of
give one's name to (2)   have one's own name be used to name something else
give voice to (2)   express something often not expressed by others
against the currents (5)   in the opposite direction
a bid for (5)   an attempt to get
hold in thrall to (5)   keep as a slave to
set on a course (6)   start going in a certain direction
put one in touch with (8)   help one to contact
pay a price (10)   suffer to gain something
account for (11)   explain
drift into (13)   slowly move without a good plan

Answer these questions.

1. How did George Eliot *give voice to* the great issues of her day?
2. What steps did George Eliot take to keep from being *held in thrall* by a male-dominated world?
3. According to the biographer, what *accounts for* George Eliot's success as a writer?
4. What was the *price* George Eliot *paid* for her fame?

IV. Focusing on Style and Tone

Good writers enliven their prose with colorful verbs and verb phrases that present a picture. They avoid flat verbs that can be vague and lifeless. For example, in paragraph 13, the reviewer says that this biography doesn't "drift into" trivial detail that "could easily have sunk" such a long book. The reader is given a picture of a boat at sea, drifting and sinking. This image gives the sentence more force than if the reviewer had used the terms *use* and *could have made uninteresting.*

Scan each paragraph indicated below for a verb that has nearly the same meaning as the listed verb but is more colorful. Use a dictionary if necessary.

1. gave (2) _____

2. lives (4) _____

3. comes out (4) _____

4. started (12) _____

5. establishes (12) _____

V. Talking and Writing

Discuss the following topics. Then choose one of them to write about.

1. Why does the reviewer admire this book? Is his opinion convincing? Would you read this book?

2. Can you think of any current women writers or artists whose lives are an inspiration to other women? How are their struggles similar to or different from those of George Eliot over a century ago?

3. The author of the biography notes that George Eliot expressed the basic moral and intellectual ideas of her day in her writing. Can you think of any writer or artist who does the same thing today?

2. Race to Save Prague's Face

Previewing the Article

Prague, the capital of the Czech Republic, is one of the oldest cities in central Europe. Relics from ancient Roman times have been found there, as well as a seventh-century cemetery. The city was established by German settlers in the year 759. Some of its structures date back to the 13th and 14th centuries. In the 1600s, Italian architects came to Prague. Some of the elaborate castles and churches they designed are still standing. Prague's nickname is "the City of a Hundred Spires."

Prague, called *Praha* in the Czech and Slovak languages, lies along both banks of the Vltava (Moldau) River. Many of its oldest castles and public buildings stand along the river. Some of the bridges that span the river were built in the 1300s and 1400s. The most famous of these is the Charles Bridge, discussed in this article.

Communist rule of Czechoslovakia ended in 1989. This peaceful change in government was referred to as the Velvet Revolution. In 1993, Czechoslovakia was divided into two countries: the Czech Republic and Slovakia.

Strangely enough, the beautiful outdoor art of Prague has suffered more damage during peacetime than it ever did during wars. Fortunately, the city has 84 skilled restorers working to save its crumbling sculptural and architectural treasures. The work is difficult and sometimes dangerous. But, as the following article demonstrates, to these workers it is a labor of love.

Before You Read

Discuss these questions and do the map search.

1. Find the Czech Republic, Prague, and the Vltava River on a recent map of Europe.

2. If you have lived in or visited Prague, what do you remember about the city and its outdoor art? Share your recollections with the class.

3. What other cities are you familiar with that have outdoor works of art hundreds of years old? Tell about them.

4. What do the following terms mean: *medieval, Renaissance, Gothic,* and *Baroque?*

5. Explain the difference in meaning between each pair of words: *sculpture* and *statue; sculpture* and *architecture; preserve* and *restore.*

As You Read

Do the following:

1. Look for information about how restorers preserve old outdoor works of art.

2. Make a list of things that have caused the structures to deteriorate.

Race to Save Prague's Face

Restorers Work to Preserve Stone from Time and Tourists

By Jane Perlez
New York Times Service

1   PRAGUE—With his red plastic bucket, some putty-like material and a spatula, Jan Branda is an expert on outdoor chins, noses, fingers and feet.

2   Lovingly, he restores glowing expressions to pockmarked cherubs, rubs down delicate hands encrusted with layers of grime and glues back feet splintered by severe weather.

3   Mr. Branda, a stonemason and sculptor, is one of the anonymous men who tend Prague's glorious collection of medieval, Baroque and Renaissance statues, monuments and buildings.

4   The other morning he was perched above the St. Matthias Gate at the Prague Castle, hidden by blue net and rusty scaffolding, touching up the mane of a royal lion and replacing an angel's chin.

5   "Rain collects on the chin and it falls off," said Mr. Branda, in blue coveralls and black beret, as he peered at a dented chin through his glasses.

6   All over Prague, it is a race against time to shore up the city's splendors before the sandstone statues crumble under the weight of pollution, the rumbling of streetcars and, most recently, vandalism by tourists who think a piece of Prague stone is a nice memento.

7   Unlike some European cities of architectural majesty, Prague emerged intact after World War II. Its curling medieval passageways and cobbled courtyards, its Gothic towers and vaults, its froth of Baroque churches and Art Nouveau mansions were unscathed by bombs.

8   But peace was not so gentle. Soot from coal-burning stoves and chemicals from factories poured down on centuries of cultural heritage. And while the guardians of Paris and Vienna were constantly retouching their beauty, the Communist would-be builders of a new worker state had less use for the heritage of a repudiated past.

9   In those years, men like Mr. Branda worked more often on projects intended for the greater glory of the state: the fixing up of statues and squares for party anniversaries and military parades.

10   "At least 80 percent of our statues and sculptures are in bad shape from assaults ranging from acid rain to mechanical damage," said Vratislav Nejedly, director of conservation at the Culture Ministry. "We have missing fingers, hands. Our roads were planned for horse carriages and now we have cars backing into statues."

11   The Culture Ministry has increased the money for restoration, partly in the belief that better-kept statues will reap an economic return from tourists.

12   Cupolas, fronts of churches and sides of buildings are swathed in protective netting as the ministry's 84 restorers tackle the city's long inventory of damaged goods.

13   For Mr. Branda and his fellow restorers, the work is less cosmetics for tourists than a passion to preserve the soul of the city. Sometimes they have to go to extraordinary lengths.

14   Many nights past midnight Mr. Branda and his colleague, Jiri Novotny, clambered onto the windswept roof of St. Salvator Church at the foot of Charles Bridge to wrap and tie up seven 17th-century stone statues of the disciples. In the dark, a crane then plucked the statues for safekeeping and repair in a workshop.

Charles Bridge is one of Prague's biggest tourist attractions.

15 "The streetcars had rattled them so much the statues were about to fall down on the people below," Mr. Branda said.

16 There were similar problems with the dagger-wielding stone giants at the St. Matthias Gate.

17 "They are replicas from 1902 of the 18th-century sculptor Frantisek Platzer," Mr. Branda said as if talking of an old friend. "It's unusual to work on replicas, but these are in a prominent place so it's important to restore them."

18 Especially, he said, since one of the outstretched arms was about to drop off.

19 Mr. Branda, who is 52, studied at the Academy of Art for six years and considers himself an artist, but he tries not to leave his own imprint on the works of some of Central Europe's finest Baroque sculptors, like Matyas Braun and Ferdinand Brokof. "I want to be the most anonymous man, to get as close as possible to the creator's work," he said.

20 The statues are cleaned with a mixture of ammonia to allow the stone to breathe. They are never stripped or painted. The restorers fret that as private buyers refurbish houses and palaces they add bright synthetic paint that suggests Disneyland elbowing its way into the old world.

21 One of the most scarred parts of Prague, Charles Bridge, is one of the biggest tourist attractions. Shoulder-to-shoulder throngs brush by 34 sandstone figures that line the parapets.

22 "Charles Bridge used to be like walking through a beautiful gallery," Mr. Branda said. "Now it's a marketplace and a dangerous place filled with gangsters. The tourists come at night and steal a halo of stars because they think it is gold. Or whole hands and fingers disappear. One of our sculptors always has several fingers ready to glue back on."

I. Getting the Message

After reading the article, indicate if each statement is true (**T**) or false (**F**). For help reread the paragraphs indicated in parentheses.

1. _____ Mr. Branda enjoys his job. (2)
2. _____ Tourists admire Prague's outdoor sculpture, so they are careful not to damage it in any way. (6, 22)
3. _____ After World War II, most of Prague was rebuilt. (7)
4. _____ After World War II, the old buildings and sculpture in Paris and Vienna were kept in better condition than those in Prague. (8)
5. _____ The Cultural Ministry is interested in preserving Prague's art treasures because they bring in tourist dollars. (11)
6. _____ Sometimes large, heavy statues are moved indoors for repairs. (14)
7. _____ After Mr. Branda restores a work, he signs his name to it. (19)
8. _____ Charles Bridge has been restored to its former beauty. (21–22)

Check your answers with the key on page 182. If you have made mistakes, reread the article to gain a better understanding of it.

II. Expanding Your Vocabulary

A. Getting Meaning from Context

Find each word in the paragraph indicated in parentheses. Use context clues to determine the meaning of the word. Match each word with its definition.

1. _____ restores (2)   a. deliberate destruction of or damage to property
2. _____ anonymous (3, 19) b. copies
3. _____ peered (5)   c. returns something to its original condition
4. _____ vandalism (6)   d. unidentified; unknown
5. _____ replicas (17)   e. looked closely

B. Reading for Suggested Meanings

Answer these questions. For help, reread the indicated paragraphs.

1. When the author writes that Mr. Branda was *perched* above a gate (4), what animal is she comparing the restorer to? What does that comparison suggest?

2. Why is it unusual for restorers to work on *replicas* (17)?

3. Why does Mr. Branda try not to *leave his own imprint* on the sculptures he restores (19)?

C. Identifying Categories of Words

Find the word or words that don't belong in each category.

1. Which one is *not* part of a building?

   cupola   spatula   tower   vault   roof

2. Which has *not* caused damage to Prague's outdoor art?

   pollution   vandalism   tourists   streetcars   colleagues

3. Which two words do *not* name figures in Christian history or literature?

   cherubs   halos   angels   gangsters   disciples

4. Which word does *not* describe some type of deterioration?

   pockmarked   scarred   unscathed   crumbled   splintered

5. Which two are *not* forms of transportation?

   cars   carriages   cosmetics   streetcars   synthetics

6. Which one is *not* equipment or supplies used by the restorers?

   spatula   netting   crane   glue   sandstone

III. Working with Idioms and Expressions

Study the meanings of these idioms and expressions. A form of each one appears in the indicated paragraph of the article.

rub down (2)   massage; rub repeatedly
the other morning (4)   a few mornings ago
touch up (4)   make small repairs (often, with paint)
shore up (6)   add support to
would-be (8)   someone who wants to be something but isn't
fixing up (9)   repairing; putting back in good condition
go to extraordinary (great) lengths (13)   go to a lot of trouble
elbow one's way into (20)   push into a place where one isn't wanted
shoulder-to-shoulder (21)   very close together

Answer these questions.

1. Do you have to touch something to *touch it up?*
2. What kinds of things do people fix? What do they *fix up?*
3. What would you *go to great lengths* to get or do?
4. When soldiers march, do they stand *shoulder-to-shoulder?*
5. Did you do anything unusual *the other morning?*
6. Did you ever *elbow your way into* a place? Why?
7. Is a *would-be* artist a real artist? Is Mr. Branda a *would-be* artist?

IV. Making Sense of Sentences

Used to (followed by an infinitive verb) tells about something that happened frequently or continued for a long time in the past. Note the use of *used to* in paragraph 22.

> **Examples:** When I was a child, I *used to take* dancing lessons.
>
> I *used to be* in dance recitals once or twice a year.

Answer these questions using *used to.*

1. Where did Mr. Branda study art?
2. What does a restorer want his restoration to look like?
3. How did Charles Bridge look in the past?
4. Where did you live as a child?

V. Talking and Writing

Discuss the following topics. Then choose one of them to write about.

1. Do you believe that a city, state, or country should spend money to restore its old buildings and sculpture? Why or why not?

2. Would you like to work in Prague as a restorer? What would you like about the job? What would you dislike?

3. Mr. Branda believes that his work is important. Do you feel that you spend your time on important things? Why or why not? Would you like to do work that you considered important? What kind of work would that be?

3. Disney Assailed for Pocahontas Portrayal

Previewing the Article

The name *Pocahontas* translates into English as "playful one." But Pocahontas, perhaps the most famous child in American history, had her serious side, too. She was a little girl with a big heart. In choosing to make a movie about Pocahontas, Walt Disney Studios took on the task of retelling a story that is both history and legend. Pocahontas was a real person, but she is also a symbol, a larger-than-life heroine.

In 1607, a British adventurer named John Smith sailed to Virginia to help establish an English colony. The colony, called Jamestown, became the first permanent English settlement in North America. After a friendly beginning, the Native American tribes of the area became distrustful of the colonists. On one occasion, John Smith was captured by the Powhatan tribe. The Indians were about to kill him. Suddenly Pocahontas, the chief's beloved eleven-year-old daughter, threw her arms protectively around Smith, laid her head beside his, and persuaded her father not to kill him. Back in England many years later, Smith wrote this account of his adventures in Virginia. The little Indian "princess" became a symbol of courage, nonviolence, and tolerance.

John Smith died in 1631, at the age of 51. Pocahontas was not so lucky. After the incident with Smith, she continued to help the colonists. She lived in Jamestown for a while, probably as a respected, well-treated prisoner. Then she married one of the colonists and traveled to England with him. There she died of smallpox in 1617, when she was about 22 years old.

Before You Read

Discuss these questions and do the map search.

1. Find the following states on a map of the United States: Virginia, Maryland, and North Carolina. Find Washington, D.C., the capital of the United States.

2. Why are Native Americans sometimes called *Indians?* What is the difference between native Americans and Native Americans?

3. What does the name *Disney* mean to you? In the headline of the article, does *Disney* refer to a person or a company?

4. What do you know about Native Americans? Discuss their lifestyles, talents, problems, and contributions to American culture.

As You Read

Look for these main ideas:

1. What changes did Disney make in the Pocahontas story?

2. Why does Little Dove Custolow disapprove of these changes?

Disney Assailed for Pocahontas Portrayal

By Anthony Faiola
Washington Post Service

1 WEST POINT, Virginia—Clouds of smoke from a roaring pit fire circle Little Dove Custolow as she weaves the tale of her tribal heroine. Here, she says, in rural Virginia just west of the Chesapeake, before the Europeans came, before the smallpox and the reservations, there was Pocahontas.

2 "She was a child of respect and honor," said Custolow, daughter of a Powhatan chief, and a village storyteller in one of the last surviving tribes descending from Pocahontas, the 17th-century child ambassador of an Indian nation. "Respect and honor were as great a part of her life as food and air. She used them as a tool to bridge the gap between peoples with different languages and different cultures."

3 Custolow recalls her dying grandfather calling her to his bedside when she was 5, commanding her to spread the tales of Pocahontas and her people "like seeds upon the four winds." That mission has consumed her. For the past 30 years—since she was a teenager—she has journeyed to schools, museums and folklore festivals to tell the tales, often six days a week, and often for free.

4 It was on a mission to colonial Williamsburg in 1992 that researchers for Walt Disney Studios spotted Custolow. Struck by her intimate knowledge of the tale and her strong Indian facial features, they brought her to California as a model and consultant for Disney's epic "Pocahontas," the animated successor to its blockbuster "The Lion King." Custolow hoped that through the 78-minute animated feature premiering June 10, she could share with the world the tales told by her grandfather.

5 But when Disney flew her to California three weeks ago to preview the film, her hopes were dashed. "I wish they would take the name of Pocahontas off that movie," she sighed.

6 Disney's portrayal of Pocahontas, she says, is a sharp departure from history. Her disappointment is being echoed by historians and Indian activists nationwide. For Custolow's people, whose ancestors spoke Algonquian—an unwritten language—the oral tradition of storytelling is considered a vital link to their past. So, by reinventing

The animated star of Disney's "Pocahontas" is the subject of much off-screen controversy.

Pocahontas, Disney in effect is reinventing and distorting the tribe's culture for future generations, they maintain.

7 Perhaps there are no people more sensitive to the story of Pocahontas than her tribal descendants, who now live in a region of rural central Virginia that stretches from the Chesapeake Bay to Richmond. About 1,000 strong, they make up the remnants of the Powhatan Nation, a confederacy of 34 tribes that once stretched from present-day North Carolina to Southern Maryland and were named after their ruler, Chief Powhatan, the father of Pocahontas.

8 Disney, which labored to avoid ethnic stereotyping by hiring many Indians for the four-year project, argues that the exact details of the Pocahontas legend remain vague at best, making it a perfect piece of history to mold.

9 "We set out to do something inspired by the legend, not to make a documentary," said Peter Schneider, president of Walt Disney Studios' animation division. "But you've got to remember something important. The history of Pocahontas is, in and of itself, a source of much controversy. Nobody knows the truth of her legend. We simply set out to make a beautiful movie about the Native American experience."

10 The conflict underscores the pressure that movie makers in the 1990s face in accurately portraying ethnic or other minorities in films. Indeed, Disney, an image-conscious company,

still carries scars from the wrath of Arab-Americans stemming from its portrayal in "Aladdin," which was retooled after those criticisms. Disney also faced an uproar over the company's approach to history at its proposed Disney America theme park in Virginia, which has been shelved.

11　To authenticate Pocahontas, Indians are used as screen voices and as consultants for the film's elaborate dance and music scenes.

12　Many of the Indians who worked on the project, including Indian activist Russell Means, who provides the voice of Chief Powhatan, applaud Disney for taking the tale of a young Indian girl to the big screen.

13　After all, they say, at its heart, Disney's "Pocahontas" is an entertaining child's film.

14　"It is the finest feature film ever done in Hollywood on the Native American experience," said Means, a leader of the American Indian Movement who, in 1973, helped lead the 71-day takeover of the Pine Ridge Reservation town of Wounded Knee, South Dakota.

15　But for Custolow, and many others, the soul of the legend has been compromised.

16　Throughout the Disney film, she says, Pocahontas is depicted not as an innocent child, but as a woman of 20, clad in form-fitting buckskin and involved in a fictitious romance with Captain John Smith. While many facts about Pocahontas remain in dispute, most historians agree that Pocahontas was about 11 when she first met the Europeans, and while she later married a white man, they say, she never romanced Smith.

17　Custolow says that early sketches of Pocahontas made her appear a child of 11. But later, Disney changed her appearance. Disney executives say that's not true. "Of course there were changes during the development of the process, but we never set out to make her look 12 years old," Schneider said.

18　Disney's film, Custolow says, also ignores significant events such as the kidnapping of Pocahontas by British settlers—a kidnapping that later led to her conversion to Christianity and her marriage to the settler John Rolfe.

19　Disney's film "may not be a feather-and-loincloth depiction of Indians as savages and heathens, but it is a disrespect for what we believe are the facts about Pocahontas," said Sonny Skyhawk, a Hollywood consultant on movies including Columbia Pictures' "Geronimo, an American Legend."

20　Hanay Geiogamah, founder of New York City's American Indian Dance Theater, worked on the Disney film as choreography consultant. He doesn't understand the fuss.

21　"O.K., so it's not historically accurate," he said. "I don't think that's necessarily bad."

22　Means said, "I can't accept all this fuss being created by these nit-picky anthropologist types. The accounts of her life were vague. And the truth is that there are some people who believe she was never kidnapped, but went to Jamestown willingly. There is no right or wrong here; it is a story that is best left up to interpretation."

23　In 1992, Disney researchers spotted Custolow and offered her a $500 consultant fee. "We felt she had the spirit of Pocahontas within her," said Disney's Schneider. "She embodied the character we were trying to create."

24　He added: "We set out to paint a very respectful, spectacular view of a culture that no longer exists."

25　But that, Custolow says, is where Disney erred.

26　"Our culture does exist; it lives through our stories," she said. "And that is why they are so important to us."

I. Getting the Message

Which of the following statements do you think Little Dove Custolow would agree with? Which ones would she disagree with? Use the letters **A** and **D** to show your answers. Then indicate if *you* agree or disagree with each statement. (Use **A** and **D** again.)

	Agree or **D**isagree?	
	Custolow	You
1. Artists have a right to work creatively with their subject matter in any way they choose.	_____	_____
2. Disney's Pocahontas is very similar to the real Pocahontas.	_____	_____
3. Disney did something good for Native Americans by creating this movie.	_____	_____
4. By changing the Pocahontas story, Disney distorted a piece of Native American culture.	_____	_____
5. The story of Pocahontas belongs to the Powhatans, and no one has a right to change it.	_____	_____

6. The real Pocahontas was probably in love with John Smith. _____ _____

7. The Powhatan culture no longer exists. _____ _____

8. Movies should not teach children inaccurate history. _____ _____

Check the answers in the first column with the key on page 182. If you have made mistakes, reread the article to gain a better understanding of it.

II. Expanding Your Vocabulary

A. Getting Meaning from Context

Find each word or phrase in the paragraph indicated in parentheses. Use context clues to determine the meaning of the word or phrase. Choose the best definition.

1. weaves the tale (1)
   a. tells the story
   b. makes the tapestry
2. intimate (4)
   a. detailed
   b. recent
3. animated feature (4)
   a. movie made with drawings, not live actors
   b. lively movie
4. vital link (6)
   a. important connection
   b. part of a metal chain
5. oral (6)
   a. spoken
   b. written
6. ethnic stereotyping (8)
   a. overgeneralizing about characteristics of racial or cultural groups
   b. making sound come from different directions
7. image-conscious (10)
   a. involved in making movies
   b. concerned about one's reputation
8. fictitious (16)
   a. real
   b. imaginary
9. in dispute (16)
   a. not agreed upon
   b. not respected

B. Defining Verbs from the Article

Match each phrase in column A with the one in column B that has the same meaning. For context clues, reread the indicated paragraphs of the article.

A

1. To *assail* (headline) someone means __h__.
2. To *spot* (4, 23) something means _____.
3. To *dash* someone's hopes (5) means _____.
4. To *echo* (6) what someone said means _____.
5. To *labor* (8) at something means _____.
6. To *authenticate* (11) information means _____.
7. To *applaud* (12) an action means _____.
8. To *compromise* (15) something means _____.
9. To *embody* (23) a character is _____.

B

a. to see it
b. to endanger its reputation
c. to repeat it
d. to approve of it
e. to give it concrete form; to exemplify it
f. to work at it; to try hard
g. to prove it is true
h. to attack the person with words
i. to destroy them

C. Using Vocabulary about Native Americans

Discuss the meanings of these words from the article. Then choose the best word to complete each sentence.

feather (19)   Indian (2)   loincloth (19)   reservations (1)

folklore (3)   legend (8)   nation (2)   tribes (2)

1. Native Americans belong to many different _____, each with its own language and culture.

2. Some Native American tribes belong to a larger group called a _____.

3. Native American men often wore a _____.

4. By the late 19th century, most Native Americans in the United States were forced to live on _____, special areas set aside for them.

5. A legend is part of the _____ of a culture.

III. Working with Idioms and Expressions _____

Study the meanings of these idioms and expressions. A form of each one appears in the indicated paragraph of the article.

bridge the gap between (2)   bring together; connect
in effect (6)   for all practical purposes; virtually
1,000 strong (7)   a group of 1,000; numbering 1,000
set out (9, 24)   start
carry scars (10)   have lasting damage
shelve (10)   postpone; put aside
nit-picky (22)   finding fault with minor details

Answer these questions.

1. What groups did Pocahontas try to *bridge the gap between?*
2. What did Walt Disney Studios *set out* to do with *Pocahontas?*
3. Do you think Custolow *carries any scars* because she's a Native American?
4. Is Custolow *nit-picky,* or are her criticisms of *Pocahontas* important ones?
5. What Disney plan was *shelved* after intense criticism?
6. Reread paragraph 3. What does the figurative comparison "like seeds upon the four winds" mean? What did Custolow's grandfather want her to do?

IV. Analyzing Paragraphs _____

Answer these questions. Indicate paragraph numbers where appropriate.

1. Which paragraphs support Custolow's viewpoint? _____ Which paragraphs express viewpoints opposed to hers? _____

2. Do you think the author gave equal space to each side? _____

3. Which paragraphs help the reader understand why Custolow feels so strongly about this issue? _____

4. Does the author of the article give his opinion about the movie? _____ If so, in which paragraph? _____

5. Which viewpoint do you agree with, Custolow's or Disney's? _____

6. Which paragraph(s) helped you reach your decision? _____

V. Talking and Writing

Discuss the following questions. Then choose one of them to write about.

1. What changes did Disney make in the Pocahontas story? Why did the company make these changes, in your opinion?

2. What arguments does Disney use to defend its movie?

3. The Pocahontas story suggests that children are sometimes kinder and more understanding than adults and can teach adults how to get along. Do you know any other stories that convey this message? If so, tell the story and the culture it comes from.

4. After an Epoch of Nagging, Christo Wraps Reichstag

Previewing the Article

Among contemporary artists, there are *rappers,* who speak in verse to a rhythmic beat. And then there are *wrappers,* who put fabric around huge structures such as buildings, bridges, and even islands. Bulgarian-born Christo Javacheff and his French wife, Jeanne-Claude, may be the world's only professional wrappers. But their temporary creations have won international attention. Their fabric or plastic wraps survive for a few weeks at most. However, in their short lifetime, they are viewed by millions of people. Many of Christo's fans are people who would never visit an art museum.

Trained in both art and engineering, Christo is sometimes called an environmental sculptor. Some say that what he creates is not art but a happening, event, or spectacle. Whatever his work is called, it is usually huge. Often, Christo hires hundreds of assistants to bring one of his designs to life.

Christo is famous for his wrappings (which have included a bridge in Paris, a mile of coastline in Australia, and islands in Florida). However, he has created many other strange works of art. In the early 1990s, for example, he built a joint work in two far-apart sites: Japan and California. At each location, more than a thousand giant (two-story) umbrellas were spread out for miles over hills and fields. These gigantic Christo landscapes cost $26 million!

In Berlin, Christo hired 1,200 monitors—mostly art students—to explain the Reichstag wrapping to visitors. When the exhibit closed, Christo and Jeanne-Claude went home to New York to work on their next projects: constructing a fabric canopy across a Colorado river valley and setting up an avenue of yellow gates in Manhattan's Central Park.

Before You Read

Discuss these questions.

1. In your opinion, is a wrapped building a work of art? Why or why not?

2. Do you think artists should be free to use any materials they wish to create their works? Why or why not?

3. Have you seen any works of art that you consider ridiculous? If so, describe them. Do you know when they were made?

4. What does the headline of this article mean? What is an "epoch of nagging"?

As You Read

Look for information that could explain why Christo fought so long and hard for permission to wrap the Reichstag. After studying the photograph, can you think of any other reasons?

After an Epoch of Nagging, Christo Wraps Reichstag

By Rick Atkinson
Washington Post Service

1 BERLIN—Nearly a quarter-century after he first sought permission to swaddle Germany's most controversial building in fabric, the American wrapmaster Christo finally began to convert his vision into art over the weekend as a team of steeplejacks began trussing up the Berlin Reichstag with a million square feet of silver cloth and nine miles of blue rope.

2 The first of 70 veils of woven polypropylene spilled down an inner courtyard Saturday while Christo's legions swarmed over the once and future German Parliament building, tugging, tucking and wrapping away. But work was short-lived on Sunday, as high winds forced the wrapping to stop.

3 Enveloping the entire building was expected to take four days, but now it may take longer.

4 The technical director, Wolfgang Volz, said Sunday: "We have been warned that winds may reach a speed of up to 60 kilometers an hour, which means we will not be able to work. We should be able to go ahead tomorrow."

5 The "Wrapped Reichstag" has long had this town atwitter with anticipation—Berlin schoolchildren have been wrapping everything from pencils to classrooms—and a sizable crowd swarmed around the project Saturday, gawking and opining.

6 Would-be critics predict the finished product, to be on display for two weeks, will resemble a vast spaceship, a silver lamé sculpture or, less generously, a diapered hatbox.

7 "You have so much empty space between the fabric and the building, and that empty space will be filled with the wind," Christo said in an interview, "The wind will make the Reichstag like a living object, like it's breathing."

8 Whatever the project's aesthetic appeal, it may not prove to be the tourist magnet predicted last winter by Berlin city officials, who rashly estimated that the event would draw 3 million to 5 million visitors.

9 For Christo, the realization of bold ambition may also prove costly. He conceded that the project—to be financed with the sale of prints and other memorabilia—was likely to far exceed cost projections.

10 "Instead of $7 million," he forecast, "it will be $10 or $11 million."

11 Denounced by some critics as a banal flimflam artist, lauded by others as an innovative visionary, the Bulgarian-born New Yorker is unquestionably audacious and persistent.

12 His "Wrapped Reichstag" proposal was rejected repeatedly by the German government during a 24-year epoch that saw the end of the Cold War, the reunification of Germany and a vote by the Bonn Parliament to move back to Berlin later this decade.

13 Refusing to take "nein" for an answer, Christo, who long ago abandoned his full name, Christo Javacheff, made more than 50 trips to Germany. With his French wife and collaborator, Jeanne-Claude, he lobbied relentlessly, personally buttonholing about 350 legislators.

14 Meanwhile, their work continued apace, including the wrapping of the Pont Neuf bridge in Paris in 1985 and the 1983 encirclement of 11 islands in Miami's Biscayne Bay with nearly 7 miles (11 kilometers) of floating, pink plastic.

15 Doggedness paid off in February 1994, when Parliament voted, 292 to 223, to permit the wrapping, despite objections from Chancellor Helmut Kohl and others who felt the project would sully the Reichstag's dignity.

16 For a majority, however, the proposal was a chance to spark a public debate about art, to affirm a symbolic rebirth of German democracy and to demonstrate a very un-German streak of whimsy.

17 Built in 1894, the Reichstag served as the legislative seat of Germany's Weimar democracy until February 1933, when a fire—blamed on the Communists but probably set by the Nazis—gutted the building and gave Adolf Hitler an excuse to impose his dictatorship.

18 Badly battered by Allied bombs and invading Red Army troops in 1945, the building later abutted the Berlin Wall, becoming a bullet-pocked emblem of the city's bifurcation. Partly restored in the 1960s, it now awaits the government's return to Berlin, and a $430 million renovation, before reclaiming its former glory.

19 The engineering work undertaken in the name of art is almost as intricate as the political maneuvering that made it possible. Lightly coated with aluminum to reflect sun and sky, the fabric was woven from 44,000 miles of yarn, then stitched together in panels with more than 800 miles of thread.

Thousands of curious visitors gather in Berlin to see Christo's wrapped Reichstag.

I. Getting the Message

After reading the article, indicate if each statement is true (**T**) or false (**F**). After each statement, write the paragraph number(s) that gave you the answer.

1. ___F___ The wrapping that Christo put on the Reichstag will remain on the building permanently. ___6___

2. _____ Christo plans to pay for this project by selling photographs and other mementos of the finished work. _____

3. _____ The Reichstag is the largest thing that Christo has ever wrapped. _____

4. _____ After the wrapping is removed, this old building will be destroyed. _____

5. _____ For 24 years, the German government begged Christo to wrap the Reichstag. _____

6. _____ Christo got permission to wrap the Reichstag by winning the approval of the German chancellor. _____

7. _____ Christo and his helpers wrapped the building in a silver-colored fabric and tied it with blue ropes. _____

8. _____ Windy weather made it difficult to wrap the building, but the artist expected the wind to enhance the effect of the finished work of art. _____

9. _____ Christo expected his two-week work of art to cost about $10 million. _____

10. _____ This article was written before the wrapping was completed. _____

Check your answers with the key on page 182. If you have made mistakes, reread the article to gain a better understanding of it.

II. Expanding Your Vocabulary

A. Getting Meaning from Context

Find each word in the paragraph indicated in parentheses. Use context clues to determine the meaning of the word. To be sure of some meanings, you may need to reread the paragraphs before and after the one that the word is used in. Match each word in column A with its definition in column B.

A	B
1. _____ swaddle (1)	a. go beyond; be more than
2. _____ swarmed (2, 5)	b. complicated
3. _____ anticipation (5)	c. artistic
4. _____ aesthetic (8)	d. looking forward to a future event
5. _____ exceed (9)	e. playful humor
6. _____ doggedness (15)	f. gathered together in large numbers
7. _____ whimsy (16)	g. envelop; wrap
8. _____ intricate (19)	h. stubbornness; persistence

B. Reading for Suggested Meanings

Often, the English language offers a writer several words that have about the same meanings. A good writer chooses words carefully, considering not only a word's *denotation* (literal meaning) but also its *connotation* (suggestions of positive or negative feelings). Find the negative word in each pair below. Discuss the associations that give each word its negative connotation. At least one of the words in each pair comes from this article.

1. nagging   complaining
2. swaddle   wrap
3. swarmed   gathered
4. gawking   looking at
5. atwitter   excited
6. denounced   criticized
7. rashly   quickly
8. relentlessly   persistently

What can you infer about the author's attitude toward Christo's artwork? Does the author's choice of words make the project and its viewers sound meaningful or foolish?

III. Working with Idioms and Expressions

Answer these questions with *yes* or *no*. Pay particular attention to the meanings of the expressions in bold print. Each expression appears in the indicated paragraph of the article.

1. Is the **once and future** (2) Parliament building being used by the German legislators at the present time? _____

2. Are **would-be** (6) critics people who currently write newspaper reviews about art exhibits? _____

3. Is a **tourist magnet** (8) something that attracts visitors to a particular place? _____

4. Does **buttonholing** (13) mean actually grabbing someone's clothing in order to keep the person near you? _____

5. If you **spark a debate** (16) do you start people expressing different opinions about something? _____

IV. Analyzing Paragraphs

A. Studying Chronological Development

Much of the information in this article is organized *chronologically.* This means that it follows the order in which the events occurred. The following chart lists three topics that are discussed chronologically in the article. Complete the chart with the numbers of the paragraphs that deal with each topic.

Topics	Paragraphs
1. the progress of Christo's wrapping	_____
2. background on how Christo got permission to wrap the Reichstag	_____
3. the history of the Reichstag	_____

B. Finding Paragraphs with Specific Topics

Some of the following topics are discussed in the article, and some are not. For those that are discussed, write the numbers of the relevant paragraphs.

1. art critics' reactions to Christo's wrapping in general _____

2. the public's reaction to the Reichstag work in progress _____

3. Christo's education and training as an artist _____

4. Christo's next project _____

5. details about the wrapping materials _____

V. Talking and Writing

Discuss the following topics. Then choose one of them to write about.

1. If you were a legislator, would you vote to let Christo wrap something in your country? If so, what structure would you recommend that he wrap? If not, what reasons would you give him for refusing?

2. What message, if any, do you think Christo is trying to convey to the public via his wrappings? Why do you think he has chosen this form of artistic expression? Do you think it is "flimflam" art or significant, meaningful work?

3. Do you have a favorite artist? If so, tell who it is and why you like this person's work.

4. Have you seen any contemporary art that you either admired greatly or hated? If so, describe it.

5A. In Stone Age Cavern, a Stunning Menagerie
5B. Stone Age Picassos: 30,000-Year-Old Trove

Previewing the Article

Thousands of years ago, before human beings could write, they were drawing pictures on cave walls. Prehistoric artists knew how to make four colors—white from pipe clay, black from charcoal, and red and yellow from ochre, an iron ore. Some artists mixed their colors with grease to make crayon-like drawing tools. Others sprayed powdered colors on the walls by blowing them through bone tubes. Most cave paintings were of animals that lived in the area.

The best examples of prehistoric cave art have been found in Spain and France. The Altamira cave in northeastern Spain was discovered in 1879. There, bumps and dents in the walls became part of some pictures, making the painted animals look three-dimensional. In 1940, the Lascaux cave was discovered in southwestern France. Its paintings are about 17,000 years old. Some of the bulls and horses stand 5.5 meters (18 feet) high. In December 1994, Stone Age paintings were discovered in the Chauvet cave in southeastern France. The hundreds of paintings in this huge cave are an extremely important find because they are very old, beautifully painted, and in excellent condition.

Three time periods are mentioned in article A. *Prehistoric* means the time before the earliest written records (before 3000 B.C.). The *Stone Age* refers to the time when human beings used tools of stone rather than metal. It began about 2.5 million years ago and ended in the Near East first, when people began using bronze tools. A few isolated societies in Australia and New Guinea are still in the Stone Age. The Stone Age is divided into three periods, which relate to toolmaking techniques. The *Paleolithic era* (or Old Stone Age) lasted until about 8000 B.C.

Before You Read

Discuss these questions.

1. What do archaeologists study?

2. What do the headlines and subheadings on the two articles mean?

3. The second article was printed almost five months after the first. By analyzing its headlines only, can you figure out what the new news is about the cave?

As You Read

Do the following:

1. As you read article A, look for descriptions of the cave paintings. Find information about their size, colors, and subjects and actions depicted.

2. As you read article B, you'll find out how old the oldest paintings in the Chauvet cave are. Look for reasons why this date is important to archaeologists.

In Stone Age Cavern, a Stunning Menagerie

Archaeologists Thrilled by Discovery of Vivid Wall Paintings in France

By Marlise Simons
New York Times Service

1 PARIS—In the mountains of southern France, where humans have habitually hunted, loved and produced art, explorers have discovered an underground cave full of Stone Age paintings, so beautifully made and well preserved that experts are calling it one of the archaeological finds of the century.

2 The enormous underground cavern, which was found on Dec. 18 at Combe d'Arc in the Ardèche region, is studded with more than 300 vivid images of animals and human hands that experts believe were made about 20,000 years ago.

3 In this great parade of beasts appear wooly-haired rhinos, bears, lions, oxen and other familiar images from the end of the Paleolithic era, large and small and variously drawn in yellow ochre, charcoal and hematite.

4 The murals have surprised specialists because they include a rare image of a red, slouching hyena and the era's first-ever recorded paintings of a panther and several owls. Specialists say this ancient art gallery surpasses in size that of the famous caves of Lascaux and Altamira, which are widely held to be Western Europe's finest collection of Stone Age art.

5 Archaeologists said they were thrilled not only by the number and the quality of the images but also by the discovery that the great underground site, sealed by fallen debris, appears to have been left undisturbed for thousands of years. They see this as tantamount to finding a time capsule full of hidden treasures.

6 One remarkable find, they said, was the skull of a bear, placed on a large rock set in the middle of one gallery against a backdrop of bear paintings.

7 "Is this some kind of altar? Someone placed the skull there for a reason," said Jean Clottes, France's leading rock art specialist. Many other skulls and bones of bears were found in the underground warren, along with bones, pieces of cut stones and remains of fireplaces, all of which archaeologists hope will provide important clues.

8 "Here we have a virgin site, completely intact," said Mr. Clottes. At all other Stone Age sites found in Europe, he said, the floor and many objects had been disturbed by explorers.

9 A measure of the importance France attaches to the find was that the minister of culture, Jacques Toubon, chose to announce it himself Wednesday at a news conference in Paris, in the company of France's top archaeologists.

10 "This discovery is of exceptional value because of its magnitude and because it was found undisturbed," Mr. Toubon said.

11 He added that the site would not be open to the public in the near future but was placed under government protection and accessible only to archaeologists.

12 *The Associated Press reported from Paris:*

13 "We have there a selection of animals infinitely more varied than the other sites and with exceptional features," said Geneviève Martin, a specialist for the Archaeological Service of the Rhône-Alpes department.

14 The paintings show standing or galloping groups of animals about 40 centimeters (15 inches) high. Some rhinoceroses were shown fighting.

15 The Culture Ministry described the find as "the only totally intact and ornate network of caves from the Paleolithic era."

16 The discovery was not announced until Wednesday so the site could be protected. The caves, yet to be named, have been secured with a heavy door and television surveillance.

17 The caves "will not be opened to the public so that the extremely fragile and precious relics can be studied," Mr. Toubon said. "Preservation is our priority at the moment."

18 The ministry said it planned to show the paintings to the public using video, CD-ROM or other multimedia techniques.

19 Jean-Marie Chauvet, guardian of about 15 caves in the area that have prehistoric artifacts, came upon the art with two assistants during an inspection tour, the Culture Ministry said.

20 Searching a narrow gallery near the cliffs of the Cirque d'Estre, the team found a shaft that led to a network of large galleries where the paintings were found, the ministry said.

Stone Age Picassos: 30,000-Year-Old Trove

Artistic Level of French Cave Paintings Stuns Scientists after Date Confirmed

By Marlise Simons
New York Times Service

1 PARIS—French authorities have announced that scientific tests have shown some of the masterfully drawn beasts discovered last December in a cave to be at least 30,000 years old, making them the world's oldest known examples of Stone Age paintings.

2 The Culture Ministry said French and British specialists had determined that charcoal pigments of two rhinoceroses and a bison found in the Chauvet cave in the southeastern Ardèche region were between 30,340 and 32,410 years old.

3 The oldest previously known cave painting was dated 27,110 before the present and shows the simple outline of a human hand. It was discovered in 1992 in France on a cave wall near Marseille.

4 Archaeologists said they were stunned by the finding. The team studying the great underground gallery with its more than 300 animal images, many of them leaping or running across great panels, said they were painted perhaps some 20,000 years ago.

5 The ministry said the test results have "overturned the accepted notions about the first appearance of art and its development," and they show that "the human race early on was capable of making veritable works of art." Until now, experts have generally thought that early drawing and painting began with crude and clumsy lines and then gradually became more sophisticated over centuries.

6 "This comes as a shock to many of us," said Jean Clottes, the French rock art specialist who has led the scientific exploration of the cave. "It upsets all our thinking about how style evolved," he said.

7 "We can no longer argue that the development of art was linear," Mr. Clottes added, "because we see now that it was not just a matter of a crude sort of art at first and then a slow improvement. This shows us that early art, just like art of the past few thousand years, had ups and downs. That there were periods when art had a heyday or was less important and that there were artists who were more backward or more gifted."

8 He continued, "Here we are talking about a time at the beginning of our species and we see that those early painters were as capable as much later artists."

9 Because the work in the Chauvet cave has proved to be so ancient, archaeologists in France and Spain, both of which are rich in Stone Age art, have said they may have to reconsider the age of artwork found in other caverns and rock shelters that has not been scientifically dated.

10 The Culture Ministry said that the surprising results had been obtained through 12 separate radiocarbon datings, made from eight samples. They were carried out recently by two French institutes, the Center for Low Radioactivity at Gif-sur-Yvetté and the Center for Radiocarbon dating of the University of Lyon.

11 Tests were also made by British scientists at the research laboratory for archaeology and art history at Oxford.

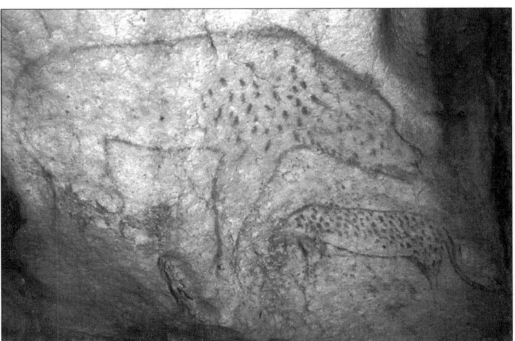

These two red hyenas are part of 300 Stone Age paintings discovered in a cave in the Ardèche region of southern France. The paintings are one of the most important archaeological finds of the century.

REUTERS/ARCHIVE PHOTOS

I. Getting the Message

A. Checking the Facts

After reading article A, indicate if each statement is true (**T**) or false (**F**).

1. _____ The newly discovered cave paintings are in very good condition.
2. _____ The artwork is very crude, proving that the paintings were made by ancient artists.
3. _____ The paintings show men and women of the Paleolithic era.
4. _____ According to the article, three colors are used in the paintings.
5. _____ Human skulls were found in the cave.
6. _____ It's possible that no one had been inside the cave for thousands of years before December of 1994.

B. Reading for Specific Details

Scan article A to find the answers to these questions.

1. Who discovered the cave at Combe d'Arc?
2. Who was thrilled?
3. What was vivid?
4. Which painted animals were fighting?
5. Which animal was slouching?
6. What was in front of the bear paintings?

Scan article B to find the answers to these questions.

7. About how old are the oldest paintings in the cave?
8. Is the artwork clumsy?
9. How did scientists determine the age of the art in the Chauvet cave?
10. Does this cave art suggest that art developed in a linear way?

Check your answers with the key on page 182. If you have made mistakes, reread the articles to gain a better understanding of them.

II. Expanding Your Vocabulary

A. Getting Meaning from Context

Match each word in column A with its definition in column B. Look in the article A paragraphs indicated for context clues. If the meaning is still unclear to you, use a dictionary for help.

A	B
1. _____ menagerie (headline)	a. bright; easy to see
2. _____ habitually (1)	b. great size; size
3. _____ enormous (2)	c. able to be entered or used
4. _____ vivid (2)	d. very large; huge
5. _____ surpasses (4)	e. delicate; easily damaged

6. _____ thrilled (subhead; 5)   f. very excited and happy
7. _____ tantamount (5)   g. a collection of animals
8. _____ magnitude (10)   h. equivalent
9. _____ accessible (11)   i. is more than
10. _____ fragile (17)   j. regularly; often

B. Identifying Categories of Words

Find the word that doesn't belong in each category. The words have been selected from both articles, A and B.

1. rock formations

   cliff   cavern   cave   gallery   mountain

2. animals

   rhinoceros   panther   hyena   ochre   bear

3. jobs

   specialist   explorer   assistant   hematite   archaeologist

4. time periods

   prehistoric   tantamount   ancient   Stone Age   Paleolithic

5. pictures

   images   murals   works of art   debris   paintings

C. Distinguishing between Similar Words

1. Discuss the meanings of these *homonyms* (words that sound the same).

   altar / alter   site / sight / cite

2. Discuss the difference between these words.

   quantity   quality

III. Making Sense of Sentences

Answer the following questions about article A. Make inferences when necessary.

1. Would you expect "well-preserved" (1) paintings to be in good condition or bad?
2. The cavern is "studded" (2) with images. Is the entire wall covered?
3. Does a "great parade of beasts" (3) refer to a lot of animals or a few?
4. Does "sealed by fallen debris" (5) mean that the cave entrance was open or closed when it was discovered?
5. What did Jean Clottes suggest about the bear skull in front of the bear paintings (6, 7)?

6. What are the guardians of the cave worried about (16)?
7. What might happen to the cave paintings if the public were allowed in (17)?

Answer these questions about article B. Make inferences when necessary.

1. The cave paintings are compared to the works of the Spanish artist Pablo Picasso (headline). What does that comparison imply about the cave paintings?

2. Why do archaeologists want to reconsider the age of paintings found in other caves (9)?

3. Why were tests to date the Chauvet cave paintings conducted in England as well as in France (10–11)?

IV. Talking and Writing

Discuss the following topics. Then choose one of them to write about.

1. Why did some prehistoric people paint pictures on the walls of caves? Do you think these pictures had some purpose, or were they just for decoration?

2. In your opinion, why are most cave paintings of animals, not people?

3. How could the cave artists have gotten enough light to paint on walls deep in caves?

Focus on the Newspaper

The newspaper provides information about events in the world of arts and entertainment. It is a handy, up-to-date, inexpensive source of information about ways to spend leisure time.

Objective Articles

Some articles about cultural events and entertainment are objective accounts, providing just the facts. This type of story tells when a particular concert, movie, play, or art exhibit will (or did) open, how long it will be in town, and how much it costs. The story also describes the content, identifies the artists, and discusses the size and scope of the show. This sort of article is likely to appear in the paper shortly before or immediately after a particular cultural event opens. At the same time, you can expect to see advertisements for the event in the paper.

Exercise 1: Comparing a News Story and an Ad about Arts or Entertainment

Cut out a newspaper article about a live performance, art exhibit, or movie that has just opened or is about to open in your city. Look for an article that is *not* a review (an evaluation) but that simply tells about the show. Then find an advertisement for the same event. Answer these questions about the article and the ad.

1. Compare the article and the ad. What are the main differences in purpose?

2. What are the main differences in content?

3. After reading the ad, did you want to see this show or exhibit? Why or why not?

4. After reading the article, did you want to see it? Why or why not?

Reviews

Newspapers often give readers opinions on various forms of entertainment. Readers want to know: Should I see this play or movie, buy this book, or visit this museum? Is it worth my time and money? Will I enjoy it or learn from it? A good review does several things: it describes, analyzes, and evaluates. Readers find out how a particular work compares to others of the same type. Readers also get an opinion about the strengths, weaknesses, and overall quality of a work.

Exercise 2: Comparing an Objective Article and a Review

Scan the newspaper for a review of the event described in your article for exercise 1. (There will probably be one within a week or so.) What is the reviewer's overall recommendation? Does the reviewer suggest going to see this event or not? Does the reviewer's judgment surprise you? Tell why or why not.

Exercise 3: Comparing a Reviewer's Opinions with Your Own

Find a newspaper review of a movie or TV show you saw, a concert you attended, or a book you read. List four of the reviewer's evaluative points and tell whether you agree or disagree with each one. Overall, did the reviewer like the event or book? Did you?

Exercise 4: Reviewing the Reviews

Look in the entertainment section of a newspaper. Select three reviews to read: they may be of movies, plays, concerts, art exhibits, or other artistic works or forms of entertainment. (Note: Some newspapers have a daily entertainment section that contains reviews. Others have a special weekly section with reviews of current entertainment or books.) Read the reviews carefully. Then complete a chart like this.

ANALYZING A REVIEW					
Type of Entertainment (Movie, Concert, etc.)	Name of Entertainment	Brief Description	Strengths	Weaknesses	Reviewer's Overall Evaluation

Exercise 5: You Be the Reviewer

Prepare a short review of some leisure-time activity you have enjoyed (or not enjoyed) recently. Tell whether or not you recommend this particular activity and why.

INTERNATIONAL Herald Tribune

Published With The New York Times and The Washington Post

SECTION 6

SCIENCE / HEALTH

1

Why Rock Fans Faint:
Science Finally Comes to Its Senses

2

In Iceman's Outfit, Cultural Clues

3

Chain Reaction in the Orbital Junkyard

4

In a Newfound Tomb in Egypt, a Fresh Look
at Ramses II's Era

Focus on the Newspaper: Science / Health

1. Why Rock Fans Faint: Science Finally Comes to Its Senses

Previewing the Article

Imagine this: You're attending a very crowded concert. The star of the show, a famous performer comes onstage, microphone in hand, and begins to sing. How does the crowd react? Several teenage girls faint.

In the United States, this kind of audience response is nothing new. It has been going on at least since the early 1940s, when a young Frank Sinatra brightened the hearts of war-weary Americans with his stylish singing and his sailor cap. During World War II, fainting was called *swooning*. Although that term went out of fashion long ago, fainting did not. The following article mentions other singers who have inspired such admiration and adoration. In the 1950s, Elvis Presley, an American whose style combined country, western, and gospel singing, became the first important rock soloist. The Beatles, a British group of four young men from Liverpool, were internationally famous by the mid-1960s. Their music was also rock and roll. New Kids on the Block is a contemporary American rock group.

Fans who attend rock concerts seem more likely to faint than those who attend events such as operas, ballets, or baseball games. Is there something about rock music that encourages fainting? Rock music has a very strong rhythmic beat; the music is often played very loudly; and the words of the songs often deal with problems or protest. Does the excitement of the music cause audience members to pass out, or is there another explanation? The following article offers a scientific opinion on the matter.

Fainting has a variety of names. The medical term is *syncope*. Nonmedical people may use the expressions *passing out, becoming unconscious,* or *losing consciousness.*

Before You Read

Discuss these questions.

1. In the headline, what does the word *fan* mean? What are *rock fans?* What is the double meaning of "Science Finally Comes to Its Senses"?

2. Have you ever fainted? When? Why? Who or what helped you regain consciousness?

As You Read

Do the following:

1. Note how many of the causes of fainting relate to breathing. Note how many relate to effects upon the brain.

2. Look for the answer to this question: Do researchers think rock music causes fainting?

Why Rock Fans Faint: Science Finally Comes to Its Senses

By Curt Suplee
Washington Post Service

1 WASHINGTON—One of the most peculiar public health hazards in post-Presley America—epidemic fainting at pop-music concerts—is a phenomenon familiar to legions of adolescents. Their parents may be less aware of the threat, which has barely engaged the attention of modern science despite decades of documentation that many a fan is prone to unconsciousness.

2 Concerned that the mechanism of mass fainting has been "neglected in the medical literature," two German physicians recently braved a concert there by New Kids on the Block and worked with first-aid staff at a Red Cross infirmary where the stricken were treated.

3 According to the doctors' report in the Thursday issue of The New England Journal of Medicine, some 400 concertgoers fainted, all of them girls aged 11 to 17. The researchers, Drs. Martin Bauer and Thomas Lempert, interviewed 40 of the victims and found that they fell into two general groups. Forty percent had lost consciousness entirely—the classic fainting condition known as syncope—whereas the rest had become faint but remained alert, if distraught.

4 Based on their observations, Drs. Bauer and Lempert discerned a "multifactorial pathophysiology of rock-concert syncope," a phenomenon certainly as old as Frank Sinatra, Elvis Presley and the Beatles, but possibly long predating rock and roll since the symptoms apparently have less to do with the musical genre than the state of the fans.

5 Fainting is a temporary loss of consciousness caused by insufficient oxygen in the brain, and can be brought on by a variety of circumstances. In the case of the German fans, the researchers found at least five likely causes:

6 • "Sleeplessness during the previous night," perhaps from the thrill of anticipation.

7 • "Fasting from early in the morning, when they had first lined up," causing low blood sugar.

8 • "A long period of standing in the arena," which reduces cerebral blood flow by causing blood to pool in the legs.

9 • "Hyperventilation, which leads to cerebral vasoconstriction"—that is, heavy breathing that produces narrowing of blood vessels that supply the brain.

10 • Abnormal pressure within the chest "induced either by screaming or reflexively by external compression of the thorax by the pushing masses."

11 The last condition resembles the effect of what is known as the Valsalva maneuver—forcibly trying to exhale through a closed mouth and nose. It traps blood in the larger veins, keeping it from entering the chest and heart and thus being pumped to the brain. This makes the victim more likely to faint.

12 The 60 percent of girls who did not faint outright experienced panic attacks from being squashed in the mob or from hyperventilation, which can reduce carbon-dioxide levels in the bloodstream, thus making the blood more alkaline and inducing faintness, among other symptoms.

13 The doctors suggest the following guidelines for concertgoers: "Sleep, eat, sit, keep cool and stay out of the crowd. But what teenage fan will do that?"

I. Getting the Message

After reading the article, indicate if each statement is true (**T**) or false (**F**).

1. _____ Four of the five causes of fainting listed in the article relate to breathing.

2. _____ All of the causes of fainting relate to effects upon the brain.

3. _____ For a long time, scientists have been very interested in studying the causes of fainting at popular concerts.

4. _____ Drs. Bauer and Lempert decided to do research on fainting at concerts because the phenomenon is extremely dangerous.

5. _____ Most teenagers who become faint at rock concerts lose consciousness completely.

6. _____ A teenager is a person between the ages of eleven and seventeen.

7. _____ More men than women faint at rock concerts.

8. _____ The study suggests that something about rock music causes people to faint.

Check your answers with the key on page 182. If you have made mistakes, reread the article to gain a better understanding of it.

II. Expanding Your Vocabulary

A. Getting Meaning from Context

The author of this article defines many of the medical terms he uses. Scan the article to find each word listed below. If a definition is given, write it down. If not, use context clues to write your own definition. Then check your work by looking the words up in an English (not a bilingual) dictionary.

1. cerebral _____

2. fainting (syncope) _____

3. hyperventilation _____

4. stricken _____

5. victims _____

6. symptoms _____

7. vasoconstriction _____

8. fasting _____

9. infirmary _____

B. Using Prefixes

Study the meanings of these prefixes. Then choose the correct prefixes to complete these words from the reading. The definition of each word is given in parentheses.

ab- away from	**multi-** many
ex- out; beyond	**path-, patho-** disease, suffering, feeling
hyper- over; excess; too much	**pre-** before
in- not	

1. _____ physiology   (diseased bodily condition)

2. _____ ventilation   (breathing too fast and too deeply)

3. _____ sufficient   (not enough)

4. _____ normal   (not normal; beyond normal)

5. _____ hale   (breathe out)

6. _____ vious; _____ date   (before or earlier in time)

7. _____ factorial   (having many causes or factors)

C. Identifying Proper Nouns

Match each proper noun in column A with its description in column B. The information in the preview section and the article will help you.

A	B
1. _____ Bauer and Lempert	a. a popular American singer, famous by the 1940s
2. _____ the Beatles	b. the first internationally known rock and roll singer
3. _____ New Kids on the Block	c. a maneuver that makes people likely to faint
4. _____ Elvis Presley	d. doctors that studied fainting at rock concerts
5. _____ Red Cross	e. an international organization that provides medical aid after disasters
6. _____ Frank Sinatra	f. a contemporary American rock group
7. _____ Valsalva	g. four British singers very popular in the 1960s

III. Analyzing Paragraphs

Find answers to these questions by rereading the paragraphs indicated in parentheses.

1. Before Bauer and Lempert's study, did scientists mostly ignore the public health problem of fainting, or did they pay a lot of attention to it? (1, 2)

2. How many rock concerts did the researchers have to attend to find 400 fainting victims to study? (2, 3)

3. About how many teenagers fainted (completely lost consciousness) at the rock concert that the two doctors attended? (2, 3)

4. What causes fainting at rock concerts: the music or the state of the fans? (4)

5. What behavior *before* the concert may lead to fainting at the concert? (5–7)

6. What kinds of actions *at* concerts are likely to lead to fainting? (8–12)

7. Now that some causes of fainting at rock concerts have been identified, do the researchers think that this public health problem will disappear? Why or why not? (13)

IV. Talking and Writing

Discuss the following topics. Then choose one of them to write about.

1. Are you a fan of any entertainer, athlete, musical group, or team? Do you spend a lot of money and fight crowds in order to attend live performances or games? If so, tell why you are such a devoted fan.

2. In recent years, many fans have been injured at professional sporting events attended by huge crowds of people. What do you think are the causes of these injuries?

3. In your opinion, why do people enjoy being fans of famous performers and athletes?

2. In Iceman's Outfit, Cultural Clues

Previewing the Article

He is one of the most famous yet mysterious celebrities of recent times. Although he has been silent for more than five thousand years, he has told us much about early European humans. He is the Iceman, the intact mummy found sticking out of the ice by a German couple hiking in the Alps in 1991. He was thought at first to be a modern victim of a hiking accident, but scientific study has proved him to be from the Copper Age. He is between 5,100 and 5,300 years old.

This article reports important facts about the Iceman, one of the oldest and best-preserved prehistoric corpses. His body was preserved by glacial ice, with its internal organs and brain intact. Although we have learned much about his clothing, his age, and his few belongings, many mysteries remain. What was he doing so high in the mountains? How did he die? Was he a holy man, an outcast, a trader?

Whatever secrets the Iceman holds, this visitor from the distant past has given the modern world a great gift: He has brought a piece of his world into our own.

Before You Read

Discuss these questions.

1. What do you already know about the Iceman?

2. Have you ever read about other well-preserved mummies? Why are many people interested in mummies?

3. Look at the picture accompanying the article. Does the Iceman's outfit remind you in any way of our own cold-weather clothes?

As You Read

As you read the extensive description of the Iceman's clothing, try to form a mental picture of both his appearance and the world he walked in.

In Iceman's Outfit, Cultural Clues

By John Noble Wilford
New York Times Service

1 NEW YORK—Still no one knows who he was or what he was doing high in the Tyrolean Alps that day 5,300 years ago, the day he died. No one can be sure of the quirks of nature that somehow mummified the corpse, then entombed it in a glacier and preserved it and his possessions so long in a semblance of a life only lately departed.

2 But scientists are now certain of one thing about the naturally mummified Alpine Iceman, whom hikers discovered in September 1991 in the melting ice on the Austrian-Italian border at an elevation of 10,530 feet (3,210 meters):

In the first genetic analysis of the body, they determined that he was European born and bred, closely related to modern northern and alpine Europeans.

3 Scientists said this finding should lay to rest lingering suspicions of a hoax. An international research team, writing in the journal Science, said the genetic findings made "the possibility of fraud highly unlikely."

4 Among the most recent results of their research is a descriptive inventory of alpine fashions in those remote times. Scientists may not be able to account for the man's presence on the mountain crest—was he a farmer, hunter, trader, prospector, village outcast or, more probably, a shepherd?—but they know what he was wearing, down to his underwear.

5 Much of the reconstruction of his apparel from the seven preserved articles of clothing has been conducted by Dr. Markus Egg, an archaeologist at the Roman-Germanic Central Museum in Mainz, Germany. The results were reported in detail by Dr. Konrad Spindler in a new book, "The Man in the Ice," translated into English and published early this year in London by Weidenfeld & Nicholson.

6 Dr. Spindler, an archaeologist at the University of Innsbruck in Austria, is directing the international team of 147 scientists investigating the Iceman. A summary and assessment of the clothing studies was included in a comprehensive review of all the research published recently in the British journal Antiquity by Dr. Lawrence Barfield,

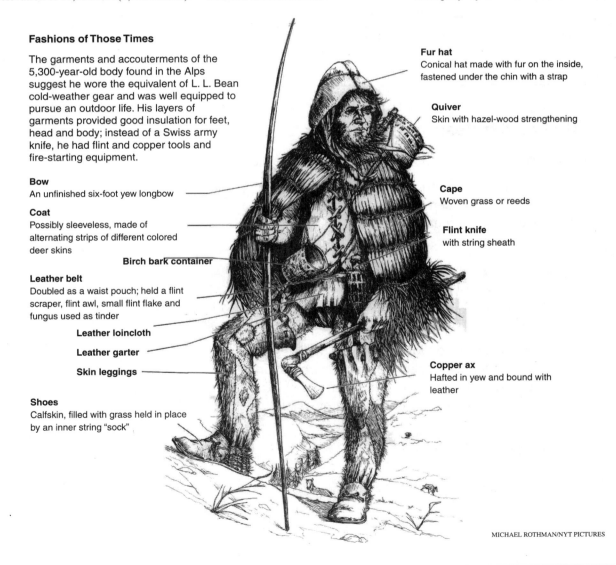

Fashions of Those Times

The garments and accouterments of the 5,300-year-old body found in the Alps suggest he wore the equivalent of L. L. Bean cold-weather gear and was well equipped to pursue an outdoor life. His layers of garments provided good insulation for feet, head and body; instead of a Swiss army knife, he had flint and copper tools and fire-starting equipment.

Bow
An unfinished six-foot yew longbow

Coat
Possibly sleeveless, made of alternating strips of different colored deer skins

Birch bark container

Leather belt
Doubled as a waist pouch; held a flint scraper, flint awl, small flint flake and fungus used as tinder

Leather loincloth

Leather garter

Skin leggings

Shoes
Calfskin, filled with grass held in place by an inner string "sock"

Fur hat
Conical hat made with fur on the inside, fastened under the chin with a strap

Quiver
Skin with hazel-wood strengthening

Cape
Woven grass or reeds

Flint knife
with string sheath

Copper ax
Hafted in yew and bound with leather

MICHAEL ROTHMAN/NYT PICTURES

an archaeologist at the University of Birmingham in England.

7 The Iceman was probably in his late 20s or early 30s and was 5 feet 2 inches (1.57 meters) tall, and in one respect, he would have been right in step with modern styles. He wore a leather waist pouch, not unlike today's popular "fanny packs."

8 His foundation garment was a leather belt that included this pouch, into which he had stuffed a sharpened flint scraper or knife, a flint awl, a small flint flake and a dark mass of organic material probably intended for use as tinder in fire-making.

9 The belt held up a leather loincloth, and leggings made of animal skin had been attached to it by suspended leather strips serving as garters. For his upper torso he had a jacket, possibly sleeveless, made from alternating strips of different colored deerskin.

10 Completing his ensemble was an outer cape of woven grasses or reeds of a type that, Dr. Barfield said, was still used in the Alps up to the beginning of this century. A conical cap, made with the fur on the inside, was originally fastened below his chin with a strap. His feet were protected from the cold by much-repaired shoes of calfskin filled with grasses for insulation.

11 Although much of the Iceman's equipment was described soon after the discovery, the list of 20 different items is now more definitive. "It is a contemporary mountain survival kit and more," Dr. Barfield wrote.

12 With the Iceman was an unfinished six-foot longbow made of yew. Why he would be on such a journey without a serviceable bow is one of the many puzzles. A quiver made of animal skin contained 14 broken or otherwise unserviceable arrows of viburnum and dogwood, two with flint tips and some with feather fletching.

13 Other contents of the quiver included two sinews, perhaps Achilles' tendons of a large animal, that probably were for the bowstring; a line made from tree fiber; a bundle of bone points wrapped in a leather thong, and a curved antler point, perhaps a needle.

14 More of his belongings included a frame made of hazel and skins, presumably a rucksack, and two sewn birchbark containers that from the blackened interior and maple leaves, may have been used for carrying embers for fire at the next campsite.

15 There were also more flint tools and knives, a fragment of string net possibly for capturing birds and two pieces of birch fungus threaded onto a leather thong. This could have been a folk antibiotic, a kind of prehistoric penicillin, Dr. Barfield observed.

16 The Iceman also had with him a copper ax with a yew haft and leather binding. At first, the ax was thought to be bronze, which would have indicated the man lived somewhat more recently, perhaps only 4,000 years ago. Radiocarbon dating of plant remains and other material finally put the date at between 5,100 and 5,300 years ago.

I. Getting the Message

After reading the article, choose the best answer for each item.

1. The main purpose of this article is to _____.
   a. prove that the Iceman's identity is a mystery
   b. describe the Iceman's clothing and belongings
   c. describe modern archaeological techniques

2. One of the mysteries surrounding the Iceman is _____.
   a. whether or not he is related to modern Europeans
   b. why he was carrying an unfinished bow and unusable arrows
   c. whether he is four thousand or five thousand years old

3. The immediate reason for this news story is _____.
   a a recent genetic analysis of the body by scientists
   b. the recent discovery of the Iceman's clothing
   c. controversy about the Iceman's profession

4. The Iceman was carrying _____.
   a. a large quantity of food
   b. a primitive kind of tent
   c. a copper ax

5. It seems that the Iceman was prepared for _____.
   a. hunting
   b. making a fire
   c. rainy weather

Check your answers with the key on page 182. If you have made mistakes, reread the article to gain a better understanding of it.

II. Expanding Your Vocabulary

A. Getting Meaning from Context

Find each word in the paragraph indicated in parentheses. Use context clues to determine the meaning of the word. Choose the best definition.

1. quirks (1)	a. frightening events	b. accidents or strange happenings	
2. semblance (1)	a. appearance	b. false imitation	
3. hoax (3)	a. trick	b. scientific study	
4. suspended (9)	a. delayed	b. hanging	
5. conical (10)	a. shaped like a cone	b. funny	
6. insulation (10)	a. protection from extreme heat or cold	b. style	
7. contemporary (11)	a. modern	b. not useful	
8. definitive (11)	a. confusing	b. complete	
9. haft (16)	a. handle	b. blade	

B. Identifying Categories of Words

Find the word or phrase that doesn't belong in each category. Look up any words you don't know in a dictionary.

1. general words for clothing

   apparel   ensemble   bow   garments

2. specific items of clothing

   embers   leggings   jacket   cape

3. tools

   ax   awl   tinder   knife

4. words used in scientific work

   genetic analysis   research team   finding   fashions

5. words used in hiking

   rucksack   survival kit   campsite   fraud

III. Working with Idioms and Expressions _____

Study the meanings of these idioms and expressions.

Idioms

born and bred (2)   by nature and by upbringing
lay to rest (3)   end
account for (4)   explain
right in step with (7)   in conformity with; appropriate for

Expressions

genetic analysis (2)   scientific testing that reveals the genetic structure of an organism
   and thus shows its basic similarity to other organisms
completing his ensemble (10)   a humorous transitional expression borrowed from descriptions of live fashion shows
fashions of those times (caption)   a humorous reference to the *New York Times* fashion section, which is called "Fashions of the Times"

Complete these sentences with idioms and expressions from the list.

1. Scientists used _____ to determine that the Iceman was a distant
   ancestor of modern northern Europeans. The test results _____ any
   idea that the Iceman is a fake.

2. Scientists are not certain how to _____ the Iceman's presence so
   high up in the mountains.

3. Even though the Iceman lived more than five thousand years ago, his waist pouch, which
   is like a "fanny pack," would have been _____ today's fashions.

IV. Making Sense of Sentences _____

Present participles are the *-ing* forms of verbs used as adjectives. They permit writers to
include more information in a sentence without the need for an additional, awkward sentence.

   Example: (Awkward): I saw a cat. The cat was sleeping.

   (Improved): I saw a *sleeping* cat. (*-ing* form used as adjective)

Past participles can be used in the same way.

   Example: (Awkward): I have a lamp. The lamp is broken.

   (Improved): I have a *broken* lamp. (past participle form used as adjective)

Find one adjective in each paragraph indicated (there may be more than one). Indicate whether it is a present or past participle; then write the word it modifies. The first two have been done for you.

Paragraph	Adjective	Kind of participle	Word modified
1. 2	mummified	past	Alpine Iceman
2. 3	lingering	present	suspicions
3. 5			
4. 9			
5. 10			
6. 13			

V. Talking and Writing

Discuss the following topics. Then choose one of them to write about.

1. The writer refers to the fact that some people thought the Iceman was a hoax. Why, do you think, did people have such suspicions?

2. Soon after the Iceman was discovered, he became a pop culture topic. He was nick-named "Ötzi" for the Ötztal Valley north of where he was discovered. Europeans created postcards, T-shirts, jewelry, and even popular songs about him. In your opinion, why was he such a celebrity?

3. If you could ask the Iceman one question about his world, what would you ask?

3. Chain Reaction in the Orbital Junkyard

Previewing the Article

When we look up at the sky, junk is probably the last thing we expect to see. But according to this fascinating and alarming article, thousands, even billions of pieces of old rockets and satellites now clutter up orbits near the Earth. These unpredictable objects threaten space programs all over the globe.

Space "litter" is different from litter on the Earth's surface in one important way: it multiplies itself. In a cycle that is never ending, one orbiting object smashes another into pieces, and those new pieces have new and dangerous orbits.

When the first satellites orbited the Earth, space seemed endless—much as the great North American forest must have seemed to the first European settlers. But we now know that each new frontier conquered by technology is accompanied by negative consequences. People must face these consequences with awareness and careful planning.

Before You Read

Discuss these questions.

1. Read the headline. What do you know about *chain reactions?* Can you think of several kinds? What picture comes to mind when you think of a *junkyard?* Why is *junkyard* a surprising word to use in talking about outer space?

2. Look at the graph illustrating the article. Is the number of objects in the "orbital junkyard" a surprise to you? Why or why not?

As You Read

Look for the following:

1. reasons why the objects in space are so dangerous

2. ideas about what can be done to "clean up" space

Chain Reaction in the Orbital Junkyard

Scientists Fear Collisions Could Multiply, Menacing Satellites

By William J. Broad
New York Times Service

1 NEW YORK—Chain reactions are commonplace on Earth. They occur in chemical plants when a single excited molecule prompts its neighbors into a cascade of combination to create plastics.

2 In nuclear reactors, they occur whenever a speeding subatomic particle slams into a heavy atom and splits it apart, releasing more particles that repeat and amplify the process in bursts of energy.

3 Now, experts say, a dangerous new kind of chain reaction is getting under way in space, where it threatens to limit mankind's endeavors beyond the planet. For instance, it could put billions of dollars worth of advanced communications and weather satellites at risk of destruction.

4 The problem is that some orbits near Earth have become junkyards of dead and active satellites, spent rocket stages and billions of bits of whirling debris.

5 The trashing of the heavens has reached the point where a speeding scrap of metallic refuse could hit a large object, shattering it into hundreds of pieces that repeat and amplify the process in a cascade of destruction. A chain reaction of this sort begins at a point known as the critical density.

6 "The consensus is that we're at the critical density, or very close to it," said Donald J. Kessler, the senior scientist for orbital-debris studies at the National Aeronautics and Space Administration.

7 "Even if we stopped putting things into orbit, you'd still see the population increase because of random collisions."

8 Several satellites lost to unknown causes over the years may well be the first victims of space junk.

9 Any chain of orbital destruction would be far slower than reactions on Earth because distances in space are so vast. Ruin on a widespread scale would take decades. But the implications for commerce, science and the military would nonetheless be enormous. Crowded orbits, which have no substitutes for some missions, would doubtless have to be abandoned to lessen the risk of collision.

10 That threat is prompting unusual action among space organizations. In the vanguard is NASA, which has raised debris mitigation to a high policy goal and is drawing up a rule book for its spacecraft designers, launchers and operators.

11 The big unknown is not so much foreign governments, which are also wrestling with the problem, but the commercial sector, which represents a growing share of the orbital pie as businesses plan new generations of communication satellites.

12 "Right now, debris mitigation is not part of the culture," said John E. Pike, head of space policy for the Federation of American Scientists, a private group based in Washington. "It's going to be like environmental regulation everywhere. First, people cry in the wilderness, saying there's a problem. Then comes the natural progression of doing the easy things, and then the harder things that tend to cost more."

13 From the start of the Space Age, orbits near Earth have steadily become more and more littered, often by the intentional discarding of debris. A different kind of intentional debris was generated in 1985 when the Reagan administration smashed a spacecraft to bits while testing an anti-satellite weapon, creating some 285 trackable pieces of whirling junk.

14 But the rubbish that is accumulating fastest today is the kind made inadvertently.

15 For instance, the third stage of an Ariane rocket engine exploded in orbit in November 1986, creating 465 pieces of speeding debris that spun about Earth. Another Ariane upper stage shattered last month, creating nine trackable items.

16 And last week, sensors on the ground detected the breakup of a Russian rocket stage. So far, that event has produced 38 observable bits of debris.

17 The problem first got serious attention in the 1980s as the tide of refuse and spacecraft became thicker. Ground-based radars, the main tool for assessing the mess, found steady rises

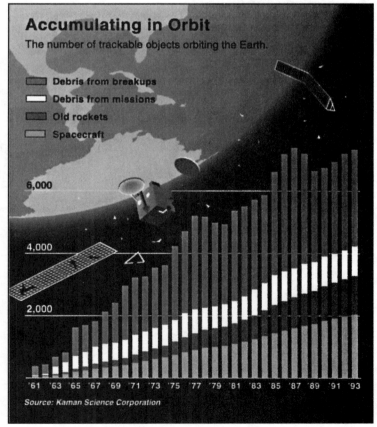

Accumulating in Orbit

The number of trackable objects orbiting the Earth.

- Debris from breakups
- Debris from missions
- Old rockets
- Spacecraft

6,000

4,000

2,000

'61 '63 '65 '67 '69 '71 '73 '75 '77 '79 '81 '83 '85 '87 '89 '91 '93

Source: Kaman Science Corporation

NYT GRAPHICS/MAPS

in large pieces of trackable debris, which ranged in size from softballs to large habitats for astronauts.

18 Scientists also began to discover that below the threshold of routine detectability was a swarm of billions of bits of speeding trash that ranged in size from small rocks to grains of sand.

19 For instance, space shuttles often came back from orbit disfigured by impact craters, as did a few satellites returned to Earth for refurbishment and evaluation.

20 After years of federal inactivity, Daniel S. Goldin, NASA's current administrator, in April 1993, spelled out a high-level agency policy "to employ design and operations practices that limit the generation of orbital debris, consistent with mission requirements and cost-effectiveness."

21 NASA also paid the National Academy of Sciences to assess the dimensions of the debris threat in a study that began last August and is to be completed this year.

22 The academy, a private group, often advises the government on science issues. The emerging consensus of the 10-member debris panel is said to be that a chain reaction is either already under way, or is likely to get started in the near future.

23 Mr. Kessler of NASA, a member of the academy panel, said the situation was so bleak that even if nothing else were launched into space, a cascade of destruction would cause a doubling of the numbers of pieces of flying debris in some crowded orbits over the next 100 years.

24 He added that if launchings continued at their current rate, each year adding to the trackable group of debris some 400 items (1,000 newcomers and 600 dropouts that burn up in the atmosphere), then the chain reaction would cause those same orbits to become 10 times as crowded.

25 "It's clearly wiser to avoid a tenfold increase," Mr. Kessler said.

26 Nicholas L. Johnson, an orbital-debris expert at the Kaman Sciences Corporation, in Colorado Springs, another member of the academy panel, said he felt there was not enough evidence to judge whether a chain reaction had already begun. In any case, he said, its repercussions might not materialize for decades.

27 "From an operational standpoint, I think we're not going to have to worry about losing satellites in my lifetime," he said. "I don't think it's imminent."

28 As for possible measures to combat space litter, one step, an expensive one, would involve moving spacecraft aside as missions are accomplished, either into less-crowded parking orbits or downward into Earth's atmosphere, where they would burn up.

29 More expensive would be to redesign spacecraft to limit debris, possibly by adding protective shields that would ward off tiny projectiles and keep a satellite from shattering.

I. Getting the Message

After reading the article, choose the best answer for each item.

1. The main problem of space junk is that it _____.
   a. ruins our atmosphere
   b. puts valuable satellites and spacecraft in danger
   c. makes astronomical observations more difficult

2. A chain reaction in space would take much longer than on Earth because _____.
   a. there is no atmosphere in space
   b. there is less gravity in space
   c. distances in space are so great

3. The problem of space junk was first noticed seriously in _____.
   a. the 1970s
   b. the 1980s
   c. the 1990s

4. Most of the destruction that space debris could cause will occur _____.
   a. over a period of many years
   b. within the next 20 to 30 years
   c. within the next 10 years

5. NASA is very concerned about space debris, but at present this concern is not shared by _____.
   a. commercial spacecraft companies
   b. foreign governments
   c. Congress

6. Unfortunately, the possible plans for combating space junk _____.
   a. would take too long to implement
   b. are too expensive
   c. require smooth international cooperation

7. According to one scientist, if satellite launches were stopped now the amount of space debris would _____.
   a. decrease quickly
   b. decrease over a period of 20 years
   c. still increase.

Check your answers with the key on page 182. If you have made mistakes, reread the article to gain a better understanding of it.

II. Expanding Your Vocabulary

A. Getting Meaning from Context

Find each word or phrase in the paragraph indicated in parentheses. Use context clues to determine the meaning of the word or phrase. Choose the best definition.

1.	prompts (1)	a. prevents	b.	urges; causes
2.	slams into (2)	a. hits forcefully	b.	surrounds
3.	spent (4)	a. used	b.	expensive
4.	consensus (6)	a. agreement within a group	b.	disagreement within a group
5.	vast (9)	a. very large	b.	very short
6.	wrestling with (11)	a. thinking hard about; trying to solve	b.	fighting in an athletic contest
7.	generation (20)	a. creation	b.	people of the same age
8.	bleak (23)	a. promising	b.	bad; without hope

B. Finding Words with Similar Meanings

Find a word or phrase in the indicated paragraph of the article that has the same meaning as each italicized word or phrase.

1. *make larger* (2) _____

2. *broke into small pieces* (15) _____

3. *far-reaching effects* (26) _____

4. *plans; solutions* (28) _____

III. Working with Idioms and Expressions _____

Study the meanings of these idioms and phrasal verbs. A form of each one appears in the indicated paragraph of the article.

Idioms

at risk (3)   in a dangerous position
in the vanguard (10)   in the lead
share of the pie (11)   piece of something
cry in the wilderness (12)   warn about the future when no one listens; a reference to the Bible (Isaiah 40:3; Matthew 3:3)
under way (22)   started; in motion

Phrasal Verbs

draw up (10)   write; create
spell out (20)   explain in detail
burn up (28)   be completely destroyed by fire
ward off (29)   protect against

Complete these sentences with idioms and phrasal verbs from the list. Use the correct form of each verb.

1. Some scientists believe that a chain reaction in space is already _____.

2. Scientists are concerned that, within one hundred years, spacecraft will be _____ because of space debris.

3. Fortunately, some space debris enters the atmosphere and _____.

4. One plan to stop spacecraft from shattering is to use shields that _____ small bits of space debris.

IV. Making Sense of Sentences _____

Some sentences that include an *if* clause are about a possibility, something that could happen in the future.

   Example: If I get a raise next year, I will move to a bigger apartment.

Other *if* statements imagine that something impossible, unlikely, or untrue happened or could happen.

   Example: If I were you, I would study harder.

Reread the *if* statements in paragraphs 7 and 23. Are they telling about something possible or impossible (unlikely)?

Complete these *if* statements about the article.

1. If humans stop sending satellites and spacecraft into space, _____

    _____

2. If humans had never sent rockets into space, _____

    _____

3. If protective shields were added to spacecraft, _____

    _____

4. If spacecraft launchings continue at the present rate, _____

    _____

V. Talking and Writing _____

Discuss the following topics. Then choose one of them to write about.

1. Have you ever seen a satellite? How can you distinguish one from an airplane or a star in the night sky?

2. Do you think satellite development should be slowed down or stopped because of space pollution? Why or why not?

3. Are the causes of pollution in space the same as the causes of pollution on the Earth? Explain.

4. In your judgment, how important is space exploration? How does it compare with other national concerns like employment, poverty, or disease? Is it as important as other kinds of scientific research?

4. In a Newfound Tomb in Egypt, a Fresh Look at Ramses II's Era

Previewing the Article

"I was struck dumb with amazement." This is how the famous archaeologist Howard Carter described his feeling on discovering King Tut's tomb in 1922.

Probably these same words could be used to describe the feelings of the archaeologists who made a more recent discovery—a giant tomb, far bigger and grander than any other in Egypt, uncovered only a short distance from the King Tutankhamen site. Tomb 5, as it is called, promises many important insights into the reign of Ramses II, a famous and very powerful pharaoh of ancient Egypt.

Kent Weeks and other archaeologists found Tomb 5 in the Valley of the Kings, the necropolis ("city of the dead") near the ancient Egyptian capital of Thebes. Here, in underground tombs, are the remains of many royal Egyptians buried between 1600 B.C. and 1000 B.C. The area has been so thoroughly studied that many researchers thought that nothing new could be found. This recent discovery is therefore a tremendous surprise to archaeologists.

Before You Read

Discuss these questions.

1. What do you know about how the Egyptian pharaohs were buried?

2. Why are people all over the world so interested in ancient Egypt?

3. Look at the picture of the writing in the tomb. What are *hieroglyphics?*

4. Look at the map of the Valley of the Kings. Why is the Nile River so important in Egyptian history?

As You Read

Try to draw a picture of the shape or layout of Tomb 5 on a sheet of paper.

In a Newfound Tomb in Egypt, a Fresh Look at Ramses II's Era

By John Noble Wilford
New York Times Service

1 RAMSES II, one of ancient Egypt's greatest pharaohs, is said to have fathered more than 100 children, including 52 sons. Archaeologists have now discovered an enormous mausoleum with at least 67 chambers, the largest tomb ever explored in the Valley of the Kings, and they think this was the resting place for most of those royal sons.

2 Working their way through a narrow entrance in the limestone hillside, archaeologists were astonished to find a central hall with 16 pillars, a passageway to a statue of the god Osiris, and other corridors leading to many separate chambers. In the dim light, they could glimpse wall decorations and alabaster fragments carrying inscriptions with the names of four sons of Ramses, and sarcophagus pieces, mummy fragments and statuary strongly suggesting that the tomb was used for their burials.

3 The sons never attained the power of their father, whose reign lasted 66 years, and their elaborate burial place is not likely to yield treasures similar to those in the tomb of Tutankhamen, the young King Tut. But the newly explored tomb, archaeologists said, promised invaluable insights into Egypt's royal family at a crucial period in ancient history.

4 The discovery was described on Monday by Kent R. Weeks, a professor of Egyptology at the American University in Cairo, who directs a project to map the monuments at the ancient Egyptian capital of Thebes, 300 miles (485 kilometers) south of Cairo. The tomb is part of the necropolis, known as the Valley of the Kings, where monarchs and nobles were buried from 1600 B.C. to 1000 B.C. The site is on the west side of the Nile, across from the ruins of Karnak and Luxor.

5 "It's like no other tomb I know of anywhere in Egypt," Mr. Weeks said in a telephone interview.

6 Most ancient Egyptian tombs consist of only a few chambers, and these are small and laid out along a single axis. Tomb 5, as the new find is designated, not only has at least 67 cham-

An inscription in the tomb with the name of Ramses II's first son.

bers arrayed in a complex plan, but stairs and sloping corridors—yet to be explored— apparently lead to even more rooms on a lower level. These lower rooms may be the actual burial chambers, Mr. Weeks said, and the total number of chambers could exceed 100.

7 Peter Dorman, an archaeologist from the University of Chicago who works across the river at Luxor and has visited the site, praised the discovery as "a very significant find, very impressive and certain to give us a much clearer picture of the family of Ramses II." He also noted that the tomb's architecture was "completely unlike any other tomb" in Egypt.

8 David O'Connor, an Egyptologist at the University of Pennsylvania's University Museum, said the grandeur of the tomb complex "seems to say something important about the status of royal princes during the Ramses reign." Princes usually rated much more modest burial places.

9 Mr. Weeks wondered if there could be other multiple burials for the families of other pharaohs that have gone undetected.

10 "Tomb 5 raises many questions about what else the Valley of the Kings

and other areas at Thebes may have to offer," Mr. Weeks said in a statement issued by the American University of Cairo. "It is an entirely new type of New Kingdom burial structure."

11 Egypt and a large part of the region in the 13th century B.C. were dominated by the long reign of Ramses II. He was one of the most powerful rulers in antiquity and a prolific builder of monumental architecture. His empire extended from Libya east to the valleys of the Tigris and Euphrates rivers, from Turkey south to Sudan. His charioteers fought many battles against the Hittites, archenemies in what is now Turkey and Syria. Tradition has it that Ramses was pharaoh at the time of the Exodus of the Israelites from Egypt.

12 According to the Book of Exodus, the first son of the pharaoh was killed by God. In Chapter 11, Verse 5, it says: "And all the firstborn in the land of Egypt shall die, from the firstborn of Pharaoh that sitteth upon his throne, even unto the firstborn of the maidservant."

13 The eldest son of Ramses II was named Amon-her-khepeshef. He is one of the sons whose names are inscribed on the walls of Tomb 5.

14 The tomb occupies a prominent place in the necropolis, 100 feet (30 meters) from the tomb of Ramses II himself and not far from King Tut's. In fact, when the English archaeologist Howard Carter excavated Tut's tomb, he unknowingly piled dirt and debris over Tomb 5's entrance, further obscuring it.

15 That entrance was discovered once in 1820 by an English traveler, but he explored no farther than the three outermost chambers, which were unprepossessing and had been damaged by flood waters. In the 1980s, Mr. Weeks and other archaeologists rediscovered the hidden entrance by studying the diaries of 19th-century travelers. They also followed the lead of an ancient papyrus now in a museum in Turin. It described the trial of a thief in 1150 B.C. who was caught trying to rob the tomb of Ramses II and also one "across the path," presumably the one now called Tomb 5.

16 Cutting test trenches on the slopes near the Ramses tomb, they uncovered the narrow entrance and did some preliminary investigation. But debris washed in by floods hampered exploration. Only in February were Mr. Weeks and his team able to remove debris blocking the door leading off the grand hall with 16 pillars.

17 Once through the door, they found less water damage and one surprise after another. They followed the passageway leading past 20 doors of smaller chambers and ending at the statue of Osiris, god of the underworld. Two branching corridors each had 20 doors to other rooms. The smallest rooms were about 10 by 10 feet: the largest was 60 by 60 feet.

18 This was when Mr. Weeks realized he had entered, as he said. "The largest tomb in the Valley of the Kings and maybe the largest ever found in all Egypt." It was certainly more complex and extensive than the standard royal tombs, which are simple structures with a single corridor leading to a main burial chamber.

19 In an interview with the Reuters news agency in Cairo, Abdelhalim Nourredin, head of Egypt's Supreme Council for Antiquities, described the structure and the many chambers as magnificent, even if some of the rooms were badly damaged by water, and important because of its "unique design and size from a crucial period in ancient history." The Egyptian government worked with Mr. Weeks in the explorations.

20 Mr. Weeks speculated that the rooms on the main level were used for religious ceremonies and making offerings to the dead, with the lower rooms set aside for the burials.

21 The floors were littered with thousands of pieces of pottery, statue fragments, jewelry, beads, pieces of wooden furniture, stone sarcophagus fragments, inscribed stone vessels, bones from offerings of cooked meat, and pieces of mummified human bodies. Mr. Weeks said there was no indication that looters had penetrated the back chambers or been anywhere in the tomb since antiquity.

22 Close examination revealed the inscribed names of four sons of Ramses. Decorations in the small entrance rooms included the names of Amon-her-khepeshef, the firstborn, and the second son, whose name was, in effect, Ramses Junior. A piece of alabaster jar bore the name and titles of another son, Sety. Outside the entrance, archaeologists found a piece of limestone on which was written the name of Mery-amon, the 15th son.

23 Historians know the names of all 52 sons, but little else about them. They had previously been able to identify the burial sites of only two of them. Mernepteh, the 13th son, succeeded his father as pharaoh and so built his own tomb in the Valley of the Kings. The fifth son, Khaemwase, is thought to be buried at Saqqara, south of the pyramids of Giza.

24 It is entirely possible, Mr. Weeks and other archaeologists said, that all 50 of Ramses' other sons were laid to rest in Tomb 5. Explorations are scheduled to be resumed in July.

NYT GRAPHICS/MAPS

I. Getting the Message

After reading the article, choose the best answer for each item.

1. This newly discovered tomb was a surprise because _____.
   a. archaeologists thought they already knew where all of Ramses' sons were buried
   b. it is so large and in a much-studied location
   c. it is similar to the tomb of Tutankhamen

2. The size of the tomb indicates that _____.
   a. princes were more important in Ramses' time than at other periods of Egyptian history
   b. Egyptian knowledge of architecture was more extensive than previously thought
   c. lack of space was a factor in the Valley of the Kings during Ramses' rule

3. One of the exciting questions this discovery raises is whether or not _____.
   a. other pharaohs' sons are buried in the tomb
   b. there are more large tombs yet to be discovered
   c. Mernepteh, the son who succeeded Ramses as pharaoh, is buried in the tomb

4. Most royal tombs are _____.
   a. simple with a single corridor leading to a main burial chamber
   b. complex, with a large central room and many corridors branching off from it
   c. the same shape as Tomb 5, but larger

5. The archaeologists discovered the tomb by _____.
   a. exploring every inch of the Valley of the Kings
   b. studying the diaries of 19th-century travelers
   c. learning to read obscure markings on monument walls

6. The tomb was hard to find because _____.
   a. the entrance was covered with debris
   b. the Egyptian government discouraged the archaeologists from digging
   c. it was far from the other tombs in the Valley of the Kings

Check your answers with the key on page 182. If you have made mistakes, reread the article to gain a better understanding of it.

II. Expanding Your Vocabulary

A. Getting Meaning from Context

Find each word in the paragraph indicated in parentheses. Use context clues to determine the meaning of the word. Choose the best definition.

1. astonished (2)	a. surprised	b. exhausted
2. designated (6)	a. made	b. named
3. inscribed (13)	a. written	b. hidden
4. unprepossessing (15)	a. not interesting	b. not large

5. preliminary (16)   a. early   b. thorough
6. crucial (19)   a. hurtful   b. important
7. speculated (20)   a. looked   b. guessed
8. looters (21)   a. thieves   b. explorers

B. Identifying Categories of Words

Find the word or phrase that doesn't belong in each category.

1. names for royalty

    monarchs   nobles   princes   charioteers

2. words related to ancient Egyptian burial

    sarcophagus   necropolis   cremation   mausoleum

3. words related to archaeology

    explorations   excavation   telescope   test trenches

4. ancient Egyptian structures

    basilica   pyramid   monument   tomb complex

5. archaeological sites in Egypt

    Majorca   Thebes   Luxor   Valley of the Kings

III. Analyzing Paragraphs

Paragraphs usually have one main or key idea. Match each of these main ideas with one of these paragraphs: **11, 14, 15, 21,** and **23.**

Main Idea	Paragraph Number
1. Part of the tomb has been damaged, but other parts are apparently untouched.	_____
2. The tomb of the pharaoh's sons is in an important location, near the tomb of their father.	_____
3. Research into old writings led archaeologists to discover the tomb.	_____
4. Researchers think many of Ramses' 52 sons may be buried in Tomb 5, but at least two of them are not.	_____
5. Ramses II is very important not only because he was a conqueror and builder, but also because he ruled for so long.	

IV. Talking and Writing

Discuss the following topics. Then choose one of them to write about.

1. What do you know about other important archaeological sites? Choose one and explain why it is important.

2. No people in the world today have the spectacular burial practices of the ancient Egyptians, but many people do bury the dead in special monuments. What do you think of this practice? Why?

Focus on the Newspaper

Newspapers print articles on scientific topics when the information is of interest and/or importance to the general public. The discovery of a new chemical element, research leading to new insights about disease, analyses of the causes of an earthquake or volcanic eruption, predictions about future conditions on Earth—all these matters of "hard" science need to be explained to the general reading public in understandable, nontechnical ways.

The social sciences are also frequent topics of newspaper articles. Social sciences deal primarily with people and how they live now or lived in the past. Fields such as psychology, sociology, and anthropology examine how people function individually and in groups. Archaeologists study past cultures, often digging up artifacts and ruins to piece together information about the characteristics and lifestyles of ancient peoples. As you can see, science articles in a newspaper may cover a wide variety of topics.

Explanations in Science Articles

Journalists must be careful to make technical material meaningful to readers who are not specialists in the field. Science-related articles often include definitions, examples, comparisons, reasons, and statistics (numerical facts) to help readers understand scientific findings.

Exercise 1: Dissecting a Science Article

Find an article about a science or social science topic in the newspaper. Number the paragraphs in the article. Then read it, looking for the information to complete the chart.

ANALYZING A SCIENCE ARTICLE

Did you find . . .	Yes	No	Paragraph number(s)
1. a definition?			
2. an example?			
3. a comparison?			
4. a reason?			
5. a result?			
6. a statistic?			
7. a problem?			
8. a solution?			
9. a discovery?			
10. a recommendation?			
11. contrasting points of view?			

Articles on Ecology

Ecology is the branch of science that deals with the relationship between living things and their environment. In recent years, there has been a lot of public concern about the environment throughout the world. Newspapers frequently print articles about air, water, and land pollution and about damage to plants and animals. These articles can be divided into two main categories: (1) those that tell about present or future harm; and (2) those that tell about efforts to improve the environment.

Exercise 2: Articles about the Environment

Find a newspaper article on some aspect of ecology. Then answer these questions about it.

1. What is the main idea of this article? State it in one sentence.
2. Who or what is affected by the subject of the article?
3. Does this article make you feel optimistic or pessimistic about the environment on Earth in the future?
4. What is the source of the information in the article?
5. Do you think this is an objective source, or does this person, group, business, or industry have a bias? Would the person or group benefit from making things sound better or worse than they really are?

Articles on Health Care

Newspapers often print news stories about the latest in medical research and treatment. Many papers also print regular columns by physicians and other health-care experts. In these columns, the experts answer questions from readers and give advice about physical and mental health.

Daily newspapers are an important source of information about advances in the field of medicine. Newspapers perform a great service by telling people how to take better care of themselves.

Exercise 3: It's Your Health

Scan the headlines of three newspapers, looking for articles and columns about health care. Select two articles or columns to read and analyze. Write this information about each article:

1. What is the most important scientific fact stated in the article?

2. Did you know this fact before reading it here?

3. Is there a stated or implied recommendation about changing behavior to become healthier (for example, avoid smoking or eating fats)?

Herald INTERNATIONAL **Tribune**

Published With The New York Times and The Washington Post

SECTION 7

SPORTS

1

A Novice Angler in Arctic Russia

2

Rodeos of the American West Spur Imitators
Far, Far South

3

An Adventurer's Life: Always New Heights

4

Bannister and Peers: Heroes Made by Dreaming
the Impossible Dream

Focus on the Newspaper: Sports

1. A Novice Angler in Arctic Russia

Previewing the Article

Most of us have a memorable sports "first"; the first time we golfed, or skied, or bowled, or simply watched an unfamiliar sport on TV. But few people have had a "first" like this author's: fishing for salmon above the Arctic Circle in the summer, when the sun never sets.

Learning a new sport as an adult is very different from learning one as a child. Most adults are embarrassed to show their lack of skill and knowledge in a world of other adults who have been doing a sport for years. This author entered several new worlds at once—salmon fishing, the Arctic, and a select group of people who love to fish. As a consequence, everything about her trip—the daily routine, the conversation, the equipment, the living conditions—became vividly memorable.

Before You Read

Discuss these questions.

1. What sports "firsts" have you had? How old were you at the time?

2. Do you fish? If so, where and when do you do it?

3. Salmon are very interesting fish. What do you know about them?

4. The title of this article uses the word *angler* for a person who fishes. Another common word is *fisherman.* Why do you suppose *angler* is used here?

As You Read

Essay writers use various forms to organize their material, such as narration, comparison, cause and effect, description, and definition. As you read, try to discover which of these forms the author has used in this article.

A Novice Angler in Arctic Russia

By Malabar Hornblower

1 PONOI, Russia—I was sitting in the dark cabin of an Aeroflot helicopter 5,000 feet over the barren tundra, flying 185 miles southeast from Murmansk to the Kola Peninsula in the northwestern corner of Russia. My fellow travelers and I were crammed together on two benches that ran the length of both sides of the helicopter, our mountain of baggage on the floor between us. Our ears were stuffed with cotton to reduce the helicopter's piercing whine, and conversation was futile. Everyone else eventually dozed. But, claustrophobic and apprehensive about the week ahead, I stewed.

2 I was here because my new husband's greatest joy in life is fishing, particularly salmon fishing, and he would like to make a fisherman of me, too. Thinking that I should try at least once to like it, I had even attended the Wulff School of Fly Fishing on the Beaverkill River in Lew Beach, New York, to learn to cast. Half the time, I could get the fly into the water at a point close to where I wanted it but not at any great distance.

3 I was still very short on experience, though, when I journeyed above the Arctic Circle in June 1994 to fish a portion of what many claim is one of the world's greatest salmon rivers. I later learned that in the first six weeks of the 1994 season, more than 4,000 fish were taken (and released).

4 We would be staying at a camp on the river run by the Ponoi River Company, which has a 10-year lease on the fishing rights from the sea to the river's headwaters, about a 100-mile stretch. For $7,500 a person (raised to $7,990 this year), the company would house and feed us for the week, take us to different spots on the river by helicopter and boat, supply licenses and experienced guides, and generally keep the clients content.

5 Many in our group were repeaters, eager to try the river in different seasons under different conditions. They talked of nothing but salmon, rods and flies.

6 We were 18 men and 2 women, myself and an Irish banker who later became the life of the party. She was already an excellent angler—a point my husband used to encourage me. During our six days, she caught two of the largest fish, a 25- and a 23-pounder.

7 Most of the men were over 50 and notably affluent (fishing the choice corners of the world costs dearly). Not content with fishing during the day, they would take advantage of June's nearly constant daylight and the proximity of what was called the "main pool" (actually, the only pool in the river accessible by foot) to fish all night, too.

8 Our helicopters—one with our group and our luggage and the other with food and supplies—landed at 6 P.M. on a plateau just above the camp, a white-tented village. We were comforted to see smoke from the wood stoves, considering the damp and cloudy 38-degree-Fahrenheit weather.

9 Our 16-by-12-foot tent included two bunks with sleeping bags, a stove stocked daily with wood, table and chairs, a water dispenser that acted as a faucet over an improvised sink, an electric heater and one light bulb that would be extinguished when the generator shut down at 10 P.M. The floor was wooden, not dirt. Once filled with wood, the stove kept the tent cozy for about an hour. After that, the northern cold took over and the sleeping bag proved the best bet. Hot showers were in a separate building.

NYT GRAPHICS/MAPS

10 Meals were served in the main building, a frame structure, and were the scene of much comparison each night over drinks and dinner. (Where were you? How many did you catch? What size? Using what flies?)

11 The Finnish chef, Mika Repo, cooked imaginatively and well. Salmon was the only local food, and its use was limited, as the camp sticks religiously to the catch-and-release philosophy; all but enough fish for supper are returned to the river. There was a different salmon dish nightly, followed by heaping platters of meat, potatoes and vegetables, topped off with dessert, such as apple pie and carrot cake baked at the camp. Vodka accompanied dinner at no extra charge, with moderately good Russian wine available for a modest price.

12 For the fishermen, the days quickly assumed a pattern. They went out in any weather, well insulated with multilayered clothing. The day's fishing assignments would be posted at 9 A.M., after an abundant breakfast (fruit, juices, cereal, eggs, bacon, pancakes, toast and muffins). Without hesitation, the crowd arose and gathered their rods and reels, backpacks, sweaters, cameras and binoculars. A moment later, there were cries of "good luck," "get a big one today," and my favorite, "tight line," repeated over and over until all had disappeared.

13 Along a 100-mile stretch of river, the camp has 15 fishing locations, all with different characteristics so that the frustrations—or joys—encountered one day won't be repeated the next. Each locale has its own guide with his own approach to the river and to fishing, so that the fisherman can constantly learn new techniques and theories. Under the poor conditions of our visit, we did not do badly. Among 20 rods, we caught a total of 757 fish (of which 328 were grilse, small salmon that have spent less than a year fattening up in the sea, and 137 kelts, older fish that came to the river to spawn and never left). The top rod caught 66 and the lowest (other than mine) 27. I came in last with 5 grilse, each weighing about 5 pounds. Minnows really.

Malabar Hornblower, a food and travel writer who lives in Cambridge, Massachusetts, wrote this for The New York Times.

I. Getting the Message

After reading the article, choose the best answer for each item.

1. The fishing trip that the author took _____.
   a. is enjoyed by thousands of anglers every year
   b. is common for first-time anglers
   c. is expensive so only a few can enjoy it

2. The writer began fishing because _____.
   a. her new husband wanted her to
   b. she had always wanted to do it
   c. all her friends were anglers

3. Since it was summer in the Arctic, _____.
   a. people did not need to wear coats
   b. sunlight lasted all night long
   c. the campers swam a great deal

4. The anglers reached the camp _____.
   a. by boat
   b. in off-road vehicles
   c. by helicopter

5. After the anglers caught the fish, they _____.
   a. cooked and ate them all
   b. released most of them back into the water
   c. shipped them for sale by the fishing industry

6. The author of the article _____.
   a. caught more fish than she thought she would
   b. caught more fish than her husband did
   c. caught the smallest number of fish

Check your answers with the key on page 182. If you have made mistakes, reread the article to gain a better understanding of it.

II. Expanding Your Vocabulary

Find each word in the paragraph indicated in parentheses. Use context clues to determine the meaning of the word. Choose the best definition.

1.	barren (1)	a. unfruitful; unproductive	b. filled with vegetation
2.	futile (1)	a. useless	b. interesting
3.	apprehensive (1)	a. worried	b. excited
4.	affluent (7)	a. happy	b. wealthy
5.	dearly (7)	a. a lot	b. affectionately
6.	proximity (7)	a. inconvenience	b. nearness
7.	improvised (9)	a. carefully made	b. made from available materials
8.	cozy (9)	a. warm and comfortable	b. hot and uncomfortable

III. Working with Idioms and Expressions

Study the meanings of these idioms, phrasal verbs, and expressions. A form of each one appears in the indicated paragraph of the article.

Idioms

short on (3)   lacking in; not having much
best bet (9)   best solution to a problem
assume a pattern (12)   take a shape; form a schedule

Phrasal Verbs

stick to (11)   refuse to change
top off (11)   complete; finish

Expressions

the life of the party (6)   the most entertaining person at an event
corners of the world (7)   distant or remote parts of the world; often written as *the four corners of the world*

Answer these questions. For help, reread the indicated paragraphs.

1. Who was *the life of the party* (6)?

2. Why are most people who fish the choice *corners of the world* affluent (7)?

3. Why was the sleeping bag the *best bet* (9)?

4. What *topped off* the meal (11)?

5. Why did the days quickly *assume a pattern* (12)?

IV. Making Sense of Sentences

In a basic English sentence, the subject comes first, followed by a verb. When the verb is a form of *to be,* an adjective or adjective phrase often follows.

subject verb   adjective phrase

Example: Mary is kind to all her neighbors.

However, several sentences like this in a row produce a choppy effect.

Example: Mary is kind to all her neighbors. She is popular. She has many friends.

To make their sentences flow smoothly, good writers vary the word order. Two or more sentences can be combined by using an adjective phrase in front of the subject.

Example: Popular and kind to all her neighbors, Mary has many friends.

In each paragraph listed below, find a sentence that begins with an adjective phrase. Write the adjective phrase and the subject it modifies.

Paragraph	Adjective Phrase	Subject
1	claustrophobic and apprehensive about the week ahead	I
2		
7		
9		

V. Talking and Writing

Discuss the following topics. Then choose one of them to write about.

1. What aspects of this fishing trip would you enjoy? What aspects would you dislike?

2. This is obviously an expensive way to fish. Can you name some other expensive sports? If you had enough money, would you pursue these sports?

3. Is there a particular "corner of the world" that you would like to visit? Where is it? Why would you like to go there?

2. Rodeos of the American West Spur Imitators Far, Far South

Previewing the Article

Among the many cultural exports of the United States are Hollywood movies, rock music, designer jeans, and fast food. One of the newest and most colorful exports is the western rodeo. This article examines the rise of the rodeo in an unlikely place, Brazil. Here people crowd into arenas to watch athletes ride wild horses, rope cattle, and perform other skills developed in the American Wild West of the 1800s.

The author explains how the image of the rugged American cowboy has created a whole new identity for some Brazilians—as well as creating an industry that supplies Brazilians with western-style fashions and music. He also shows how a phenomenon such as this can reveal much about a country's culture in general.

Before You Read

Discuss these questions.

1. What do you know about rodeos? Have you ever been to one? Have you ever seen one on TV or in a movie?

2. Do you like American cowboy movies? What do you think people like about these films?

3. Do you ever wear western-style clothes? Why or why not?

As You Read

Look for the author's answers to these questions.

1. Where in Brazil is the rodeo becoming most popular? Why?

2. Is the popularity of the rodeo in Brazil related to changes in the economy and the kind of work people do?

Rodeos of the American West Spur Imitators Far, Far South

By James Brooke
New York Times Service

1 PRESIDENTE PRUDENTE, Brazil—Shane Sanders had barely hung on for the regulation eight seconds on the bare back of a bucking bronco, but the scrappy Texan was grinning as he packed his car in the rodeo parking lot here.

2 "A guy can make more money on the rodeo circuit down here than at home," the 24-year-old rodeo rider said, as Portuguese-speaking women in cowboy hats warmed up their quarter horses for the races.

3 American-style rodeos are sweeping Brazil's cattle country like a brush fire. Fifteen years ago, Brazil's pioneer rodeo, in nearby Barretos, was a dusty stock-lot affair, offering black-and-white television sets to winning cowboys.

4 Today, the prizes are new cars, and the contest in Barretos takes place in a 35,000-seat, horseshoe-shaped arena designed by Oscar Niemeyer, the architect of Brasilia.

5 Here in Presidente Prudente, a railroad junction 560 kilometers (350 miles) west of São Paulo, the annual June rodeo was broadcast live by two television networks to a huge swath of Brazil's farm belt.

6 "We started the rodeo here as a joke—no one really believed it would catch on," said Adauto Peretti Jr., a quarter-horse breeder.

7 On the opening night of the rodeo, two weeks ago, a line of cars more than three kilometers long snaked toward the stadium.

8 Outside the covered arena, sales clerks in a trailer rented by Smith Brothers Roping Supplies did a brisk business selling hats, ropes, boots, blue jeans, checked shirts, belt buckles, and chewing tobacco—all imported from the United States.

9 Taking advantage of a rural Brazilian thirst for all things from the American West, the Denton, Texas, company has opened stores here and in three neighboring Brazilian states.

10 Guto Medeiros, the mustachioed owner of Cowboys, a locally owned rival Western goods store here, said after watching a roping contest: "We now sell to 190 stores in Brazil. Presidente Prudente is the center of western style in Brazil."

11 Gradually, the American Western-gear industry is discovering that rodeo's geography—which had already expanded to Western Canada and Australia—now includes Brazil. Eying Brazil's growing market, this rodeo season a Texas hat manufacturer is sponsoring Adriano Moraes, a rugged São Paulo state farm boy who has become a top-ranked bull rider on the U.S. circuit.

12 In part, rural Brazil's passion for the American West goes with the national fascination with the United States.

13 "They want to be more like Americans," said Gary Don Hopkins, a Texan who has watched the rodeo phenomenon for the last two years as manager of King Ranch do Brasil, an American-owned horse and cattle ranch near here. "Cowboys are idealized, and people want to be like that."

14 With modern agricultural methods bringing a new affluence and a new worldliness to Brazil's rural midwest, many ranchers and farmers seem to be searching for a more dynamic identity than the old rural stereotype of the languid coffee baron in a white linen suit.

15 Part of this new rural pride involves looking down on Brazil's crowded coastal cities. Digging into a T-bone steak at an eatery here, José Eduardo Pinheiro, a local rancher and rodeo organizer, said that he could not care less that animal protection groups had recently won bans on rodeo from left-leaning city administrations in most of metropolitan São Paulo.

16 Waldemar Ruy dos Santos, a retired bull rider who now commands legions of fans as a rodeo announcer, likes to tell the story of how he handled a Rio de Janeiro resident who had described ranchers as "dumb hicks."

17 "I shook a stuffed stork in his face and told him, 'without the ranchers, you'd be eating fish and birds,'" he recalled.

18 Country chic has national appeal. Brazil's top country singing duo, Chitaozinho and Xororo, routinely rank among the nation's top performers.

19 In this city, where newspaper front pages always carry yesterday's beef prices, social columnists vied recently for tidbits of gossip emanating from the rodeo boxes for which local cattle and horse breeders pay $1,150 for the four days of events.

20 Located slightly above a boisterous sea of white cowboy hats, one box featured ruddy-cheeked men with fist-sized silver belt buckles. They swigged Jack Daniels from hip flasks while their wives, wearing cowboy hats, chatted about American Airlines' new direct flight from São Paulo to Dallas. Outside, a barbecue chef roasted a freshly butchered pig on a skewer.

21 Before ducking into a box, Domingos de Souza Medeiros, a leading quarter-horse breeder, said in Texas-accented English: "This isn't fad or fashion—this is our life."

I. Getting the Message

After reading the article, choose the best answer for each item.

1. The author explains the importance of rodeos to Brazilians by _____.
   a. describing one rodeo as an example and interviewing people
   b. presenting research on the history of the South American rodeo
   c. visiting many rodeos in Brazil over several months

2. Rodeos are popular _____.
   a. all over Brazil
   b. mainly in rural Brazil
   c. mainly in Brazil's coastal cities

3. Presidente Prudente's annual rodeo is _____.
   a. broadcast only over the radio
   b. broadcast by two TV networks
   c. ignored by most rodeo fans in Brazil

4. The rodeo is popular in Brazil because _____.
   a. it is an age-old Brazilian tradition
   b. rural Brazil has always been known for its cowboys
   c. Brazilians are fascinated by American culture

5. The popularity of the rodeo in Brazil is a sign that _____.
   a. Brazilian culture is changing
   b. the rich are getting richer and the poor are getting poorer
   c. animal-rights groups are becoming more powerful in rural areas

Check your answers with the key on page 182. If you have made mistakes, reread the article to gain a better understanding of it.

II. Expanding Your Vocabulary

A. Getting Meaning from Context

Find each word in the paragraph indicated in parentheses. Use context clues to determine the meaning of the word. Choose the best definition.

1. _____	bronco (1)	a. an untamed horse	b. an expensive horse
2. _____	scrappy (1)	a. made of small pieces	b. eager to compete or fight
3. _____	sweeping (3)	a. moving quickly across	b. cleaning
4. _____	swath (5)	a. area	b. cloth
5. _____	dynamic (14)	a. energetic	b. old-fashioned
6. _____	tidbits (19)	a. false information	b. small pieces of information
7. _____	vied (19)	a. competed	b. wrote
8. _____	boisterous (20)	a. loud	b. wet

B. Using Colorful Vocabulary

The word *spur* in the headline is a good example of colorful word choice. A *spur* is a small, sharp metal object attached to the heel of a rider's boot; the rider uses it to urge his horse forward. Thus *spur,* used as a verb, means "to push something forward quickly."

Write one sentence using the word *spur* as a noun. Write another sentence using *spur* as a verb.

III. Working with Idioms and Expressions ⎯⎯⎯⎯⎯⎯⎯⎯⎯⎯⎯⎯

Study the meanings of these phrasal verbs and expressions. A form of each one appears in the indicated paragraph of the article.

Phrasal Verbs

hang on (1) hold tight to something
catch on (6) become popular
take advantage of (9) use for one's own gain or profit
go with (12) be part of; be a result of
look down on (15) feel superior to
dig into (15) eat with enthusiasm
duck into (21) enter quickly

Expressions

make money (2) earn money
farm belt (5) an area noted for farming
dumb hicks (16) *(not polite)* unsophisticated people from the country

Complete these sentences with phrasal verbs and expressions from the list. Use the correct form of each verb.

1. The rodeo rider ⎯⎯⎯⎯⎯⎯⎯⎯⎯⎯ for eight seconds, the required time for a successful bronco ride.

2. American-style rodeos have not ⎯⎯⎯⎯⎯⎯⎯⎯⎯⎯ in Brazilian cities.

3. Many rodeo fans from the rural areas of Brazil ⎯⎯⎯⎯⎯⎯⎯⎯⎯⎯ people who live in the cities.

4. While ⎯⎯⎯⎯⎯⎯⎯⎯⎯⎯ a steak, a local rancher talked to the author.

IV. Making Sense of Sentences ⎯⎯⎯⎯⎯⎯⎯⎯⎯⎯⎯⎯⎯

Many *appositives* are used in this article. An appositive is a word or phrase placed just after a noun that identifies or renames the noun. Appositives convey important information briefly, without the use of a new sentence.

appositive
Example: ". . . designed by Oscar Niemeyer, *the architect of Brasília.*" (paragraph 4)

Match each appositive phrase in column B with the noun that it identifies in column A. For help, reread the indicated paragraphs of the article.

A	B
1. _____ Presidente Prudente (5)	a. an American-owned horse and cattle ranch near here
2. _____ Guto Medeiros (10)	b. a railroad junction 560 kilometers (350) miles west of São Paulo
3. _____ King Ranch do Brasil (13)	c. a leading quarter-horse breeder
4. _____ José Eduardo Pinheiro (15)	d. a local rancher and rodeo organizer
5. _____ Domingos de Souza Medeiros (21)	e. the mustachioed owner of Cowboys

V. Talking and Writing

Discuss the following topics. Then choose one of them to write about.

1. The author says that Brazilians have a "national fascination with the United States." Is the same true of people from other countries you know about? Why or why not?

2. Is a sport from another country becoming popular in your country? How does the popularity of a sport spread from one country to another?

3. What do people admire about cowboys? Why are cowboys considered symbols of the U.S. character?

3. An Adventurer's Life: Always New Heights

Previewing the Article

"Because it's there."

This is the classic answer that mountain climbers give when asked the question, "Why did you climb the mountain?" Reinhold Messner, the fascinating adventurer profiled in this article, is no exception: "I don't suppose I will ever know, deep down inside myself, why I do it."

Messner's explanation may be unsatisfying, but his achievements are incredible. He was first to climb the highest mountain in the world, Mount Everest, without oxygen to help him breathe in the thin air. Then he climbed all the highest mountain peaks of the world without the food stations or external assistance that many climbers rely on.

Reinhold Messner's life is an exciting story of human courage in the face of great challenges. He is now retired from climbing, but he still goes on dangerous expeditions. He also works to combat a problem never faced by earlier climbers: trash. Climbing is now so popular that Mount Everest, for example, has on its slopes thousands of tons of trash discarded by climbers. Messner has created an organization that encourages people to leave the beautiful places they explore as they found them.

Before You Read

Discuss these questions.

1. What do you know about mountain climbing? Can you name any famous mountain climbers?

2. Have you ever climbed a mountain? If so, describe the experience.

3. How high are the world's highest mountains? Where are they?

As You Read

Make a list of questions you would ask Reinhold Messner about his life if you were interviewing him.

An Adventurer's Life: Always New Heights

By Roderick Conway Morris
International Herald Tribune

1 SULDEN, Italy—Reinhold Messner spent his 26th birthday lying in a Munich clinic. Several weeks before, he and his brother Günther, having been invited to join a German expedition, had reached the summit of Nanga Parbat in Kashmir. During the descent, amid continual avalanches, Messner lost contact with Günther, who was never seen again.

2 The South Tirolese climber combed the mountain for two days and nights searching for Günther. By the time Messner literally crawled, and was finally carried by mountain farmers, back to civilization, he was so badly frost-bitten that he lost half a dozen toes, and was lucky not to lose several fingers. When he emerged from the clinic he was penniless and, in his own words, "a cripple."

3 "It was clear that I would never be able to climb again," said Messner. "For practical reasons, because of the amputations I had undergone, but also for psychological reasons. But after a while I realized that by staying at home and continuing to try to study for a profession—I was doing architecture at Padua University at the time—I could not bring my brother back to life again. He was dead.

4 "So I went back to what was my real life before, my life as an adventurer. Because, by then, it was too late—that was my life. I could have become an unhappy and unsuccessful architect—but there were already plenty of unhappy and unsuccessful architects."

5 Within a decade, Messner was the first (with Peter Habeler) to climb Everest without oxygen and, soon after, the first to scale the mountain solo. By the mid-'80s he had become the first to scale all 14 of the world's 8,000-meter (26,250-foot) peaks—all without oxygen. Having crossed Antarctica and Greenland, unsupported, Messner, who last September celebrated his 50th birthday (perhaps, when one studies the history of his hair-raising exploits, his most improbable achievement of all), is due to set off at the beginning of March on what he reckons will be the biggest challenge of his career—crossing the pack ice and ice barriers of the Arctic Ocean (with his doctor-brother Hubert) from the New Siberian Islands to Cape Columbia in Canada via the North Pole, "by fair means," without any air support, food depots or external assistance.

6 By the time Messner came on the scene, the world's highest peaks had been conquered, but no climber of previous generations could have conceived that a single individual would be able to scale every one of them in a lifetime. But then nobody before Messner—who was born into a family of nine children in a tiny mountain village in the Italian South Tirol, and had no prospect of raising the massive sums required by earlier Himalayan expeditions—imagined that it might be possible to tackle these giants in what Messner has called "alpine-style" ascents.

7 "Everest was climbed, so it was not important to go there any more, to climb it again and again," he said. "What was interesting was to see whether it was possible to climb it without oxygen. Because, as I came to realize, if you could, expeditions would be far less expensive. Doing Everest solo, or in a two-man or three-man team would cost peanuts.

8 "Before you needed a lot of money, a lot of time and faced huge logistical problems, with dozens of porters, moving tons of material. The good weather time is very short, and the more material you have, the more people on the expedition, the chances of reaching the summit get less and less."

9 The medical establishment, however, was unanimous in arguing that spending extended periods at high altitude without oxygen would lead to permanent brain damage. "I could not be sure, but I did not believe that this was true," Messner said. "I knew that a British climber, Colonel Norton, had gone up to nearly 29,000 feet in 1924. He approached the summit of Everest, though he didn't reach it, without suffering any ill effects—and lived to be an old man. And I personally had done three 8,000-meter peaks without oxygen. I did not feel perfect, but I knew that I could go higher."

10 Although triumphantly proving conventional medical wisdom incorrect, Messner has nonetheless had some extraordinary experiences along the way: "On Nanga Parbat in 1970, I had a clear out-of-body experience. I had the feeling that I could see my own body rolling down the mountain. I was flying above myself—maybe six or seven meters above—and I could observe every move I was making. And it was a very painful moment when I came into my own body again."

11 "Yet I think these hallucinations are logical things," he said. "If you go for days and days at high altitude, exposed to the limits of your endurance, you begin to seek out other human beings. The main difficulty is not the lack of oxygen, not the climbing, the cold, the storms—but to be so far away from other human beings. And, in reality, human beings should not be up there, and we know it when we are up there. So we create others, or even see our-

Reinhold Messner at his museum.

selves, so that for an hour or two we are not entirely alone. And these visions help us to survive."

12 The chances of being alone in some places in the Alps, Himalayas and other ranges where once Messner wandered alone or in the company of one or two fellow climbers have, alas, seriously diminished. Peaks that could be climbed 50 years ago by fewer than 20 mountaineers, he said, are now accessible to several thousand. The result has been the despoilation of once virgin wilds—on the slopes of Everest alone there are thousands of tons of discarded oxygen bottles and other refuse.

13 In response, Messner has set up an international organization, Mountain Wilderness, aimed at preserving remote landscapes and encouraging climbers to leave the places they visit as they found them. He hopes too to set an example by his own practices.

14 Messner now combines his life as adventurer with that of a farmer (he is particularly proud of a new breed of cattle he is developing, by crossing yaks and Scottish Highland cattle, able to live outside all year round, which could make very high alpine farms economically viable). He has also bought and restored, in the village of Sulden, an old building where local mountain guides used to wait to take well-heeled amateur climbers on excursions in the surrounding peaks, and turned it into a singular and amusing museum, illustrated by more than 100 pieces from his own collection.

15 The museum's central theme is "the gulf between thought and deed to be found in even the best mountaineers."

16 Now considering himself "a walker rather than a climber," Messner said: "I'm not an ambitious climber any more—and anyway, I'm too old to compete. But I am not running out of possible adventures, only running out of time."

17 He does not pretend to be without apprehensions about his 1,250-mile (2,000-kilometer) polar trek.

18 "I often feel afraid before I go," he said. "But once I am out there I feel quite well, and I go step by step to see if I can reach the goal. I'm still quite strong, and still feel the necessity to do it. But I don't suppose I will ever know, deep down inside myself, why I do it."

I. Getting the Message

After reading the article, choose the best answer for each item.

1. In the author's opinion, Messner's most amazing achievement is _____.
    a. climbing Mt. Everest without oxygen
    b. creating an ecologically conscious organization for mountain climbers
    c. surviving to age 50 despite all the risks he has taken

2. At age 26, after Messner recovered from a climbing disaster, _____.
    a. he tried to study to be an architect
    b. he immediately returned to mountain climbing
    c. he became a farmer

3. At the time Messner climbed Mt. Everest, doctors thought that _____.
    a. the thin air would kill climbers
    b. the lack of oxygen would cause brain damage
    c. the weak air pressure at the top would make climbers sick

4. Messner says he no longer competes at mountain climbing because _____.
    a. he lost six toes while mountain climbing
    b. he is too old
    c. he now dislikes the sport

5. To Messner, the hardest thing about mountain climbing is _____.
    a. the weather at high altitudes
    b. the danger
    c. the absence of other human beings

Check your answers with the key on page 182. If you have made mistakes, reread the article to gain a better understanding of it.

II. Expanding Your Vocabulary _____

A. Getting Meaning from Context

Find each word in the paragraph indicated in parentheses. Use context clues to determine the meaning of the word. Choose the best definition.

1. combed (2)   a. researched   b. searched
2. literally (2)   a. exactly; actually   b. according to literary sources

3. reckons (5)   a. destroys   b. thinks
4. prospect (6)   a. view   b. hope or chance
5. unanimous (9)   a. all agreeing   b. all disagreeing
6. hallucinations (11) a. unreal pictures in the mind   b. memories
7. singular (14)   a. unusual   b. unmarried
8. despoilation (12)   a. restoration   b. ruin

B. Identifying Categories of Words

Find the word or phrase that doesn't belong in each category.

1. dangers of mountain climbing

    avalanches   frostbite   hallucinations   external assistance

2. aids to mountain climbers

    high altitude   porters   food depots   air support

3. ways of climbing mountains

    alpine style   polar style   three-man team   solo

4. crossing of remote wilderness areas

    sightseeing   expedition   excursion   trek

5. parts of a mountain

    slope   valley   peak   summit

III. Working with Idioms and Expressions _____

Study the meanings of these idioms, phrasal verbs, and expressions. A form of each one appears in the indicated paragraph of the article.

Idioms

come on the scene (6)   arrive
cost peanuts (7)   be very inexpensive

Phrasal Verbs

seek out (11)   look for
aim at (13)   have as one's goal or purpose

Expressions

lose contact with (1)   be unable to communicate with
bring back to life (3)   make a dead person live again
medical establishment (9)   the prominent doctors and medical groups that determine
   accepted medical practices
out-of-body experience (10)   a feeling of seeing oneself from outside one's body,
   often produced by a life-threatening situation
well-heeled (14)   rich

Complete these sentences with idioms, phrasal verbs, and expressions from the list. Use the correct form of each verb.

1. Messner thinks his _____ resulted from being so far away from other human beings.

2. After Messner _____ his brother, he searched frantically for him.

3. At the time that Messner climbed Mt. Everest, the _____ believed that doing it safely without oxygen was impossible.

4. Before Messner _____, no one imagined that one person could scale all fourteen of the world's highest peaks.

IV. Analyzing Paragraphs _____

Reread the indicated paragraphs. Choose the answer that best completes each sentence.

1. Paragraphs 1 through 4 do all but _____.
   a. describe a tragic incident in Messner's life
   b. tell why Messner continued climbing after his brother's death
   c. explain the history of Messner's museum

2. Messner's remarkable achievements include all but _____ (6–8).
   a. conquering high peaks without oxygen
   b. being the first to scale Mt. Everest
   c. showing that spectacular climbs could be done cheaply

3. In paragraphs 10 and 11 Messner explains in his own words all but _____.
   a. his idea about the role of hallucinations in survival
   b. what his out-of-body experience was like
   c. his fears about crossing the Arctic

4. Currently Messner does all but _____ (14).

    a. compete in climbing the world's tallest peaks

    b. run a mountaineering museum

    c. develop a new breed of cattle

5. Paragraphs 16 and 17 show that Messner feels all but _____.

    a. apprehensive about his trip across the Arctic

    b. optimistic about his future as an adventurer

    c. depressed about his past injuries

V. Talking and Writing

Discuss the following topics. Then choose one of them to write about.

1. Reinhold Messner says, "I don't suppose I will ever know . . . why I do it." In your opinion, why does he live the life of an adventurer and take the risks that he does?

2. A famous song by Richard Rodgers and Oscar Hammerstein II contains the words "Climb every mountain . . . till you find your dream." Reinhold Messner has actually done this. What "mountains" do *you* have to climb in your own life to find your dream? What can you learn from Messner's example?

3. What other kinds of exploration of our world do you know about? Which ones are most appealing to you? Why?

4. Which of the great explorers of the past and present do you most admire? Why?

4. Bannister and Peers: Heroes Made by Dreaming the Impossible Dream

Previewing the Article

What is "impossible" for the human body? Do physical boundaries limit most sports achievements? For many years, people believed that no human could run a mile in less than four minutes. Roger Bannister, an English medical student, broke this invisible barrier in 1954. Since then, the record for the mile has moved steadily downward.

This sports column describes a gathering to celebrate the 40th anniversary of Bannister's achievement. At the gathering, several runners who have broken the four-minute mile speculated on what the final record might be. The author uses their comments to discuss the wisdom of setting limits in any sport. Bannister and the other runners dared to think that they could do what was considered impossible. It is strange, the author argues, that they are now discussing limits to what other athletes can achieve.

Before You Read

Discuss these questions.

1. What other athletic records can you think of? Is breaking any of these records impossible?

2. Why is it sometimes hard to determine what is genuinely impossible for the human body?

3. Do you know anyone who achieved a goal everybody said was impossible?

4. What limits do you have in your own life—socially, financially, physically, or artistically? How can you overcome these limits?

As You Read

Try to discover the author's attitude toward these famous runners. Does he admire them? Does he disagree with them? What lessons does he draw from their discussion?

Bannister and Peers: Heroes Made by Dreaming the Impossible Dream

By Ian Thomsen
International Herald Tribune

1 LONDON—The smartest people do this. They try to tell you what is impossible. Then they go on and on explaining why, like politicians on the eve of a tax increase.

2 In this case, it has to do with the lung membrane. "There are only two sources of energy," said Peter Snell on the way to explaining—on the 40th anniversary of Roger Bannister's four-minute mile, ironically—why it would be impossible to run the mile any faster than the fastest man today.

3 This is getting away from the lung membrane, or perhaps it isn't, but when Bannister was a child, the four-minute mile was supposed to be an impossibility. Sir Roger is 65 now, and the world record of Noureddine Morceli is 15 seconds faster than the impossible time of 3:59.4 he ran on May 6, 1954. Morceli and 13 preceding world-record holders gathered here on Friday to celebrate.

4 "I'd like to pay tribute to the anonymous person who said the four-minute mile was impossible," said Herb Elliott of Australia, who ran the mile in 3:54.5 in 1958. "Do you know who it was who said the four-minute mile was impossible, Roger?"

5 Sir Roger did not know.

6 "If it weren't for him, we all wouldn't be here," Elliott said at a press conference.

7 At this point, seven of them began debating the difference between what is impossible and what is not. Six of them should have known better. Morceli predicted he would cut two or three seconds from his record of 3:44.39, and agreeing with him was Arne Anderson, the 76-year-old Swede, who ran 4:01.6 in 1944. Bannister, who retired from running to become a neurologist, set the bar at 3:30 and doubted whether anyone would better that. Jim Ryun doubted he would live to see the man who did it.

8 Snell's theory of the lung membrane had to do with the limits of oxygen. The lung membrane can only deliver so much of it to the muscles, and he said the interface has already been maximized by athletes born and trained at

On May 6, 1954, 24-year-old English medical student Roger Bannister crashed his way into athletic history by running a mile in 3 minutes, 59.4 seconds.

high altitudes. Snell is the 55-year-old New Zealander whose time of 3:54.1 was a world record in 1964, and of Morceli he said: "I think I've seen the fastest mile ever."

9 There also was discussion of the potential genetic variations offered by China and India, as well as the necessity of a global environment free of war, and as these athletes, these jocks, went back and forth, I began to wonder whether there was more intelligence at this one table than in all of the football locker rooms of America. And then Elliott said this.

10 "I think I'm the only dreamer. I think

we're only on the verge of understanding the interface between the mind and the spirit and the body. I think a quantum leap is there to be made someplace."

11 I had been thinking of the American football coaches, the coaches in every team sport, who direct their players to avoid mistakes. There is so much negativism in sports. So many coaches create "systems," judging athletes by the most rudimentary statistics. Ultimately, a coach reveals only that which he doesn't understand. The great teams, the great performers, are propelled by a genius that no one can predict. The

losers tend to think there's a recipe, and they stumble around the kitchen, refusing the spices. They never understand the faith of a winner who never can say how he's going to win exactly.

12 "I'm thinking about my coach," said Ryun, the 47-year-old Kansan. "After my fourth high school race, we were riding home and my coach—after I had run the blazing time of 4:21—took me to the back of the bus and proceeded to tell me that he thought I could be the first high school boy to run the mile in under four minutes."

13 What was unthinkable, impossible, was actually within his reach. By the time he was 19, Ryun had set the world record in 3:51.3. In the following year, 1967, he was improving it by 0.2 seconds on a slow cinder track in a performance that will always stand out, according to Bannister, no matter how many times the record is broken.

14 The barrier of four minutes was dismantled by a medical student. Often Bannister could only spend a half-hour each day in training, which today would inspire a lack of confidence. But he spent that time preparing only what the mile required of him. He was among the first to institute interval training, and he had the confidence in himself that the future doctor would demand of his patients. The self-doubts, the second-guessing of experts that quells so many athletes today, played little role in his development.

15 Yet he is now as unwarily guilty of establishing barriers as the naysayers who unwarily made him famous. No one was predicting the changes in training and the rivalry with John Landy of Australia that drove Bannister. Based on his understanding, on what he has come to believe, anything faster than 3:30 is unattainable. The lesson of his own run 40 years ago is that he should know better.

16 "There are all sorts of alternative medicines becoming available, and medical treatments for illnesses based upon the communication between the mind and the body in some way," Elliott said. "I think there is some real power there that we haven't touched yet. Through medical stimulus, I think we'll understand that link."

17 He was coached in Australia by Percy Cerutty, who preached yoga as a means for overcoming the weaknesses of body. It was common to call Cerutty crazy. But his method produced Elliott, who was undefeated in the 1500 meters and the mile, who won the Olympic 1500-meters gold medal in 1960 by 2.8 seconds, and who might be the greatest miler of them all.

18 Considering that we learned of our own evolution only 135 years ago, isn't it likely that we have a lot more still to understand? Jim Ryun, against his own better judgment, became the first high school boy to run the mile in under four minutes, after Roger Bannister had run through a wall. The biggest fools create tomorrow's heroes.

I. Getting the Message

After reading the article, choose the best answer for each item.

1. The author believes that _____.
   a. runners will never be able to run much faster than the fastest runner today
   b. coaches should set sensible limits for athletes so they can train wisely
   c. it is foolish to use the word *impossible* in relation to sports records

2. The main purpose of the article is to _____.
   a. describe a meeting of famous runners
   b. present the author's opinion on an important aspect of a sport
   c. give a profile of a famous runner

3. According to the author, Roger Bannister set a record for running the mile _____.
   a. through a combination of training and confidence
   b. by training longer and harder than anyone else
   c. by making a career of running

4. According to the author, most of the athletes at this gathering _____.
   a. were not very knowledgeable or intelligent
   b. weren't able to support their opinions with reasons
   c. were wrong about setting limits

5. Peter Snell believes that _____.
   a. the fastest mile has not yet been run
   b. Herb Elliott is right about the future of running
   c. the ability of the lung membrane to bring oxygen to the muscles limits speed

6. According to the article, _____.
   a. coaches have little influence on an athlete's performance
   b. coaches have a great influence on an athlete's performance
   c. coaches should direct athletes to avoid mistakes

Check your answers with the key on page 182. If you have made mistakes, reread the article to gain a better understanding of it.

II. Expanding Your Vocabulary

A. Getting Meaning from Context

Find each word or phrase in the paragraph indicated in parentheses. Use context clues to determine the meaning of the word or phrase. Choose the best definition.

1.	peers (headline)	a. friends	b. equals	
2.	interface (8)	a. point of contact; connection	b. two parts of something	
3.	quantum leap (10)	a. slow improvement	b. very big change	
4.	rudimentary (11)	a. basic; elementary	b. complicated; complex	
5.	dismantled (14)	a. reached	b. taken apart	
6.	second-guessing (14)	a. confident decision-making	b. questioning of conclusions	
7.	quells (14)	a. stops	b. helps	
8.	alternative (16)	a. traditional	b. nontraditional	

B. Defining Useful Vocabulary

Match each word in column A with its definition in column B.

A		**B**
1. _____ unwarily		a. future ability
2. _____ stumble		b. slow change
3. _____ potential		c. unknown
4. _____ naysayer		d. begin
5. _____ institute		e. nearly fall
6. _____ anonymous		f. not reachable
7. _____ evolution		g. skeptic; disbeliever
8. _____ unattainable		h. unconsciously

III. Working with Idioms and Expressions

Study the meanings of these idioms and expressions. A form of each one appears in the indicated paragraph of the article.

dream the impossible dream (headline) dare to do what others say is impossible
pay tribute to (4) thank; honor

set the bar (7)   declare the limit
go back and forth (9)   discuss an issue
break a record (13)   do the best in some aspect of a sport
stand out (13)   be very noticeable or memorable
run through a wall (18)   achieve something that seems impossible

Complete these sentences with idioms and expressions from the list. Use the correct form of each verb.

1. One runner wanted to _____ the person who first said that no human could run a mile in less than four minutes.

2. Only one of the runners refused to _____ for running a mile at any particular time.

3. _____ is a way of thinking that can help an athlete succeed.

4. To _____ is probably a goal for anyone who wants to be remembered for a great achievement in a sport.

IV. Analyzing Paragraphs

Reread the indicated paragraphs. Choose the answer that best completes each sentence.

1. Paragraphs 1, 2, and 3 include all but _____.
    a. the reason for the meeting of the famous runners
    b. one runner's explanation for why there will never be a new record for the mile
    c. the author's main idea about how limits affect athletic performance

2. Paragraphs 14 and 15 do all but _____.
    a. show the author's admiration for Roger Bannister
    b. express the author's agreement with Roger Bannister
    c. give reasons why Bannister was able to run the mile in less than four minutes

3. Paragraphs 16 and 17 explain all but _____.
    a. why Herb Elliott believes the final limit for the mile will soon be reached
    b. how coach Percy Cerutty influenced Elliott's success
    c. why the author admires Percy Cerutty

V. Talking and Writing

Discuss the following topics. Then choose one of them to write about.

1. Do you agree with the author that setting limits to athletic performance keeps athletes from great achievements? Do you think setting limits can inspire athletes to achieve greater success?

2. Have you ever done something that others told you was impossible? If so, describe your experience.

Focus on the Newspaper

Who won the Monte Carlo road rally? What teams will be the strongest in the next World Cup soccer tournament? Currently, who is the world's fastest human? Most newspapers have a daily sports section that answers questions like these.

Contents of Sports Articles

Much of the information on the sports pages is transitory: it is of interest for the current day and may be of little interest the following day. Sports articles tell the results of yesterday's games and the prospects for today's and tomorrow's games. Sports feature articles, however, tackle larger issues, such as the roles of business and politics in sports. Other feature articles give insight into the sport itself or into the people who play the sport.

Exercise 1: Who's the Winner?

Choose two or three articles from the sports section of a newspaper and analyze their contents. Decide what type of article each one is, and answer the appropriate questions.

ANALYZING A SPORTS ARTICLE

1. What is the sport?
2. What's the headline? What key words helped you predict the content of the article?
3. Does a photo accompany the article? If so, what does it show?
4. What is the purpose of the article? Does it report the results of a contest or analyze one about to take place? Or is it a feature article?

Articles on Sports Results
1. What was the contest?
2. Where and when did the contest take place?
3. Was there a key play or player?
4. Is the contest discussed in strict chronological order?

Articles on Future Sports Events

1. What is the contest?

2. Where and when will the contest take place?

3. What are the predictions for the outcome?

4. What is the importance of the contest?

Sports Feature Articles

1. What is the topic of the article?

2. Does the article address issues other than sports (for example, finances or health)? If so, which ones?

Profiles of Sports Figures

1. Why did the newspaper print a feature about this person at this time?

2. Does the article portray this person sympathetically or unsympathetically?. What sentences give you the best clues?

3. Does the article make you want to read more about this person? Why or why not?

The Language of Sports

Exercise 2: Sports Vocabulary

Each sport has its own terminology. Pick a sport that you know. Look at several newspaper articles about the sport. Make a list of terms relating to the sport. Arrange them in categories such as the ones listed below. Add or delete categories as appropriate.

positions on the field _____

plays _____

verbs (action words) _____

slang _____

other _____

Share your list with your classmates. Compare your list with those of other students who chose the same sport.

COMPREHENSION CHECK

Answers to "Getting the Message" Exercises

News/Features

Article 1 (page 4)
1. b
2. b
3. b
4. a
5. c
6. b

Article 2 (page 10)
1. b
2. c
3. b
4. c
5. b

Article 3 (page 14)
1. T
2. F
3. F
4. T
5. T
6. F
7. F
8. F

Articles 4A/4B (page 19)
A. 1. The Dalai Lama hopes to recover Tibet from the Chinese and return home someday.
2. The Chinese government, which overtook Tibet in 1959, will not allow the Dalai Lama to return to Tibet.
B. 1. home
2. irrelevant
3. home
4. home
5. monastery
6. monastery
7. irrelevant

Opinion

Article 1 (page 29)
1. b
2. b
3. a
4. c
5. c
6. c

Article 2 (page 34)
1. F
2. F
3. T
4. T
5. F
6. T
7. T
8. T

Article 3 (page 39)
A. 1. c
2. b
3. a
4. b
5. b
6. c
B. 1. The title doesn't seem completely appropriate because it doesn't mention the Indians who live in the rain forest. The article focuses more on the harm being done to them than on the destruction of the rain forest itself.
2. The authors put their thesis statement at the end as a conclusion to the arguments they present in the article.
3. This is a strong beginning because it captures the reader's interest and shows both the historical and current significance of the topic.

Article 4 (page 44)
1. c
2. a
3. b
4. c
5. c
6. b

Business

Article 1 (page 53)
1. b
2. c
3. a
4. a
5. c
6. b

Article 2 (page 59)
1. b
2. c
3. a
4. a
5. a
6. b
7. b

Article 3 (page 64)
A. 1. F
2. T
3. T
4. F
5. T
B. 1. yes
2. no
3. yes
4. no
5. no
6. yes

Article 4 (page 70)
1. F
2. T
3. F
4. T
5. T
6. T
7. T
8. F

Profiles

Article 1 (page 78)
1. c
2. a
3. b
4. b
5. c
6. a

Article 2 (page 83)
1. a. M   b. T
2. a. M   b. T
3. a. T   b. M
4. a. T   b. M
5. a. M   b. T
6. a. T   b. M

Article 3 (page 89)
1. F
2. F
3. T
4. F
5. F
6. T
7. T
8. F
9. T
10. F

Article 4 (page 95)
A. 1. F
2. T
3. T
4. T
5. F
6. F
B. 1. yes (1)
2. no
3. no
4. yes (11)
5. no
6. yes (21, 30, 32–33)

Arts/Entertainment

Article 1 (page 103)
1. a
2. c
3. b
4. a
5. c

Article 2 (page 109)
1. T
2. F
3. F
4. T
5. T
6. T
7. F
8. F

Article 3 (page 114)
1. D
2. D
3. D
4. A
5. A
6. D
7. D
8. A

Article 4 (page 120)
1. F (6)
2. T (9)
3. F (14)
4. F (18)
5. F (12)
6. F (15)
7. T (1)
8. T (2, 7)
9. T (6, 10)
10. T (2, 3)

Articles 5A/5B (page 126)
A. 1. T
   2. F
   3. F
   4. T
   5. F
   6. T

B. 1. Jean-Marie Chauvet and two assistants
   2. archaeologists
   3. the cave paintings
   4. rhinoceroses
   5. a hyena
   6. a bear skull
   7. about 30,000 years old
   8. no
   9. with radiocarbon datings
   10. no

Science/Health

Article 1 (page 133)
1. F
2. T
3. F
4. F
5. F
6. F
7. F
8. F

Article 2 (page 138)
1. b
2. b
3. a
4. c
5. b

Article 3 (page 144)
1. b
2. c
3. b
4. a
5. a
6. b
7. c

Article 4 (page 151)
1. b
2. a
3. b
4. a
5. b
6. a

Sports

Article 1 (page 160)
1. c
2. a
3. b
4. c
5. b
6. c

Article 2 (page 165)
1. a
2. b
3. b
4. c
5. a

Article 3 (page 170)
1. c
2. a
3. b
4. b
5. c

Article 4 (page 176)
1. c
2. b
3. a
4. c
5. c
6. b